Targeting the
Nation's Youth

Targeting the Nation's Youth

The Bold Assault by Woke Politicians, Teachers Unions, and Other Predators

Bruce J. Gevirtzman

ROWMAN & LITTLEFIELD
Lanham • Boulder • New York • London

Published by Rowman & Littlefield
An imprint of The Rowman & Littlefield Publishing Group, Inc.
4501 Forbes Boulevard, Suite 200, Lanham, Maryland 20706
www.rowman.com

86-90 Paul Street, London EC2A 4NE, United Kingdom

Copyright © 2022 by Bruce J. Gevirtzman

All rights reserved. No part of this book may be reproduced in any form or by any electronic or mechanical means, including information storage and retrieval systems, without written permission from the publisher, except by a reviewer who may quote passages in a review.

British Library Cataloguing in Publication Information Available

Library of Congress Cataloging-in-Publication Data Available

ISBN 9781475863031 (paper) | ISBN 9781475863048 (ebook)

Contents

Preface..vii

Acknowledgments...ix

Introduction: Apologize!...................................xi

Chapter 1: Targeting Your Children...................1

Chapter 2: Old. White. Dead Men.....................13

Chapter 3: Bizarro..33

Chapter 4: Diversity Wears No Clothes............51

Chapter 5: The Math Doesn't Add Up...............63

Chapter 6: The War on Boys Massacre.............77

Chapter 7: Me-Too for Kids..............................89

Chapter 8: Rewriting History..........................101

Chapter 9: Speak Only What I Want to Hear...123

Chapter 10: Political Correctness, a Laughing Matter...141

Chapter 11: Teaching Science: An Exercise in Hypocrisy...153

Chapter 12: Graduate Woke.............................169

Chapter 13: COVID-19 Rides to the Rescue....181

Chapter 14: Under the Gun, Getting It Done...193

Bibliography..205

Index	217
About the Author	223

Preface

On November 9, 2021, the Superintendent of Detroit's public schools bragged, "Our curriculum is deeply using critical race theory, especially in social studies, but you'll find it in English language arts and the other disciplines. We were very intentional about . . . embedding critical race theory within our curriculum."[1]

No secrets here, despite what they tell you. Woke ideas are buried in the *curriculum*. They have crept insidiously into every part of American education. Sometimes it's subtle; sometimes it's not. Sometimes they admit it; most of the time they don't.

I've been in education for nearly fifty years. I finally got to the point where I thought, *What the heck . . . at my age, I have nothing to lose. I'm going to tell the truth here, and I'm going to tell it in a way that actually* sounds *like it's the truth*.

I did not want to write a narrative (one of too many, I am sure) focusing on the infusion of Critical Race Theory into American institutions, including K-12 schools. I work in education. I am a teacher. I am blessed to have been a teacher for so *long*. I write about what I know, and I know curriculum, pedagogy, and children.

My expertise does not lie with sociological problems regarding race, law enforcement, and science. *Education* has forever been my thing. I've had experience in helping other teachers become better at their craft. I've authored several books on that. I've offered a hand in developing secondary school curriculum and setting learning standards for public schools in the state of California.

What I initially wanted to discuss in this book is the rapidly changing curriculum, pedagogy, and lesson planning in schools across the nation. That is what I wound up doing, despite all the hysteria surrounding CRT.

This book is not solely about Critical Race Theory; it is about the tentacles of woke dogma as they have become interwoven into the changing curriculum being offered to our children. The impact of these cunning changes can't be overstated. In the year that it took me to reach the final chapter, teachers' unions, radical politicians, and special interest groups have come a long way in managing to get their foot in the door. Since, they have squeezed a lot more through that door than a foot.

Those educators that *could* persuasively fight this are not in a position to do so. They *can't*. Although it is a "free speech" America they live in, they must keep their mouths tightly shut. It's one of the most unfortunate characteristics of the woke assault. They scare people. They cancel people—good people, professional people, people that have served children and society for decades. These good folks are afraid to say anything, to speak even the obvious, and it is sickening. Listening to someone apologize to a woke makes me nauseous.

My vast experience as an educator puts me in the best position to report to you, no holds barred. After we have discussed the facts, you be the judge of what's happening. Your opinion matters more than mine. The deconstruction of your children is underway.

NOTE

1. Nikolai Vitti, "Superintendent Says Detroit Schools 'Deeply Using Critical Race Theory,'" Fox News, December 1, 2021. https://www.foxnews.com/us/superintendent-says-detroit-schools-deeply-using-critical-race-theory

Acknowledgments

Thanks to Tom Koerner at R&L for helping to get this project off the ground. Thank you to Carlie Wall at R&L for helping to see it through, with her helpful suggestions and careful editing. I also want to acknowledge my walking buddies and good friends, Eugene Leydiker and David Yungman, for allowing me to bounce my ideas off them, and in several instances, for their tossing those ideas right back into my face, a necessary part of this process.

In addition, I owe an immeasurable amount of gratitude to those that allowed me to interview them, either anonymously or otherwise. I appreciate their courage and input. (Where appropriate, their names have been provided in the endnotes at the ends of chapters.)

What I can't do justice to here is an expression of the love and admiration I have for my A+ wife, who is also the best teacher in America (not kidding about that)! And the two most delightful children in America, my twenty-one-year-old daughter and nineteen-year-old son. They think this book might not be a good idea; they worry about my safety. I'm a tough old geezer, though. And their support is enough to guide me through anything (that, and a Big Mac–Coke combo).

Finally, even though these publications, media outlets, and individuals may never know how much they helped and inspired me, without them I would have wound up with . . . nothing: thanks to Candace Owens, the *National Review, PJ Media, RedState, The Federalist,* the *New York Post,* the *Washington Times,* Tucker Carlson, Larry Elder, Glenn Beck, Laura Ingraham, Dennis Prager, the *Washington Free Beacon,* the *Epoch Time*s, the *Wall Street Journal,* Greg Gutfeld, and Adam Carolla. I am sure I missed a few. My apologies.

Introduction
Apologize!

RATE OF CHANGE

"The parents just don't know," Seattle radio host Jason Rantz claimed on nationwide television. "But as their kids are sitting around the living room on their laptops, the parents are starting to hear, and they are beginning to wake up."[1]

Rantz's comments were broadcast on October 5, 2020, in the midst of the confusion over what to do about our kids and their schools during the coronavirus pandemic. At the time, most of our children were on laptop computers, involved in distance learning (roll of eyes). Parents had direct access to what their kids were learning in their "classrooms." Parents could even make audio or video recordings of the lessons.

Frankly, this sudden invasion of the sanctity of the learning environment could not have happened at a better time.

America's educators have never sounded more militant about making sweeping changes in classroom curriculum and social pedagogy in our schools. A vice chairperson for the National Teachers Association, wrote in September of 2020, "The nation is speaking up. This time [it is] the people that are lending their voices. . . . Systemic racism in America must end. . . . As teachers, We will exercise our power to make the necessary changes, to be anti-racist. . . . [It] begins with our children, and in our schools."[2]

Americans are not unnerved by the nation's preoccupation with ending racism. To end racism would be a good thing, a *very* good thing. But constantly sermonizing to children that America is *inherently* racist, and that our schools, churches, businesses, law enforcement agencies, government bodies, military personnel, entertainment industry, and other great institutions are codified in bigotry is woefully inaccurate and dangerously counterproductive.[3]

Those that may otherwise claim to be victims of racism have some surprising concerns. Serious misgivings are voiced by parents like Scarlett Johnson, a Hispanic-American whose children are taught Critical Race Theory in Wisconsin's Mequon-Thiensville district. She worries that [her] children are being exposed to a curriculum that claims the U.S. is an oppressive country, which denies [her kids] the ability to learn about history and have hope for their own success, no matter what the color of their skin.[4]

Ms. Johnson embraces America. She boasts of her gratitude for a nation that has welcomed her and generations of her family. She feels lucky that she was not one of the unfortunates that stalled dead at the Southern Border or did not make it all the way to the promised land on a boat.[5]

At this writing, the only thing left certain is that there is *no* certainty. Teachers, administrators, parents, the general public—and, mostly, our *children*—face challenges that no other generation has had to deal with in over 160 years. While it may be true that children are the least harmed *directly* by the ravages of COVID-19, kids are the most vulnerable to strange new policies, ill-motivated manipulations, and "strategically" funneled curricula in the schools. And even these tactics keep changing and may wind up causing far more harm to our children than the coronavirus.

The newest progressive education movements are soundly organized and well-funded; they are currently on overdrive. They include tactical organizations that lobby politicians and the teachers' unions; they have become emboldened by special interest groups that have been around for an eternity. (Interestingly, the major teachers' unions are now among those powerful special interest groups.) They boast of grass roots organizations made of the public, regular people, many of whom do not have any children in the schools. And they are driven by our political leaders, men and women that foster notions about race and gender and history and science that none of them would have held as truths ten years ago, lest they be laughed out of town.

The American Association of School Administrators (AASA) boldly proclaimed, "AASA's work on equity must go further and become actively anti-racist."[6] Which sounds like an appealing idea, until one begins to critically analyze just what that really means. (It may sound appealing even after we know what it means, but we should have the opportunity to be *informed*.) Being informed sounds like a cool idea, too, until we realize that the specific details of what it entails to be "actively anti-racist"—and exactly how the nation's school children would be taught to be "actively anti-racist"—offer up more education minefields than meet the eye.

That you would dare to question what a term like, "actively anti-racist," actually means, might compel others to consider *you* a racist, simply for asking a question about a definition! As ludicrous as this may sound, it is the truth: Ask a question, risk going to racism purgatory.

These confusing and—at least, on the surface—well-meaning, and unquestionably moral platitudes are emerging every day, faster than a normal human being can possibly digest, much less critically analyze. What complicates matters is increasingly visible evidence of changes, or proposed changes, to the curriculum in America's schools in every nook-and-cranny of the education spectrum.

It runs the gamut: from white privilege, to subliminal racism; from the obliteration of biological sciences in the first grade, to a broad spectrum of gender studies in high school; from the reordering of American history, to the rethinking of American social, cultural, and political values; from the compulsory study of social justice principles, to the dismissal of free speech, the nuclear family, and American sovereignty—as outdated, outmoded, and out of touch with a preferred one-world view.

And that is just the tip of the iceberg.

STRAINING YOUR CREDULITY

Those that work in the system today—teachers, teachers' assistants, administrators, counselors, school psychologists, special needs directors, nurses, secretaries, custodians—know the direction in which we are headed. The people that operate on the inside have an inkling of the trouble ahead. That's their burden. They may not be in the loop, but they see changes happening, some of them precipitated by the reality of COVID-19, and some not.

Even from inside the education establishment, disagreements over the direction of schools frequently occur. Sometimes the disagreement is subtle, quiet, and subdued; other times, the disagreement is vehement, confrontational, and bombastic. But change has swept through the schoolhouse door, while educators may have turned their backs on the children they are entrusted to protect.

I taught English for over three decades. I presided over a championship speech and debate team, directed theater, and coached high school baseball. For the past ten years, I have taught communications at California State University in Fullerton, a diverse city in Northern Orange County, a place with a perennially conservative face. My wife teaches high school level English to adults; my children attend college. I am privy to what's happening in our schools.

Because of challenges related to the coronavirus pandemic, along with upheavals in American cities that have affected society and its culture, there is currently an incentive to produce a flood of information about the changes that are taking place—or will soon take place—in the schools. Some of the philosophies are hysterical (as in funny) or produce hysteria (as in panic). Other ideas appear to be whacky; they nurture an atmosphere of disbelief, creating surreal discussions about history, math, and science—and just about every other subject taught in American education. Suggestions for advancing new curricula into the schools resemble *SNL* sketches. I keep telling myself, "You can't make this stuff up!"

SORRY FOR WHAT MY PEOPLE DID

Up until recently, public and private schools hesitated to deal with topics related to race. Even public schools that were predominantly Black or Latino steered away from racial issues for two main reasons: (1) They distracted from a curriculum that teachers were mandated to follow, which, during those times, had little to do with racism, except on a peripheral level. Novels like *To Kill a Mockingbird* brought on discussions of race, but once students left the classroom, that was usually the end of their racism ponderings. (2) A curriculum that entailed analyses of race issues would be controversial, and given that race relations in America were in repose, educators denied the usefulness of stirring up a hornets' nest.

This nation elected a Black president to not one, but *two* terms, and any discourse about race in in the United States would probably wind up being counterproductive. Educators, and some politicians, had been validated. Racial strife in the United States—though many individual racists still existed—had been an ugly sore on our country's past; at least, most Americans perceived it that way.[7]

This text goes into some depth about how the new woke books, ideologies, workshops, seminars, rehabilitation and recovery centers (punishment for one's poor racist attitudes), had charged—sometimes covertly—into the schools.

A bizarre concept captured the limelight: the relatively new, at least, in its contemporary context, notion of *white privilege. White privilege* has been contextualized. I remember hearing the term—though not often—while I was teaching high school. I didn't pay much attention to it then, which, some would argue, is the crux of *my* problem: the inattentiveness of people like me to these types of brilliant, innovative, racial narratives. I never entertained the idea that I was a racist. Listening to theories about how my being a white guy made me a racist guy or, at best, a spoiled brat of a guy that took his good fortune for granted, didn't interest me for a millimeter of a second, even from an academic standpoint.

Of course, that was *then*.

Merriam-Webster defines *white privilege* as, "*inherent* [italics added] advantages possessed by a white person on the basis of their race in a society characterized by racial inequality and injustice."[8] As a long-time high school and college debate coach, I could raise cogent arguments that attack the fabric of that definition. I might express doubts about the logic inherent in the concept of "white privilege," while refuting the notion of white privilege itself. *White privilege* conjured up visions of Caucasians that flattered no one.

I could not identify. If "white privilege" meant having been adopted at three days old by a loving mother and father that had managed to escape the Holocaust, then, yes, I qualified. My father never earned more than a hundred bucks a week; my mother never worked outside the house. She didn't drive a car and chose to walk around the house all day in an apron, while carrying a dust cloth. We didn't have much, but we were happy. We loved each other; we sacrificed for one another. My parents were not exactly Romeo and Juliet, but through a minor amount of marital turbulence, they stayed together, aware that a two-parent home gave their children greater odds to succeed in their lives. In that sense, we were privileged. And, yeah, white.

A few years ago, a new book appeared on the scene. The author intended to teach the world, specifically, people like *me*, because I am of Italian/European heritage, that my good fortune in life had manifested itself into something more sinister than just that little ol' white privilege thing.

It goes like this: Not only have millions of white people in this country benefited from their "privilege," these same white people are racists. But we may *possibly* give them the benefit of the doubt by claiming that they don't know they are racist; they are *subliminally* racist, *subconsciously* racist. Or they commit micro-aggressions, which are *insidiously* racist. And even if none of these is true about them, they are not *actively anti-racist*, which makes them racist.

Sorry, I am just explaining. . . .

Author Robin DiAngelo capitalized financially on all this talk of white people being in positions of power and superiority and not realizing it, or realizing it and not caring, in her 2017 best seller, *White Fragility: Why It's So Hard for White People to Talk About Racism*. The book did well for a while, became an easy, and provocative, radio talk show interview for DiAngelo whenever she wanted one, and then soared to the top of the *New York Times* Best Seller List shortly after George Floyd died at the hands of Minneapolis police on Memorial Day Weekend, 2020.[9]

The premise of *White Fragility* is head-scratching. At first, you want to laugh; you then get a sinking feeling and begin to recoil. Eventually, you look for something to throw. DiAngelo contends that white people who question their privilege are demonstrating their privilege. Why? They don't understand, or can't accept, their fortunate lot in life. DiAngelo dismisses criticism from "whites" as a product of their "white supremacy" or "racism" and labels it *white fragility*.

She has it both ways. If you don't accept, at the very least, that you are a subliminal bigot, one guilty of micro-aggressions, you are a racist. And if you tell off those who think you might be a racist for being ignorant about your alleged racism, then you are, indeed, a racist or a white supremacist. DiAngelo puts you in a corner and stifles you by not allowing you an escape route. "For all the white people listening right now, thinking I am not talking to you," she had a message: "I am looking directly into your eyes and saying, *it is you*."[10]

In June of 2020, *White Fragility* was the best-selling book in the United States; it was bought by school districts across the nation. Teachers freely admitted they were planning to use *White Fragility* in their classrooms. The race of the teacher didn't matter; the demographics of the students played no part in the decision. Using this book to teach kids was a done deal.

Connor Pollogar, a new fourth grade teacher in Vermont, already knew exactly how to work this text into his curriculum. He would bring it out during Martin Luther King's birthday week. That's Martin Luther King: you know, the guy that claimed *a person should not be judged by the color of his skin*. Yes, that guy.

Pollogar planned his lessons, some of which put nine and ten-year-old kids in the uncomfortable position of having to apologize to a "person of color" for being white. For this to happen, Pollagar grouped kids by their race: *All the white kids stand over there. . . . Oh, wait, you aren't sure if you're white? What did your mother tell you about being Italian? I guess that's white. . . . What? No, if I tell you you're white, you're white! Like I said, go stand over there.*[11]

DiAngelo tours the country, conducting workshops packed with ideas about how to implement *White Fragility* games into the curriculum, or, at least, how to inspire teachers to play around with *White Fragility* exercises with their first grade students: *I'm Becky, and I'm white. I'm sorry that my great-great-great grandpa owned slaves.* What could this possibly mean to a six-year-old child? And it's not altogether certain—probably not certain at all—that Becky's family, no matter how far you go down the chain, owned slaves. No matter. She's white. Guilt by association is vogue.

Imagine grouping together all the Muslim kids in the classroom and explaining to them that they should walk around the room, apologizing to their classmates for the events of 9/11! School officials would be rightfully horrified by such an activity. Antiracism activism used to be directed towards people who were . . . you know, racist. Now, the idea of all white people being racist is championed around the country, most notably in academia. You don't have to nurse a hatred of Black or Brown people to be racist. All you must be is white.

The public has the right to know what is being taught in America's schools by teachers, administrators, and special interest groups. Startling revelations appear every day. It has become mind-boggling, actually. It is a world turned upside down, backwards, and inside out.

To a fault, our schools ignored race issues, except for the obligatory mentioning of Martin Luther King's birthday, the weekend when mostly everyone seized an annual opportunity to visit shopping malls. Or Black History Month, which most teachers scribbled on their calendars and then forgot about it. The wrangling started when teachers figured *other* teachers would handle this celebration of Black culture in their classrooms, with, of course, the proud—though often gratuitous—references to Rosa Parks. But many teachers allowed Black History Month to slide by without mention.

That was then.

Now, the pendulum has begun to swing the opposite way, in the direction of a new obsession with one's personal culture, and the power of its movement can't be overstated.

A TALE OF MUDDLED MOTIVES

While teaching high school AP and Honors English (which I had done for over three decades), I began each semester by telling my students something like, "We're going to study literature that you would never pick up at the library in order to meet your entertainment needs for the weekend. The writing may not be compelling; the style of the author is often dull and convoluted, and the vocabulary ridiculously difficult, but we will read it because it *matters*."

We are currently discovering what "matters" has changed. It used to be that I, the instructor—within certain limitations, of course—decided which literature pieces I would be teaching to my students. Literature impacted them; it stretched them; it helped them to figure out who they were; it sparked discussions—inside and outside the classroom—of core values that every civilized country required for it to survive, and for its people to thrive.

Now, other things matter. If I do my own thing, stray from the so-called norm, I am a renegade teacher, a rebel—and worse: I am a racist, a misogynist, a homophobe—or all the above. Maybe I am evil.

Except for when the cat knocks my computer from the desk while I am working on something, and I may have *thoughts,* I am not evil. A professional conflict may arise because my criteria for what "matters" is different from the woke efforts to alter the curriculum offerings in American schools. That is not evil. That is a long-time teacher making well-intentioned decisions.

The style of organization of this book helps to clarify a complex content. I tell you in chapter 2 (Old. White. And Dead) what English teachers *used* to impart to their students and why; we then contrast that curriculum with what students are learning now, and what lies on the horizon. This is loosely the organization for each of the chapters in this book: *then, now, later*. And let me tell you: the *later* part is indefinite, open-ended. I can hear clamors for additional curriculum changes in our schools, as I type this. And I'm not exaggerating!

Phil Nei, author of *Was the Cat in the Hat Black: The Hidden Racism of Children's Literature, and the Need for Diverse Books*, spoke to the *Washington Post* about a "problem." "Representation is about power. If you are mainly reading books about straight white boys and men, the message you receive is that straight white boys and men are—and should be—at the center of the universe."

Your children are the outlet, the itinerary, the pipeline to societal changes. "They" get to the kids first, and all the rest follows. Where are the kids? In the schools, of course. *How do we get to the kids through the schools?* We use the teachers and coaches, of course: teachers present the information that helps to mold the children. What kids used to think and believe can—and often *does*—change. Those changes start in the schools.

SCIENCE TAKES A HIT

On second thought (or third thought—or whatever), maybe the bad stuff does not start at school—not all of it. There's a chapter in this text entitled, "Teaching Science: An Exercise in Hypocrisy," that examines forever-changing science theories and tries to make logical sense as to why, one day, we honor knowledge solidly based in science, and on the next day, not only have those scientific principles gone cuckoo, but only cuckoo people seem to believe in them.

Beginning with kindergarten, your children are being warned about climate change (yes, gently, but vicious vernacular about mucking up the environment is often hurled at youngsters by teachers, administrators, and guest speakers in the schools). Alternative theories about climate changes have been largely ignored, statistics have been manipulated or altered to suit a political end, and mind-boggling stuff about melting glaciers being linked to incandescent light bulbs is being peddled to our kids.

Branch Cody of the All-Dead Society, said in December of 2019, "Politicians have visited schools and scared children with their over-the-top doomsday predictions. . . . Yesterday, Congresswoman Alexandria Ocasio-Cortez [spoke at] a grade school in Detroit and told third graders they would all be dead in about fifteen minutes, unless their parents and other adults did something *big* to stop the erosion of the environment."[12]

I doubt that these eight-year-olds processed words like "erosion" or "environment," but they had an inkling what "dead" meant and probably figured their parents and teachers weren't doing enough to keep them from ending up that way. "Are you trying to kill me, Mommy?" "Yeah, kid, now turn off the lamp and shut up, so I can sleep!"

The argument that Ocasio-Cortez launched at third graders was for them (and, by transfer, for *us*) to trust the scientists. She claims that over 99.9 percent of the world's scientists fall somewhere in line with her doomsday climate scenarios. She dismisses the "few scientists that disagree" as kooks, beholden to big business, or supporters of President Trump, alluding to each category with disdain, but mindful of rising to a special degree of loathing for people who had voted for Trump in 2016.[13]

I experienced the wrath of other teachers who had worked the threats of human-caused climate change into their curriculums (not just science classes). They wanted me to feel like an outcast, because I hadn't yet confessed to being alarmed by the dangers that they saw. I always thought science was *science*, and science was *fact*, and that fact was, well, *fact*. When there is so much disagreement (most assuredly, more than *one hundredth of a percent*), actual *established* or *settled* science should be substituted for *controversial* science while teaching kids about *facts*.

Educators that cite opinion or faith or conjecture and call it *science* are missing the point about *fact*. And with the climate change issue, *fact* has not been settled. Anger has substituted for facts, especially during late-night dorm discussions and special family gatherings. Even at six feet apart, the density of emotion carries a long way before it finally comes to rest at the Thanksgiving dinner table; and by that time, many of the verbal combatants may have already deserted the dining room. At least in this setting, so-called authorities toss *both* sides of an issue around, permitting a captive audience to come to their own conclusions.

In their classrooms, our children have no defense, no safe way to question the legitimacy of the holy science being preached to them, or how to answer a teacher who snarls, "It's true! Just *listen*!"

Andrew Urevig, freelance science writer, wrote in *Ensia*, "Tim Swinehart, a social studies teacher at Lincoln High School, a public school in Portland, Oregon, has taken class groups to advocate for climate at the state capitol. He also worked alongside young climate activists to push the Portland school board to pass a resolution banning materials that cast doubt on the reality of global warming and the encouraging of a climate change curriculum."[14]

Swinehart calls this a *movement* and says that if they can't get (your) children to come to the movement, they will bring the movement to (your) children.[15] And he isn't alone—far from it.

Whenever we hear someone claim something like, "It's all about the science," we should question at least some of those claims: *whose* science, which scientists have offered the highest levels of expertise in their professional interpretations of data? *Why is one perspective more valid than another perspective*? After all, aren't we supposed to teach children how to think things through, so they may reach their own conclusions? I would argue that *educators should stay free from political propagandizing and new social engineering agendas*. Just a weird thought I had.

But then there is *that* science, the science that frees our kids to *choose* their gender. Although *that* science is embraced by the very same teachers that swear by the science of climate change, most kids ignore it. It goes against what their families and churches and synagogues and mosques have taught them since the day they were born. It also challenges what they intuitively understand. *That* science, the woke, progressive science of the New Millennium, contradicts all that our children have ever been told about girls and boys.

I want to be clear: I am not taking a position, one way or the other, on the science of gender selection. It is a delicate issue. And I'm ignorant about it. Although I'm learning, I don't know enough. But I suspect when it comes to the science of gender, some basic, long-accepted theories have been flung into the trash heap, along with some good old-fashioned common sense.

Gender biologist and theorist Arnold De Loof argues in a complicated academic article for the *National Institute of Health* that it is no longer in vogue (interesting way of referring to it: *vogue*) to believe that humankind may be divided into only two genders; that while biological *sex* many be predetermined, sex may be altered.[16] Gender, on the other hand, may be *selected* by an individual, because gender lies outside the bounds of (only) physiological considerations.

Basically, we can break it down this way: If you are born a man, your gender, if you *choose*, may be that of a woman. And there are several other options besides *man* or *woman*. But sex is science, and sex is determined by one's genitalia. The catch is if you have a penis, that penis doesn't necessarily require you to be a man; if you have a vagina, that vagina doesn't necessarily require you to be a woman. There are exceptions, combinations of genders that form creative alliterations that broadcast ways of identifying oneself—and others.

Whew! Can we explain this to our children?

We can *try*. In California, the schools are decoding these theories for kindergartners! *The Washington Post* reported, "The California guidelines are quite clear about what is to be taught and why. Page 45 of the K-3 guidelines states: 'While students may not fully understand the concepts of gender expression and identity, some children in kindergarten, and even younger, have identified as transgender, or understand they have a gender identity that is different from their sex assigned at birth.'"[17]

I must admit that when I was in kindergarten, I didn't know what *sex* meant! All I knew was that I was glad to be a boy, even though I had no idea how I had gotten that way. Nor did I care. I am sure that if I had been a little girl, I would have felt the same—fortunate to be a girl.

A nationwide, non-binary gender dogma is being taught not only in science classes, but across the curriculum—and outside the curriculum—wherever teachers can fit it in. The young, unsuspecting targets run the gamut of ages, from kindergarten through twelfth grade.

Thousands of educators view the popular changes in attitude regarding science, whether embedded in a science curriculum or as the official vision of their school, as hypocritical. In some instances, science is treated as though it emanates from God (climate change); in other instances, the theories are outright denied as science (gender selection).

A consistent case can be made for either side on these issues, but confusion reigns when it is generally the same people that swear by science in one instance (climate change) but deny science in the other instance (gender selection). Science is good, if you agree with it, or if it fits your agenda. Science is bad, if conclusions do harm to your agenda. Nevertheless, commonplace changes, some of them dizzying in their logic, have been made in our schools.

George Leef, Director of Research for the John W. Pope Center for Higher Education Policy, wrote on November 4, 2019, about even bigger curriculum changes being addressed in California: "Many schools have adopted an 'ethnic studies' curriculum, the point of which is to indict capitalism, whiteness, and Western Civilization as forms of power, privilege, oppression. Teachers revel in giving students assignments that are meant to turn them into social justice warriors."[18] When Mr. Leef wrote this, he didn't know that these kinds of ideas were being developed into courses that would, as early as 2022, become *graduation requirements*![19]

You won't be blamed for thinking the transition between the two previous paragraphs is non-existent. What is the link between gender selection and culture studies? Ta-da! According to the California Teachers Association, a state branch of the largest teacher's union in the country, a course on culture studies is *inclusive* of gender studies. After all, according to these powerful education groups, everything settles into the cookie cutter tray of equity, diversity, and inclusion. Culture is about equity, diversity, and inclusion; sexual orientation comes down to equity, diversity, and inclusion. Gender selection winds up as an issue of equity, diversity, and inclusion. For better or worse—heck, *better*, for all I know!—"equity, diversity, and inclusion" has become the hallmark of American education. If you're against it, you likely spend time breaking bread with the Devil. If you ask someone what it means, you're a bigot.

I dared to ask someone in my university's education department what equity, diversity, and inclusion meant. I was met with a bug-eyed stare that would have made for a scary "wanted" poster. I hadn't just asked the professor if she thought the Holocaust was a hoax; that would have been bad enough. But equity, diversity, and inclusion are sacred! Nobody asks about those!

Now, if only educators and political leaders could discover a conduit for carrying their messages. If only they had a way to start 'em while they were young.

NOTES

1. Jason Rantz, "The Tucker Carlson Show," Fox News, interview with Tucker Carlson, October 5, 2020.

2. Heather Howicker, *ABC News Tonight*, August 15, 2020.

3. My mother warned me of anti-semitism, especially when I began going to public school. I was the only Jewish kid in the high school until my sister arrived there two years later. I can't think of one experience during my entire schooling in which I had been a victim of anti-Jewish bigotry.

4. Rick Esenberg and Daniel Lennington, "Critical Race Theory Has No Place in American Schools," *Real Clear Education*, June 14, 2020. https://www.realcleareducation.com/articles/2021/06/14/critical_race_theory_has_no_place_in_american_schools_110595.html

5. I *gathered* Ms. Johnson's thoughts and feelings about America from her comments about the woke curriculum.

6. James Minichello, "AASA Issues Statement On Recent Events And Racial Inequality In Our Nation," *The School Superintendent's Association*, June 3, 2020.

7. During the Obama presidency, the racial temperature of the mainstream media was low. There were issues, but nothing like now.

8. *Merriam-Webster*, July 22, 2021. https://www.merriam-webster.com/dictionary/white%20privilege. This "dictionary definition" was compiled from several contributors.

9. Robin DiAngelo, *White Fragility: Why It's So Hard For White People to Talk About Racism*, (Beacon Press), 2018.

10. Daniel Bergner, "'White Fragility' Is Everywhere. But Does Antiracism Training Work?" *New York Times Magazine*, July 17, 2020, par. 1. https://www.nytimes.com/2020/07/15/magazine/white-fragility-robin-diangelo.html.

11. Hollee Actman Becker, "You Have to Watch This 8th-Grader's Viral Apology for His #WhiteBoy Privilege," July 12, 2016, *Explore Parents*. https://www.parents.

com/toddlers-preschoolers/everything-kids/you-have-to-watch-this-8th-graders-viral-apology-for-his/. View the video. Mr. Pollogar patterned his lesson after this video. It made my skin crawl.

12. Branch Cody, "Introducing 'The Squad,'" December 15, 2019. Saw this guy on a PBS station, and thought he had a good take on some of the new members of Congress, and what they might mean to the teaching of "science" principles in our schools.

13. ibid.

14. Andrew Urevig, "How Should Climate Change Be Taught in the Schools?" *Ensia*, July 10, 2019. https://medium.com/ensia/how-should-climate-change-be-taught-in-schools-across-america-4c22a577644b

15. High school teachers like Swinehart tend to be popular because they are incredibly passionate about their subject matter. I suggest that a person can be both passionate and wrong at the same time.

16. Arnold Le Loof, "Communicative and Integrative Biology," *National Institute of Health*, January 31, 2018. https://www.ncbi.nlm.nih.gov/pmc/articles/PMC5824932/

17. Henry Olsen, "California Wants to Teach Kindergartners About Gender Identity," *The Washington Post*, May 12, 2019, Op-Ed section.

18. George Leef, "A Racially Woke Agenda Is Now Hardwired in Public Schools," *Minding the Campus*, November 4, 2019. https://www.mindingthecampus.org/2019/11/04/a-racially-woke-agenda-is-now-hardwired-in-public-schools/

19. We discuss some of those courses and graduation requirements in chapter 13.

Chapter 1

Targeting Your Children

AMERICA'S MOST PRECIOUS TREASURE

Former U.S. Senator Christopher Dodd wrote, "Our nation's children are our greatest asset and our most precious treasure."[1]

The words echo: *Everything* starts and stops with children. Everything that is bad is exponentially worse when it affects children. *Evil* is more evil. *Hate* is more hateful. *Despicable* is more despicable.

Reading about the ruins of a city that has been ravaged by a 7.5 earthquake is emotionally draining; reading about that same natural disaster, and how it had violently and painfully snuffed out the lives of hundreds of *children*, is off-the-charts emotionally devastating. Experiences of children evoke feelings in us that experiences of adults do not evoke.

John Dean, an education professor of great merit but little renown, said in August of more than fifty years ago, "If you want to get to the heart of a pulsating civilization, you make the children feel safe. If they trust you, they will tell you everything. You will learn more about what matters in life from them, than they could possibly learn from you."[2]

While a few societies have indifferently cast off the value of their children, people in most cultures have historically viewed children as their most prized possessions; hence, their reverence for institutions where they send children to learn. Kids drive legislation. They depend upon us, communicate to us. Children are instruments of pathos. If malevolent forces can get to the kids, they can make changes in the basic power structures of civilizations.

NOTHING TO DO WITH DRIVING TRAINS

Most people are ambivalent about the concept of social engineering. It's not that they don't care; it's that they don't think about it. People have other things to consider: paying the bills, going to the gym, attending their friends' weddings and bar mitzvahs. Who cares what schools are teaching the kids? If other people find out and don't like it, they will do something about it. Not sure what, where, why, or how—but they will do *something* to take care of it.

Take a nap. Go on vacation. Attend a ballgame. Watch a movie. But public schools? *Why, the schools are not your domain*! What can *you* do about the public schools? Why should *you* care enough to waste your precious time and energy and—God only knows—money on this obscure idea called *social engineering* that some people seem to be throwing around?

Reluctantly, this chapter serves up a definition of *social engineering*—and "reluctantly," because doing so may make your author sound like a conspiracy theorist, which he is not. Lee Harvey Oswald *was* the lone assassin of President Kennedy; nobody fired a gun from the Grassy Knoll. And the Twin Towers fell on 9/11 as the result of an orchestrated terrorist attack on the United States by Muslim radicals, not mysterious explosive devices rigged by right wing militia groups. Tantalizing conspiracy theories rarely earn much credibility.

The imperative here is to offer a concise definition of social engineering: *the use of centralized planning to manage social change and regulate the future development and behavior of a society.*[3]

Remember that this is not an attempt to introduce a sinister conspiracy that advances harmful ideas to American education. Those that toil to introduce their woke matter into the classroom are not clandestine about it. They are in the open, wildly up front—unmistakably proud of their endeavors.

Everyone knows that America's public schools are in the business of practicing *the use of centralized planning to manage social change and regulate the future development and behavior of a society.* Duh. That's why government (and religious) schools exist. They have goals. These goals aren't necessarily bad goals or sinister goals, but they proclaim ends to be reached, whether they are through the teaching of reading, writing, and arithmetic, or the propagation of cultural ritual or patriotic ceremony.

Each day, when boys and girls of all ages stand at their desks, put their hands over their hearts, and recite by rote the Pledge of Allegiance, they are acting out the government's function of social engineering (in some form). That's not a bad thing here; in fact, it could be reasonably argued that some types of social engineering shape positive societal behaviors. Some social norms have universal acceptance. Educators teach kids to respect their elders, treat others kindly, work hard, and obey authority.

Those aren't exactly wide-eyed expectations. In fact, if families were instilling similar values in their own children, the schools would not be required to work so hard while deviating from reading, writing, and arithmetic. But not all children have decent families. Not all children are blessed by being loved and nurtured and cherished by their parents. Some kids don't even *have* parents.

COMMONPLACE SOCIAL ENGINEERING

Consider ten quick allusions to the way the schools traditionally "socially engineered" your children:

1. promoting patriotism
2. establishing hierarchy of authority
3. supporting the nuclear family
4. preferring religion
5. promoting health and safety
6. erasing racial and gender barriers
7. preaching the Golden Rule
8. favoring capitalism
9. admitting boundaries
10. reinforcing science

Mind you, these are not necessarily undesirable feats of engineering; in fact, most of them aren't undesirable at all. For the past sixty years or so, schools have been run by practical people, dedicated educators who have had the best interests of your children at heart. You decide whether that is still true. But note how the past rises gently into that discussion, just before it is about to erupt into turmoil, when comparing what educators are endorsing today.

PROMOTING PATRIOTISM

Love of country is an abstract concept, but most people know it when they feel it. The men that fought in the Second World War (and other wars) gave their lives for the United States of America. Whether they did it because they believed they were fighting for freedom, or they had been drafted and forced to participate in that horrific spectacle, those that survived had come back—almost to a man—gushing with pride in themselves and for their country. It was, after all, primarily the United States that had ultimately freed Europe, liberated the concentration camps, and prevented Hitler from taking over the world.

As the education system progressed through the 1950s, a mandate for teaching kids to love their country went naturally with that progression. Possessing a sense of communal pride and a shared sense of gratitude was part of a seamless transition from war to peace. It wasn't hard; everyone agreed.

American schools have fostered love of *patria* from the turn of the nineteenth century.

In the 1950s, school children sometimes said the Pledge, in unison, two or three times a day. Okay, maybe that was excessive, but even throughout the political and social turmoil of the last several years, parents expected their children to believe in the concept of *country*, and they also expected their public schools to stand as a bulwark for national pride and as a source of dignity.

ESTABLISHING HIERARCHY OF AUTHORITY

Most schools are connected by a structure of authority that is brandished from the top (greatest power) to the bottom (the least powerful); thus, principals sit at the top of the authority pyramid (or district superintendents), down to students, who wield the least amount of authority in a school.[4]

The nation's schools have differing views about those in charge, and what is assumed about their most basic functions. Teachers lead their classrooms. Students in those classrooms sometimes pilot groups that have been assigned to do research or solve problems. Public schools, as do private schools, perpetuate the view that parents have control over their own children; at least, they used to. You might say public schools "engineer" children into believing they should respect authority, that certain people have dominance over them, and even the highest authority (except maybe for God) must deal at one time or another with individuals that are at least equal to them in power. Children are taught that this is necessary—and *good*.

SUPPORTING THE NUCLEAR FAMILY

Some sociologists and anthropologists consider the nuclear family as the most basic, and effective, form of social organization. By its purest definition, a *nuclear family* consists of a married mother and father and a couple of children. Of course, divergences from this format have sprung up, but two parents, living together with their children, model for one of America's simplest, most widely accepted social constructs.

At one point, educators assumed that all children who attended their schools were living in that type of family: Dad went to work; Mom stayed home. Two children toddled off to school every day. When they came home, Mom stood at the door to greet them, holding freshly baked chocolate chip cookies and a glass of cold milk.

Everyone doesn't sign on to this paradise. Dave Brooks wrote in the *Atlantic* in March 2020, "[The nuclear family] gave the most privileged people in society room to maximize their talents and expand their options. The shift from bigger and interconnected extended families to smaller and detached nuclear families ultimately led to a familial system that liberates the rich and ravages the working-class and the poor."[5] You may have noticed a trend. Wokes constantly make everything about *privilege.* Those who *have* must feel guilty about that.

HIGHLIGHTING RELIGION

The separation of church and state has been a backbone of American political rhetoric. The school is a primary breeding ground for issues to arise regarding that separation. Christmas carols, trees, and decorations in the classroom are perennial signs of festivities of the holiday season. They are considered cornerstones during this special time of year. Children forget their differences with their peers to bring holiday cheer and celebration to one another. Often their parents—and maybe a few fuddy-duddies in the community—look askance at them, but the sheer joy of Christmas dominates the mood of most American schools.

The schools, and society at large, are filled with sourpusses and ne'er do wells. But most Americans come up with ways of sustaining their own joys, and reaching out to the downtrodden at a time when Christmas can perform its greatest miracles. The schools don't only tolerate these kinds of experiences; they *promote* them, even in full view of the grumpiest and most cynical of the so-called adults in the room.

The emphasis on diversity has promoted different religious and racial/cultural celebrations in the schools. Education institutions, while supporting religion, do not favor one domination to the exclusion of others. Most of the celebratory occasions are secular experiences. That said, educators usually send a clear message that even the barest of religious expression is generally a good thing.

PROMOTING HEALTH AND SAFETY

Schools at all grade levels teach kids that they should eat healthy, stay clean, and be cautious. Lessons in the primary grades have forever emphasized these admonitions. They are continuous. In secondary schools, public or private, children take courses in health and safety, drug and alcohol abuse, and sex education, which are treated as health experiences, rather than moral lessons. During the various peaks of the COVID pandemic, educators claimed that they would not invite children back to the classroom until they could guarantee their safety; children's health was their priority. Health and safety have always come first, sometimes to a fault; there is a distinction between being cautious and being ridiculous.[6]

ERASING RACE AND GENDER BARRIERS

For the most part, the schools have emphasized the need for racial tolerance. Especially since civil rights laws were passed sixty years ago, the school, even as an extension of the force of government, has been in the forefront of a battle for equality. The intensity of this effort varies state by state, but the conspicuous inclination of educators to teach fairness doesn't go unnoticed. If America's children have been brainwashed or "socially engineered" in this realm, it's been a positive thing. The children have consistently been taught valuable lessons in civil rights, nondiscrimination, and equal *opportunity*. What could be bad about those?

PREACHING THE GOLDEN RULE

The Golden Rule is something all people understand. *Following* the Rule is another discussion, but the schools have waged war against parents who have not prepared their own children "to do onto others as you would have them do onto you." One thing that gets through to children is when they must walk around for a while in someone else's shoes to understand the plights of others. This doesn't require much thinking on the part of kids; children, especially the younger ones, tend to be empathy magnets.

FAVORING CAPITALISM

Even while being critical of American policies at home and abroad, teachers admit that America is the best place on the planet. With all its flaws, America still beats the rest. A popular history teacher asked his students which they thought was better: socialism or capitalism. Before listening to his students' answers, the teacher taught them that socialism promotes *equity*, and capitalism encourages *competition*.

With socialism, the teacher said, everyone is about the same; everyone has something, though no one has too much. With capitalism, everyone strives for the most they can get; the sky is the limit. In doing so, people might obtain everything they have ever wanted, and then some. Or they might wind up with nothing.[7]

Teachers in the public school system do not defile capitalism. Sure, they may critique it, analyzing its flaws. But teachers, as a rule, promote capitalism, from aggressively singing its praises, to encouraging their students to join clubs, in which they buy and sell stock or figure out how to make a profit marketing lemonade on their street corners.

ESTABLISHING BOUNDARIES

At a given point, there is a line you may not cross, a place you may not go. Adults get certain privileges that children do not. Better students earn favors for having gotten good grades; lesser students do not receive these privileges.

You may write for the school newspaper, take photos for the annual yearbook, or carry signs protesting the insipid-tasting food on campus. The powers that be at the school tell you that you can't jot down certain inflammatory words in the school paper; you may not post yearbook pictures of a student sneaking a joint near the boys' locker bay. And those protest pickets about food are not allowed near the cafeteria, where, presumably, they would have their most potent effect.

Incessant bell ringing signifies the beginnings and ends of classes. You need a hall pass to wander over to the bathroom. You might even live under the tyranny of a dress code that prohibits you from exposing your navel. Social engineering at its best teaches order for the good of the many; social engineering at its worst teaches order to make it easier for lambs to be led to slaughter.

REINFORCING SCIENCE

Little children are told about science from a very early age. Their curiosity about what goes up must come down reaches a crescendo when they topple off a windowsill or try to sail through the air like Superman, discovering that flying is a lot harder than it looks.

Teachers usually criticize those that attack science or are unaccepting of its precepts. "How dumb those early explorers had been! They thought the world was flat!" Or, "They swore that the sun goes around the earth!" The scientists that were originally wrong in their calculations are considered archaic, short-sighted, old and feeble. They have been replaced by better scientists and updated—even hipper—theories.

Most teachers convey that science is the gospel; renown scientists are on the same rung of the reverence ladder as Jesus. The schools reinforce scientific theories, providing a foundation for a student's possibly becoming a successful scientist. Teachers point out to their students the importance of hard work and developing a driving curiosity for understanding why everything works the way that it does. Teachers want their students to realize there are smarter people in the world than they are, who work harder than they do, and have discovered answers to questions no one else before now has been able to find.

American schools have always "socially engineered" children. In the past, however, parents were on board with the results of that "engineering." Recent curriculum changes and woke pedagogy may be changing all that.

THE MYTH OF OPEN-MINDED DISCUSSIONS

Hey, sweet, blue-eyed little girl; hi, rambunctious, energetic, well-meaning adolescent dude: *They want you.*

Nancy A. Thomer wrote in 2018, "Children in our public schools are being pummeled with political correctness. Specific assignments and class discussions are designed purposely to promote specific political viewpoints which may seriously oppose those of their parents. This new political correctness is carefully woven through textbooks and classroom assignments starting in kindergarten and reaches its apex in college."[8]

Woke organizers target kids; by virtue of specific strategies, they aim at American children as their bullseye. And they have reasons:

Children carry the torches of tradition. Those traditions are generational; they may cross over several decades of living and loving and yearning. If you teach a 60-year-old something, he may die in five years and, likely, what he has been taught dies with him. If you teach a child something, she has the potential to pass it on to untold numbers of others—and so on down.

Children live to be malleable. The younger the children, the easier it is to work inside their heads, hearts, and souls. Parents teach right from wrong, but not all children have parents; and even among the kids that do, those parents may lack the necessary skills or willingness to impart moral wisdom.

From the day they are born, children are empty vessels. They will fill up with *something*; ideally, they fill up with the *good* stuff. As far as information and knowledge are concerned, kids know little by the time they get to kindergarten. With both parents working, one-parent families ubiquitous, or narcissistic parents roaming free to produce as many children as they can without having learned how to parent even one child, the sky is the limit for those inside (and outside) education that wish to "mold" young minds.

Society trusts the schools. At least, they did before the coronavirus fanned the flames of fear. With teachers' unions dictating the direction of American schools—and much else—it wasn't hard for public opinion to polarize for, or against, the education establishment.

Before recently, however, teachers had been revered. To be a teacher was to be in a noble—albeit underpaid—profession. America respected its teachers. Parents liked teachers, especially their own kids' teachers. In the past, movements by groups outside the mainstream of education spurred controversy with their demands for sex education, drug and alcohol awareness, and behind-the-wheel driver training. Occasionally, a parent protested a particular book being taught in a literature course or a lesson in a science class (evolution comes to mind). For the most part, the community had faith in its educators to make decisions that were for the good of their children and in the best interests of America.

Children absorb—and believe—what is taught to them. The trust factor permeates all aspects of culture, and nowhere is it more apparent than in the schools. Because kids are easy to influence, educators exert almighty power that often defies the imagination. This may be compared to advertisers that go after consumers, mainly children. Whether it is a cereal commercial on television, or a new video game being hyped on Instagram, corporations know that music, movies, games, and food are easy to push on youngsters.

It isn't that kids are gullible; they are, um, *enthusiastic*. *Media Smarts* reported in April 2021, "Kids represent an important demographic to marketers because in addition to their own purchasing power [which is considerable], they influence their parents' buying decisions and are the adult consumers of the future."[9]

It's easy pick-ins, too. When a corporation (or union leader or political special interest group) pays close attention to kids' needs and wants, they bolster the self-esteem of those kids (and their parents). According to the book *Kidfluence*, "A school setting delivers a captive youth audience and implies the endorsement of teachers and the educational system."[10]

However, more than just *implying* its influence, it *states* that influence. It is an *absolute*. Schools influence their clients (students), their hired professionals, their communities, and their societies. It *starts* with children. They are the target, the mark, the goal. Get 'em while they're young; the effects may carry on for generations.

WOKE SHOOTS ITSELF IN THE FOOT

International influencers have identified themselves and readily admitted that your children are ideal agents for change. The globalist view of American education has been around for a while.

Sometimes special interests pop up, and no one knows why they exist or what they do. It is clear, however, that they have designs to make a lot of money, and they sell themselves in bulk to the schools. Reading their ads, you would see that they don't try to disguise themselves. It's as if they have no shame. And never did. From an advertisement brochure: their marketing pitch to what usually begins as a naive, initially well-intentioned, school district: *Teach Woke is a global education consulting company that provides race and equity workshops to teachers, leaders, and schools to develop antiracist agents of change.*[11]

They offer a short justification for their initial statement:

> Educators play a crucial role in helping students talk openly about the historical roots and contemporary manifestations of systemic racism and social inequality. Racism and injustice are still prevalent in our modern-day school system.

These workshops for educators start out benign. Usually heading the agenda is a noninflammatory discussion about the economic inequities that plague the schools. No surprises arise from that bout of rhetoric. But then this: *Children of color score lower than white kids and Asian kids on standardized tests; let's figure out why. . . .* At this point in the conversation the terrifying ordeal begins.[12]

What has begun as (that familiar) four-hour workshop at which a thirty-year-old middle school teacher sneaks away from his campus and enjoys a cup of coffee and a donut two or three times during the in-service, eventually blows up into something more. Much more.

Again, from the advertising brochure for *Teach Woke*: "Many educators avoid talking about race and racism because it calls for skills few of us possess. *Teach Woke* is helping solve this problem!"[13]

The *Teach Woke* folks provide the strategies all right; they use the same innate skills that most teachers already possess—their professionally honed instructional skills—to convey their beliefs about the newly ordered curriculum.

Those "skills" they're referring to? *Just teach*. Adhere to the fresh curriculum guidelines in almost every subject matter, at every grade level in the public schools and—and *woke*! The result is that your children are guided, mostly by the professionals they already know and respect, to hate the United States of America.

The truth of the matter—this can't be emphasized enough—is that rank-and-file teachers love the schools in which they teach; they love their curriculum, and they love their students. Kids *do* come first. Listening to these teachers' leaders, though, paints a different portrait of educators. The Chicago Teachers' Union issued this statement on December 24, 2020: "The push to reopen schools is rooted in sexism, racism, and misogyny."[14]

Perhaps, that is all you need to know about the Chicago Teachers' Union. Notice there is no mention of the emotional, mental, physical, or intellectual suffering of Chicago's children, the kids that are being taught by members of the Chicago Teachers' Union. Those students languish at home in front of their computer screens (if they are fortunate enough to have one), trying to learn in a mode that doesn't suit them. And that lasted for over a year!

How many of Chicago's parents that could not go back to work because their kids had been stuck at home said, "Well, good, I'm glad that my kids' teachers aren't going back to the classroom; it is antiwomen and racist to expect the teachers to go back to work!"?[15]

Distorted logic like this confounds parents. Intelligent, educated people such as teachers, counselors, and heads of major lobbying groups believe that they can coyly sneak through a few suggestions for monumental cultural changes in American society. They mark children as their agents to initiate those changes. Astonishingly, the wokes had convinced each other—and themselves—that the parents of America's kids wouldn't notice anything. But they *have* noticed. Quisha King's rallying cry in front of a school board: "I really think at this point the only thing to do is have a mass exodus from the public school system—that's it."[16]

That is the frustrated proposition of a *parent*, a mother of a grade-schooler: everyone should walk out on the public schools! You may hear it again; it is only the beginning of parents' noble and strenuous efforts, cautiously celebrated in chapter 14.

It used to be that school meant a sanctuary for children. Yeah, a certain amount of social engineering took place. But parents didn't care, because the vast majority of them were on board with promoting patriotism and family and capitalism. They *wanted* their children's education at school to buttress what they were teaching their kids at home. *They still do.* Children of all races and creeds, cultures and nationalities, genders and sexual orientations want the adults in their lives to *lead*, and they want to be able to trust them.

NOTES

1. Christopher Dodd, "Franklin Child Development," *The Franklin Health Department*, 2021. franklinchilddevelopment.com. Senator Dodd said these words in

a discussion about proposed education legislation. His words have become famous and are posted on numerous education websites.

2. John Dean, Professor of Education, Whittier College, course: *Methods in the Secondary School*, August, 1971.

3. *Lixico*, 2021, https://www.lexico.com/en/definition/social_engineering

4. During the 1960s and 1970s, many schools experimented with various types of authority allocations; sometimes they experimented by awarding students unusual amounts of power. Those experiments usually failed.

5. David Brooks, "The Nuclear Family Was a Mistake," *The Atlantic*, March, 2020 Issue, p. 1.

6. Mike Stobbe and Collin Brinkley, "Vaccinated Teachers and Students Don't Need Masks, CDC Says," *AP*, July 9, 2021. https://apnews.com/article/lifestyle-science-health-education-coronavirus-pandemic-a65c9c0375ce441fcd10866eb8ea990b

7. In order to use the actual names of those involved in stories, interviews, and examples for this book, I asked for written consent. Also, I had to be careful about divulging the locations of specific schools and school districts. Sometimes fictitious names were used; other times, no names were used.

8. Nancy A. Thormer, "Social Engineering-Transferring Parental Control Of Children To Teachers," *The Heartland Institute*, January 24, 2018, par. 1. https://www.heartland.org/news-opinion/news/social-engineering---transferring-parental-control-of-children-to-teachers

9. Barbara A. Martino, "How Marketers Target Kids," *Media Smarts*, 2008, par. 1. https://mediasmarts.ca/digital-media-literacy/media-issues/marketing-consumerism/how-marketers-target-kids

10. ibid., par. 7

11. *Teach Woke*, July 24, 2021, par. 1. https://www.teachwoke.com

12. In 2020, the University eliminated the Scholastic Aptitude Test (SAT) and other standardized tests as a condition for admittance, citing "inequitable" performances among Blacks and other persons of color on the exams. Translated: the SAT is racist.

13. ibid., par. 3

14. Robby Soave, "Chicago Teachers Union: 'The Push To Reopen Schools Is Rooted in Sexism, Racism, and Misogyny,'" *Reason*, June 20, 2020, https://reason.com/2020/12/06/chicago-teachers-union-reopen-schools-sexism-racism-misogyny/

15. This comment from the teachers' union is replete with non-sequiturs: for example, what does a teacher returning—or not returning—to work in her classroom have to do with sexism, racism, or misogyny? Seriously. I must have missed that little tidbit.

16. Sam Dorman, "Florida Mom Gets Standing Ovation," Fox News, October 8, 2021. www.foxnews.com/us/florida-mom-virginia-mass-exodus-public-schools

Chapter 2

Old. White. Dead Men

RACIST CARL

Most people know next to nothing about one of America's most influential poets, Carl Sandburg. If taught correctly to high school students, Carl Sandburg's poetry may entice children away from their iPhones and video games long enough for them to notice that poetry ain't all that bad; in fact, a poem by Carl Sandburg has the potential for crawling into their psyches and piquing their curiosities about subjects they didn't know they cared about. With teenagers, topics like poverty, self-discovery, and war usually prevail over poems on trivial topics, like trees and roses.

Most of Sandburg's antiwar rants happened during, and shortly after, World War I. Sandburg's poetry easily rivaled the works of Allen Ginsberg or Leonard Cohen,[1] but whereas Ginsberg and Cohen, hippies of the 1960s, entertained despair and death, Carl Sandburg, a hippie of years before, embraced optimism and life.

Recently, woke censors have spearheaded attempts to remove the works of, among others, Carl Sandburg from the secondary school curriculum—in some cases, even from school libraries. In a few states, Advanced Placement English exams may not be covering Sandburg's works. Soon California's students may not be able to distinguish Carl Sandburg from Colonel Sanders.[2]

Targeted pieces include the likes of *The Leaves of Grass*, "The People, Yes," "Fog," "Threes," and countless other poems that captured the essence, the soul of America, during times of great divide. Who could read "Chicago" and not come away in wonderment over Sandburg's ability to personify a magnificent city, to the point in which it seems to want to jump off the page and into your soul!

Matthew Priggue, dutifully reported in the *Milwaukee Journal*, on May 29, 2018, "Sandburg was much more than just a poet. He wrote novels and children's stories, recorded folk music, and published an exhaustive six-volume biography of Abraham Lincoln. Later in life, he appeared regularly on television and became the first white man ever to receive the *NAACP's Silver Plaque Award for his work for the Civil Rights Movement* (italics added)."[3]

Sandburg also won a few Pulitzer Prizes, two for his poetry and one for his biographies of Abraham Lincoln. Why was this great poet being ousted from its scholarly midst in American secondary education?

On April 21, 2020, Asante Lake commented on an online platform that published Sandburg's controversial poem, "Nigger." Not surprisingly, in the year the poem was written, 1916, only a modest controversy ensued. Today, the poem falls into a narrative of either overt racism, or racism of a more subdued, subliminal variety. Lake writes, "When this poem was written, racism was a taken-for-granted reality in an America that was built on a solid pillar of racism."[4]

She is referring to slavery here; no one would disagree with her assessment of an America that was *then* built on a "solid pillar of racism." Lake continues, "To suggest that Carl Sandburg was *not* racist is to suggest he was immune to the pervasive racism he was immersed in as a white man."[5]

Lake implies that Carl Sandburg was racist, because he could not be anything else *but* racist. (How does one go about refuting *that*!) If Sandburg had written from his own experiences, he would have recognized his "white male privilege." Sandburg could have denounced that privilege. Or he would have apologized for it. Or maybe he should have died before he had written anything else controversial. His poem's title would not have contained the N-word.

Most of those that actually *read* the poem, understand that it shows Sandburg had sympathy for Black people—more than most people back then had sympathy for Black people. (His future works, mainly his biography of Lincoln, confirmed this.) Sandburg appeared to be about as much against racism as you can get.

A segment of the population, along with literary and social critics, want more from people who aren't racist. They want more than sympathy: They want *empathy*. If you don't show empathy, you don't understand. You *can't* relate if you are white. So white people are inherently incapable of not being racist.

Join the group, Carl.

In some school districts, Carl Sandburg can't join the group. He has been banned. To be fair, it is worth noting that except for a few crackpots that sit in high offices of teachers' unions, school districts, or state legislatures, Carl Sandburg is still widely recognized for his tolerance: his affinity for the downtrodden, his love of nature, his standards of fairness for racial minorities, his compassion for immigrants, migrants, and marginalized workers.

Yet, despite this, Sandburg's use of one word—a hundred years ago, widely uttered to disparage African Americans—has obliterated an understanding of Carl Sandburg's true worth in the classroom, and has, at the very least, marred some educators' and historians' perceptions of any positive traits to his character.

OLD DEAD WHITE MEN

Progressive educators and some parents have categorized Carl Sandburg classified as an "old dead white man," and this is the *real* reason his works have been slowly disappearing from libraries, anthologies, and classroom bookshelves in the public schools. Old dead white men are *out*. Old dead white women, like Kate Chopin, Emily Dickinson, and Willa Cather, have a feeble chance to survive, though Cather's themes may be a bit too traditional for advancing the culture, for fostering antisexist attitudes in young America.[6]

Here are a few reasons wokes believe kids should not study the works of old dead white men.

1. The authors are *old*. Kids in school are *young*. Younger authors relate better to children, and vice-versa: children relate better to younger authors. Why is all this relating good? Younger authors know how children feel; children tend to trust younger authors—or younger people, in general. What do kids want with some writer that looks like he belongs in a Fox News commercial?
2. They are *dead*. Some kids will tell you that there is something icky about reading stuff written by dead people. Dead people aren't just *old*, they are *really* old; in fact, they are so old . . . they are dead and have been dead for a long time. Reading dead people is not hip. Dead people aren't hip, unless, of course, they are vampires or zombies.
3. They are *white*. Society constantly tells its children that a person's skin color should not matter in determining the quality of their art or the content of their character. But educators have so repeatedly trumpeted to kids about the beauty of racial diversity, they have become confused about that ol' "skin color shouldn't matter" thing.
4. They are *men*. It is now vogue in education to teach that men are bad, or that boys can't measure up to girls. The patriarchy runs the show, and negative associations—there are many—with anything male shapes reactions to male authors.

Old. White. Men. When you put them all together . . . *bippity-boppity-boo*! The Cancel Culture hat trick! *Three strikes, and you're out*! That's enough;

that's all that it takes. Add *dead*, and it cranks up the negativity. Literature doctors diagnose the *symptoms* of old dead white men, authors of yesteryear, and their findings are straightforward: racists, out of touch, outdated vocabularies, old-fashioned, outmoded values and morals, lacking diversity in their works. The grim truth is these guys gotta go. They are old, dead, white, and men: the four deadliest sins.

Not all those writers are heterosexual Christians: Walt Whitman's homosexuality and his agnosticism are now well known. But agnostic and homosexual writers, even Whitman, are not immune to attack. They are still casualties. They are old and white and male and dead. They need to move over, make room for a cooler, hipper breed of gay authors.

Benjamin Haber, high school English teacher and curriculum designer (which is a new one), wrote, "The kids' eyes gloss over every time I introduce a new book to them . . . I can feel the stagnation in the classroom . . . as my students do quick mental comparisons to some of the comedians they admire or the musicians they like . . . all of whom are young . . . men and women of color . . . mostly women."[7]

Which is a tricky point, because this teacher insinuates that most boys like entertainers that are mostly women. This may, or may not, be true, but it is quite a leap to go from old dead white men are boring to . . . *gee, I wish we could read writers that are more like the hot* chicks *in the entertainment industry. . . . Lady Gaga comes to mind.*

If there is a commentary to be made on the gender of the writers and the lack of diversity in assigned literature—this is true in grades K–12—that commentary would focus on the lack of interesting literature for *boys*. Young boys tend to disdain picture books that highlight little girls frolicking in flowery meadows, or in a more formal setting, such as a bunch of young women studying in a classroom. (Young boys may disdain any association with *anyone* studying, but that's an issue to be taken up at another time.)

The literature for older kids is not as blatant in its lack of boy appeal, but most short stories in anthologies that have become a part of textbook adoptions in the past forty years cater to girls, not the least of which are *Twilight, The Hunger Games*, or *Romeo and Juliet*, which has been around since the beginning of time. Your author is sorry for having to say this, but few boys he taught expressed any affection for this play, about two prepubescent, lovestruck children, compelling themselves to suicide after a brief dramatic fling. Boys, on the other hand, enjoyed Shakespeare's *Julius Caesar*, because it was about power and loyalty and vengeance—violent stuff—which young men tend to prefer over sappy romantic fiction.

Getting boys to read has been a source of perpetual annoyance. Boys don't read. They don't like to read. They like to destroy things, while moving around a lot. A boy's hesitancy to dive into a piece of literature is not because a bunch of old dead white men wrote most of the books being taught in schools. Boys require more stimuli than most books can provide them.

If teachers are going to capture the attention of boys, something interesting must instantly pop out at them. Whatever form that "something" takes, it may have little to do with the color of an author's skin, or the number of wrinkles on his forehead.

Old dead white men also tend to be—if you pay attention to the critics—misogynists. Depending upon whose definitions of *misogyny* strike you as suitable, you may find old dead white guys perfect templates for misogyny and sexism. Definitions play an important role in determining labels, like misogyny or homophobia or racism. But if you're in a hurry, and your audience is young and wide-eyed and trusting, who *needs* to create an objective template! Simply, label people as you see fit, and call those who disagree with you *bigots* of one kind or another.

Sexism and misogyny are embedded in lists of "what's to be worried about" by those who are perennially appalled at what society is doing to its children, *your* children: that teachers give them study materials and books that are mostly written by old dead white men.

Oh, the humanity!

Books of old dead white men still sit in the libraries and bookshelves of the public schools. With some exceptions, even the most adamant progressive educators do not want to ban completely a slew of books of one entire race or age or living status. The consensus, says James Seltzer of the American Book Academy, is for *adding* more pieces written by women, gays, LGBTQs, and authors of color. Groups exist for the sole purpose of doing just this: diversifying the overall pickings, opening the canon to all writers.[8]

Maybe a greater range of selections would attract more kids, particularly boys, to a reading culture. Maybe pushing for diversity, inclusion, and equity in literature for secondary and primary students is just the right formula, after so many years of stagnation.

Maybe. But before fully examining this concept, your author would like to look at a few examples of "cancel" that don't pull back when they throw a punch: the call to reject, not to add or push gently aside, a few of the most notable American authors of all time—and why these old dead white men are walking the literary plank.

John Steinbeck

The alleged racism of old dead white men pops up, while some modern critics examine the words of John Steinbeck. You've heard of that guy, right? He wrote *Of Mice and Men*, *The Grapes of Wrath*, and *East of Eden*. Oh, let's not forget *Tortilla Flat*, in which his depiction of minorities had later become an embarrassment to him, or so he said.[9]

Since its publication, Steinbeck scholars have grown "increasingly uneasy [and even embarrassed] about the portrayal of the *paisanos* in *Tortilla Flat*," writes Thomas French in his study of the author. "*Tortilla Flat* stands as the clearest example in American literature of the Mexican as jolly savage . . . . The novel contains characters varying little from the most negative Mexican stereotypes."[10] And in 1973, critic Philip D. Ortega concluded that *Tortilla Flat* was "a sad book in more ways than John Steinbeck may have ever imagined."[11]

Steinbeck's most popular novel, *Of Mice and Men*, has for decades warded off allegations of racism. Because of Steinbeck's depictions of minority stereotypes, and frequent use of the N-word, parents and community groups met last year to discuss the continued use of Steinbeck's story of friends, and wanderers, George and Lenny, as they try to figure out how to survive during the Great Depression.

The issue has become a simple one: Should America's teachers stick with *Of Mice and Men* in their classrooms? Most educators seem to think so, but if parents have the power of sway, they need to be smart. Covering one of these "important people" discussions for TV-FOX in Grand Rapids, columnist George Bovia wrote on February 23, 2020, "It's important for parents to familiarize themselves with material before diving into conversations about literature, and [parents are encouraged] to read literature from different perspectives and experiences."[12]

Eric Washington of Calvin University spoke of the use of the N-word. He mused, "Well, it's not right; it's never been right, but people [have to understand . . . context]."[13] That word—or any word—can be used properly, or improperly, depending upon the factors in the story that surround its use. Without an understanding of those factors, John Steinbeck would, indeed, sound like a racist. *With* the reader's understanding, Steinbeck clearly is not a bigot; he is the opposite.

e.e. cummings

It may take a special brand of scholar to view America's premiere modernist poet, e.e. cummings, as a racist. But there are those that would do just that; they would argue this position based on one poem, written long before cummings had become popular. The poem itself was untitled, but that was the only saving grace. Published in *The Atlantic*, on May 25, 2011, entertainment journalist, Ray Gustini, shared this view: "We now know that [cummings] did not like Black people."[14]

And Gustini then supported his statement with this shocker: "Author and poet James Dempsey has unearthed a long-lost cummings poem, which he found in a folder of the poet's correspondence, while doing research for a biography. . . . To call the untitled work, with its repeated use of the N-word and overall feeling of racial panic, a 'problem poem' would be an understatement."[15]

There are seven uses of the N-word. In context, or out of context, it's an ugly read. You might try to defend the poem as literature that can be deconstructed for purely academic reasons, as Ted Burke attempted to accomplish in his article, "Was e.e. cummings a Racist?" Burke wrote, "I suspect he meant [the N-word] to be a synonym for *night* or a term equally nocturnal: A quiet winter night in winter, snow on the houses, the lights are out. There is a subtext here, to be sure, the obvious ones being the sexual attraction of whites to Blacks, but there are nearly always subtexts and ambiguity in poems. cummings purpose is not to offend, but to create tension, denoting abstract virtues of black and white."[16]

Even so, once readers get past the highfalutin, esoteric, artistic jargon, they may wind up with a nagging feeling that cummings could have written this poem without using such a galling word, one offensive to most of his readers. Defenders would claim that at the time, the N-word was not offensive, but descriptive, and its use to introduce startling metaphors into the writing was nothing more, or nothing less, than a powerful writing tool.

The bottom line: Using that word, in that context (or, currently, in *any* context), is not a way to ensure one's own commercial or artistic longevity.

Arthur Miller

This old, dead, white writer may be the greatest American playwright in history. The *Telegraph* speculated in July of 2020 that Miller and Shakespeare share the stage for being the greatest playwrights ever. "His plays, with their strong emphasis on family, morality and personal responsibility, were seen as epitomizing the splintering fragments of American society and speaking to those living the broken promises behind the American Dream."[17] Kevin McCaffrey, in the same publication, goes on to say, "The complex bonds and conflicts between Willy and Biff Loman are universal. It is sad that such a powerful voice as Miller's has passed into silence."[18]

The praise for the works of Arthur Miller, for seventy years a mainstay in the libraries and classrooms of high schools and universities all over America, is endless. There are no accusations of racism, misogyny (though Linda, in *Death of a Salesman*, is a doting wife, the housewife/mother that puts the needs of her husband and sons before hers. Some may consider that sexist, white privilege, or antiglobalism, or some other *anti* or *ist* thing.) If you dig deeply enough into the bowels of literary criticism, you would be able to find, among scattered banter, men and women that accuse Miller of being a racist or misogynist—or worse, a true believer in the American Dream and American exceptionalism. But Miller's works deny the tenability of those notions.

Miller's future in the literary canon is dismissed not because he is racist, misogynistic, or materialistic; Arthur Miller is doomed because he is old, dead, white, and male. Never mind that "his works are timeless for all ages." He has been around for too many ages. He is boring. And he isn't boring because he is classically dull; he is boring because he is old, dead, white, and male, a benefactor of white privilege. Seventeen-year-old Hispanic kids can't relate. Time to go.

These are but few of the old dead white men (and in a few cases women), whose novels sit in libraries, reeking with a stench that reminds educators of old people. Plenty of old dead white women books also lie on endangered species lists, but you hardly ever get the sense of foreboding when it comes to pieces of literature by female authors, no matter what their age.

Five classic young adult novels that have been *loved* by those seventeen-year-old Hispanic kids, among others, were challenged last year in a Burbank, California, school district: Harper Lee's *To Kill a Mockingbird*, Mark Twain's *The Adventures of Huckleberry Finn*, John Steinbeck's *Of Mice and Men*, Theodore Taylor's *The Cay,* and Mildred D. Taylor's Newbery Medal-winning *Roll of Thunder, Hear My Cry*.[19] (The latter book was written by a Black author.) Dorany Pineda of the *Los Angeles Times* reported, "Unless teachers have been specifically trained to teach these texts through an antiracist lens, they are probably reinforcing racism rather than dismantling it."[20] ("Atticus, are you a nigger lover?" "Yes, I am, Scout. I love all people.")[21]

The argument has been made for compromise. After all, many claim there's room in the schools for *all* books. For years, educators have accomplished diversity in literature. Sandra Cisneros, Amy Tang, and Gary Soto have brought laughter and tears to the lives of school children. Why not introduce additional writers of color? Simply factor in the pieces that bring more diversity into education, and problem solved!

One problem arises when teachers don't know how to handle (or teach) the themes presented by woke authors—dealing with police brutality, institutional racism, transgender self-discovery, abortion, and teenage sexual relationships. Though it is not cool for them to admit it, most teachers would rather talk about the friendship bonds between George and Lenny.

GAY INFUSION, GENDER CONFUSION

Schools, with their emphasis on heterosexual writers, most of them old, dead, white, and male, shrank from the responsibility of taking on the problems of gay children; after all, gay was out, especially gay boys. Children maligned other children and saved an especially savage dose of teasing for those with "gay-sounding" voices and "gay-looking" mannerisms. Most teachers critically observed this disturbing behavior in their students; some teachers didn't appear to be bothered by it.

GLADD spokesperson Allie Conway posed a remedy: "Older kids need to read about other kids who are like they are. . . . Younger kids should learn not to judge other kids that are different. . . . Literature for children of all ages should sometimes be written by gay authors."[22]

The broader issue of sexuality and the attempt to alter kids' understanding of it, and to illicit reactions to it, is handled in other chapters of this text. Here, however, the actions, trends, and movements regarding the introduction of a Language Arts curriculum that includes plentiful discussions of homosexuality are dissected. Here it comes and in a flurry. Take a deep breath:

The Use of Pieces Written by LGBTQ Authors

From 2006–2012, several new self-proclaimed gay authors of poetry, novels, books, magazine articles, newspaper columns, pamphlets, short stories, and so on, were *introduced* [italics added] to school children. Their works were officially adopted by school boards. Unofficially, teachers introduced other artists' creations, including paintings, drawings, sculptures, and music pieces. From 2012 to the present, more gay writers (and nongay writers that wrote about gay characters or topics surrounding homosexuality) have been adopted.[23]

The New York City schools distributed materials for the current (20–21) school year: "Since 2015, Lambda Literary and the NYC Department of Education have worked together to bring LGBTQ writers into classrooms across New York City. The LGBTQ Writers in Schools Program provides critically necessary, safe spaces for students to talk about books, queer life, and how to thrive as a LGBTQ person."[24]

Self-help in this arena has also become popular in the schools. For high school, *Queer: The Ultimate LGBT Guide for Teens*, by Kathy Belge and Marke Bieschke, argues that different sexual and gender orientations exist out there, and that kids, as well as their families, are dealing with it the best they can. The book comments, "Teen life is hard enough."[25]

Fawn Naverreti reviews: "*Queer* is a humorous, engaging, and honest guide that helps LGBT teens come out to friends and family, navigate their new LGBT social life, figure out if a crush is also queer, and revolt against bigotry and homophobia. *Queer* also includes personal stories from the authors and sidebars on queer history."[26]

This was not exactly the type of self-help literature that your author had offered to his students back in the day.

Diana Souza's *Heather Has Two Mommies* came on the scene more than three decades ago and is now a mainstay in elementary school classrooms around the nation. *Thrift Books* reported in 2020, "The Thirty-year Anniversary release is a reissue of the classic children's story that tells the simple and straightforward tale of a little girl called Heather and her upbringing by two lesbian mothers. Originally published in 1990, to considerable controversy, it has now established itself as part of the cultural lexicon."[27]

According to teachers that use this book, the writer implies that "two Mommies" sometimes just happens. It's different, though, even cool; and in the story, while Heather must deal with a lot of questions, some of them of her own making, she does just fine.

The Emergence of LGBTQ Clubs on Campuses

During the 1990s, clubs were formed on high school campuses solely for the purpose of supporting gay kids. Teachers involved in your author's school's Gay Alliance Club spoke glowingly about how well their students got along. The children claimed they finally had discovered somewhere to go, a place in which they felt comfortable around peers that would not judge them.

By the end of 2019, most high schools in the United States had boasted of gay identity clubs of one kind or another. They were increasing, notably at middle school campuses. Several elementary schools formally organized clubs for children who thought they might be gay or had "odd" feelings and desires they could not explain, which most adults couldn't explain either, so everyone was confused.

Curriculum Alterations to Include LGBTQ Discussions

Sometimes teachers mentioned to their students that Whitman was gay. Whether or not teachers told their students of Whitman's sexuality sometimes had to do with pushing a social agenda; oftentimes it had nothing to do with this. Innocuous enough, teachers sometimes taught Whitman, with the sole intent of getting their students interested in *this* poet: surely, a gay man, writing about being a medic in ferocious Civil War battles, would intrigue them, would obliterate the stereotype!

Sometimes it did; sometimes it didn't.

That kind of discussion would today be mandatory in most of the public schools around the United States.

Several teachers, acquaintances of your writer—not all of them teach literature—have assigned or recommended to their students books, movies, TV shows, animation series, and video games featuring L-lesbian, B-bisexual, G-gay, T-transexual characters. Are these teachers trying to push their agendas, or are their motivations less selfish and more on the benevolent side?

One local teacher, now retired, had a reputation for asking her high school literature students to read, and report on, books like *Warrior Women* (lesbian main characters, all in positive relationships), *The Dark Light Years* (gender-shifting aliens, gay male characters), *All the Birds in the Sky* (nonbinary asexual characters), *2312* (genderqueer major characters society in which nonbinary fluid gender and sexuality are embraced).[28] That teacher has familiarity with a website, in which you may view a list of over a hundred pieces of fiction containing LGBTQ main characters and themes. A few years ago, even *one* of these books would have driven most parents to a Monday night local school board meeting.

Why had this teacher been so adamant about suggesting LGBTQ literature to her students? She pointed out that she currently had gay or bisexual students in her classes. She also indicated she had a hunch one of her students was a transgender kid.

Mary Miller and Bonnie Blackburn explained, "Though the classroom may not be a completely safe place, creating a safe enough place can allow students opportunities to approach, discuss, and enjoy LGBTQ-themed literature and have an impact on the many LGBTQ students who experience unsafe and discriminatory school environments."[29]

Most educators would now label this new emphasis on gender introspection an act of tolerance or open-mindedness: Allowing opposing viewpoints, a description—even a study—of different lifestyles and genders and sexualities is compassionate; it is enriching for students that are not LGBTQ or don't know anyone who is—or haven't been familiarized with the topic.

The National Council of Teachers in 2013 passed a resolution advocating, "strengthening teacher knowledge of gay, lesbian, bisexual, and transgender issues."[30] Studies have shown that the more teachers become acquainted with these issues, and how to teach them, the more sympathetic—and in some cases empathetic—they grow. [Empathy is] the big step, one hoped for by advocates and supporters of the schools, leading the way in making social changes.[31]

Miller and Blackburn claim that teachers should incorporate LGBTQ material into their curriculum, not just for the purpose of making kids feel better about who they are; *they want the schools to social engineer*. They are clear about this. It's not just about the children; it's about changing society.

They continue, "Teaching is inherently political, and it is necessary for teachers to take a stance that explicitly and actively advocates for LGBTQ students. LGBTQ-themed literature addresses issues of identity relatable to all students, and conversations on equality and action are transferable to other conversations on civil rights and *social justice* (italics added)."[32]

OUT WITH THE OLD, IN WITH THE NEW

One shouldn't be too quick to pass over a couple of other areas in the English/Language Arts curriculum in the schools, and how they have been affected by more recent movements that have succeeded in making changes in what American kids are learning.

Teaching Writing Content

Teachers used to teach writing in terms of, well, teaching *writing*: enhancing creativity, getting started, internally organizing, developing sentences, having a voice, obtaining a style, summarizing thoughts, using supporting evidence, clarifying ideas, and using proper grammar and punctuation. Nowhere on this list is there something about *reinforcing writing content via the teacher's personal biases*.

The following comment comes from a high school (or former) student, Bryce:[33]

> I don't dare give a speech on why I would vote for Donald Trump in 2020. If my teacher doesn't flunk me, my classmates will harass me.

An online high school teacher in Colorado dismissed a male student from his virtual class, because the boy sat flanked by posters of President Trump.[34] In a highly charged political climate this kind of behavior by a teacher is not unusual. Most students do not want to report incidents of overt bias, because they fear grading reprisals. To be fair: most teachers can contain their prejudices and don't react unreasonably toward their students while editing and scoring writing assignments. But today's curriculum crusades are potent, and their effects long-lasting. So, some topic choices require a special brand of fortitude.

Teaching Grammar

English grammar tickles some teachers' fancy. Because they are sticklers for proper word usage, sentence construction, rules, and punctuation, they sometimes become irritated when their students let them down by getting sloppy in their word usage. And then there's the teacher that annoys students with verb-subject agreement, tense consistency, and properly matching pronouns with their antecedents:

> *If a **stranger** walks up to you, and **he** demands that you hand **him** your wallet, just give it to **him**.*

The antecedent *stranger* is a singular noun. The pronoun must agree with its antecedent in *number*. In order to do this, you use the singular/neuter pronoun *he*. *He* is also singular. So why use the masculine pronoun? In this context, *he* is not masculine; *he* is neuter. *He* just sounds masculine. This sometimes lands teachers in trouble, because the unspoken rule is to use the combined *he/she* or *him/her*. Or they like to use *he or she* or *him or her*. Adherence to those traditional stipulations send messages to the woke watchers. And they're not good ones. Those teachers signal to their union leaders that they are sexist.

Today the key challenge isn't getting the gender right. The key challenge is not to worry about pronoun antecedent agreement when it comes to number. The politically correct grammar cops now want people to say, *if a stranger walks up to you and asks you for your wallet, just hand it to **them***.

Most people would see nothing wrong with that sentence. But agents of the grammar *Gestapo*, would see a lot wrong with it: how on grammar's green earth may a *plural* pronoun (them) be matched with a *singular* antecedent (stranger)? There is only *one* dang stranger! How can you hand the wallet to *them*?

Call in the progressive grammar gods. Hans Roscoe Finkelstein wrote, "They proclaim that it is admissible to break the chain of traditional grammar rules . . . because [of the need to] . . . strike a fair balance in their march toward gender inclusion."[35]

Huh?

Maybe he is (*they* are) arguing, that in the scheme of things, it is okay to twist, or change, old-fashioned rules in grammar for the purpose of making people of all genders feel included. What many people have noticed is weird pronoun spellings and awkward syntax have become commonplace in the last few years. The LGBTQ Resource Center recently helped out on that: "*Ze* is pronounced like 'zee,' can also be spelled *zie* or *xe*, and replaces she/he/they. *Hir* is pronounced like 'here' and replaces her/hers/him/his/they/theirs."[36] Just the antecedent please! (Ash ate Ash's food because Ash was hungry.) Some people prefer not to use pronouns at all, using their name as a pronoun substitute. *Jeb is hungry. Please pass the plate of mashed potatoes to Jeb*, said Jeb. One may hope there is not another Jeb in the room, for fear that the original Jeb might starve to death.

These lessons are not only *coming* to the schools. They are already here, and in some sections of the country, they have been here for a while. Pronouns may be delicately handled by schools, businesses, and government employees. As a college instructor, when your author signs his name, he is expected to sign, *Bruce J. Gevirtzman, preferred pronouns he/his/him*. Supposedly, this is a mere safeguard, just in case people can't figure out what he is. As he gets older, he has more empathy for that position, and doesn't blame someone else if *they* can't figure out what the heck he/she/it is, either.

Teaching Public Speaking in the Classroom

In recent years, changes have come to the public speaking curriculum in American education.

Selecting topics for a classroom speech is dicey, because speeches, unlike essays, are delivered in a public forum. It used to be that students selected speech topics on anything they wanted. Of course, there were those pesky rules of decorum, but students rarely selected topics that were inappropriate for the classroom, such as how to make a bomb, how to grow marijuana in your backyard, or how to get a woman to have sex with you.

Because teachers occasionally lambasted students for their inappropriate choices, most students had grown wiser from another's, or their own, experiences. Students practiced free speech—within reason—and chose their positions on whatever topics they wanted. They kept away from profanities and racial slurs. "Freedom means responsibility,"[37] was taught to children; most kids figured that out when it came to their public speaking classes.

Today many public educators stifle students' expression of ideas. Here are some real-world examples of prohibitions and mandates, those that are initiated by teachers, administrators, boards of education, members of state and federal legislatures, political leaders, and the public, most of whom adore free speech and honor its Constitutional protections . . . except for those instances in which they disagree with what is being said.

- inappropriate pronoun gender uses
- negative references to homosexuality, bisexuality, or transgenderism
- selective criticism of affirmative action, quota systems
- "improperly," or "inaccurately," referencing American history
- selective criticism of religion, *except for Christianity* (italics added)[38]

- praise for patriarchal run societies
- arguments in favor of marriage
- arguments against marriage between two men or two women
- criticism of alternative lifestyles, such as cohabitation without marriage
- expressions of dismay or disagreement with modern feminism
- criticism of transgender athletes
- invalidation of the coronavirus vaccines
- using certain terms or words is out: Muslim terrorists, shit-hole country, illegal aliens, third world country, colored person (as opposed to person of color), boomer remover, senior deleter (even in jest, they are prohibited, and if you laugh at this gallows humor, you must be an insensitive oaf), old people, Chinese Virus, thug, looter/rioter/arsonist (as opposed to protestor) and many more.
- questioning of the outcome or the legitimacy of the 2020 Presidential election
- support for American exceptionalism or nationalism
- support their right to speak: Milo Yiannopoulos, Ann Coulter, Ben Shapiro, etc.
- praise for certain celebrities: Rush Limbaugh, Tucker Carlson, Laura Ingram
- criticism of the "Me-Too" movement
- support for the presumption of innocence concept, via Brett Kavanaugh hearings
- during the worst times of COVID crisis, any criticism of mask wearing
- minimizing the extent or harms of the coronavirus
- criticism of non-Western cultural traditions
- criticism of *White Fragility*, the book
- debunking the theories of white guilt, white supremacy, white power, white privilege
- taking a stand against the intrinsic value of diversity
- against reparations for slavery
- agreeing with the verdict in the Kyle Rittenhouse trial
- criticism of President Obama or Michele Obama
- denying there was an "insurrection" at the Capitol on January 6, 2021
- praise for Dr. Laura
- taking a one-sided view (in favor of) the Electoral College
- denying theories that support human-caused climate change
- denying that all cultures are equally good or moral
- support for ex-President Trump
- express superiority of the Republican Party over the Democratic Party
- express that men are discriminated against, not women
- questions about the legitimacy of Black Lives Matter

- cops are basically good
- arguing against multiculturalism in education
- defending the National Anthem, "Under God" in the Pledge of Allegiance
- defending President Trump's response to the coronavirus
- express belief in natural differences between men and women
- ethnic humor or jokes
- arguing a political conspiracy to maintain lockdowns during the coronavirus
- debunking the seriousness of the Mueller investigation of Trump's ties to Russia
- accusing the Clintons of anything diabolical
- opposing coronavirus vaccine mandates

Most of these topics don't seem particularly controversial, but they have appeared on lists that educators and politicians would, for a variety of reasons, claim are too "dangerous" for speeches, debates, and other forms of oral discussions in a classroom, even at the high school level. And even in the United States of America.

Teaching Competitive Speech and Debate

American students, from grades 8 through 12, have reveled for decades in competitive speech and debate programs. Many have traveled around the country, fiercely competing in grueling tournaments. They have acquired scholarships, based on their talents and achievements, and been admitted into prestigious colleges. It is not surprising that hundreds of these children grew up and landed successful careers in law, business, politics, movies, stage, and education.

During the past five years or so, changes have come to the speech and debate world.

Some competitive events have flown the coup. Girls' extemporaneous speaking is gone for good, as is girls' oratory. The young ladies now compete in the categories of "mixed" extemporaneous speaking and "mixed" original oratory. Please don't ask what "mixed" means. The bottom line is that boys and girls are no longer divided into separate events.

Lincoln-Douglas Debate has been renamed "One-Person Debate." Considering that it takes at least *two* people to debate an issue competitively, go figure. The understanding is that issues of slavery were discussed during the original Lincoln-Douglas debates, and Douglas made a racist ass of himself. The competitive speech leagues concluded they could no longer sponsor an official debate event that was named after an allegedly foul-mouthed, bigoted guy like Stephen Douglas.

Discussions about speech and debate events on the national level, and on some state levels, have surged with references like—and this is a direct quotation: "Biases still exist. . . . 64 percent of the policy debates won at [this tournament] were by teams that had at least *one person that identifies as a male* [italics are added for emphasis], and 84 percent of those winning teams had *two people that identify as males.*"[39]

On the speech and debate circuit, these gender references have developed into formal procedures. You are not allowed to depart from this. If you question the lingo—there are plenty of other examples of curious language—you may be called a bigot.

On a Facebook site for the National High School Speech and Debate Association, a poster responded to a cheating scandal with this comment: "She [the alleged debate cheater] is propagating and producing future charlatans that might have influence in the world. It might just be a little indicative of *a toxic form of whiteness*" (italics added). What does "whiteness" have to do with a kid that may have fabricated evidence in a high school debate? There are no words to answer that question.

Anthropologist and famed author Margaret Mead took a lot of bashing from all sides of the political spectrum. She made one comment that seemed simple enough to understand but has been ominously ignored. Educators have heard her words—patterned after many others' words—echoing inside their heads for decades. They figured they could do a lot of good in their profession if they taught students according to Mead's philosophy: "It is important to know that children should be taught *how* to think, not *what* to think."

When that doesn't happen—if, in fact, the exact opposite occurs—there comes a point at which the damage done to America cannot be repaired.

NOTES

1. Ginsburg and Cohen were hailed as the most poignant and powerful among the antiwar poets of the 1960s. Because of the unpopularity of the War in Vietnam, becoming a popular antiwar poet (or musician) was not that difficult to achieve.

2. Cancel Culture still applies to literature—and in a big way. More examples of this come later in this chapter.

3. Matthew Prigge, "What You Might Not Know About Carl Sandburg's Milwaukee Roots," *Milwaukee Journal*, May 31, 2018, Culture section.

4. Asante Lake, "Analysis, Meaning and Summary of Carl Sandburg's poem *Nigger*," April 1, 2020, Comments Section, 2nd par. https://www.americanpoems.com/poets/carlsandburg/nigger/

5. ibid.

6. Cather writes about strong women, but they are traditional, optimistic women. Women portrayed by Kate Chopin are strong women, but they are not traditional women; Chopin's women hate men—or wind up hating them.

7. Haber is not this teacher's real name.

8. A Jewish American, Seltzer possessed passionate views about having a wide range of options while choosing literature; however, the quality of the literature was also of paramount consideration to Seltzer.

9. Matt Reimann, "Dead White Guy Author John Steinbeck Actually Invented The Woke Apology," *Timeline,* September 14, 2016. https://timeline.com/john-steinbeck-woke-apology-dcafe114855f

10. ibid., 2nd to last par.

11. ibid., 2nd to last par.

12. Chris Bova, "Racial Slurs In Literature Spark Conversation Between Educators, Students And Parents," Fox 17 News, February 24, 2020. https://www.fox17online.com/news/local-news/kent/racial-slurs-in-literature-sparks-conversation-between-educators-students-and-parents

13. Chris Bovia, "Racial Slurs In Literature . . . " Fox 17 News, February 24, 2020. https://www.fox17online.com/news/local-news/kent/racial-slurs-in-literature-sparks-conversation-between-educators-students-and-parents

14. Ray Gustini, "Noted McCarthyite e.e. cummings Also Apparently Racist," *The Atlantic,* May 25, 2011, www.theatlantic.com/culture/archive/2011/05/noted-ideolog

15. ibid.

16. Ted Burke, "Was e.e. cummings Racist," *Like It Or Not,* June 30, 2011, par. 2. https://www.ted-burke.com/2011/06/was-eecummings-racist.html

17. Kevin McCaffrey, "Arthur Miller's Empathy for the Common Man Has Never Felt More Timely," *The Telegraph,* June 9, 2020. https://www.telegraph.co.uk/theatre/what-to-see/arthur-millers-empathy-common-man-has-never-felt-timely/

18. ibid.

19. Dorany Pineda, "In Burbank Schools, A book-Banning Debate Over How To Teach Antiracism," *Los Angeles Times,* November 12, 2020. https://www.latimes.com/entertainment-arts/books/story/2020-11-12/burbank-unified-challenges-books-including-to-kill-a-mockingbird

20. ibid.

21. *To Kill a Mockingbird,* by Harper Lee, has forever been deemed an indictment of racism. The little girl's innocent question of her father (quoting what she has heard around town), is from a precious scene, exposing an innocent child's naivety about racism. The novel is now under fire from woke educators, who have absolutely no clue about how to see literature in a proper context.

22. Allie Conway, "The Righteous Survivor," *PBS News Briefs,* September 28, 2018.

23. Using several sources, I did this compilation. Referring to authors being "adopted": it means that school districts may have granted permission to teachers to use the literature in the classroom, or teachers unilaterally assigned the material to their own classroom students.

24. *Lambda Literary,* "Supporting LGBTQ Writers In The Schools," July 26, 2021. https://lambdaliterary.org/lgbtq-writers-in-schools/

25. Kathy Belge, Marke Bieschke, *The Ultimate LGBT Guide for Teenagers*, (Zest Books), 2011, publisher's description.

26. Kathy Naverette, "Review of *Queer*" Kalamazoo Public Library, 2021. https://www.kpl.gov/catalog/item/?i=ent://ERC_215_348/0/OVERDRIVE:f10e6ea7-389f-4365-ad92-375f2e14219d

27. Leslea Newman, *Heather Has Two Mommies*, (Alyson Publications), 2003, publisher's description.

28. List of LGBT-themed speculative fiction: These books never made my recommended reading list when I taught high school. They hadn't yet been published and, frankly, I am not sure I know what some of these descriptions even *mean*.

29. Mollie Blackburn and Katherine Miller, "Equity by Design: Teaching LGBTQ-Themed Literature in the English Language Arts Classrooms," *Midwest & Plains Equity Assistance Center*, 2017.

30. National Council of English Teachers, "Resolution on Strengthening Teacher Knowledge of Lesbian, Gay, Bisexual, and Transgender (LGBT) Issues," 2017, Resolution (Items 1–6), p. 1.

31. Mollie Blackburn and Katherine Miller, "Equity by Design: Teaching LGBTQ-Themed Literature in the English Language Arts Classrooms," *Midwest & Plains Equity Assistance Center*, 2017.

32. ibid.

33. A fictitious name has been used for this interview. For the purpose of clarity, I took the liberty of changing some words around and providing proper syntax. Without these protections, some of these subjects may take the liberty of changing my face around.

34. Avalon Zoppo, "N.J. Student Says He Was Kicked Out Of Class Over Trump Banner," October 30, 2020, *True Jersey.* https://www.nj.com/ocean/2020/10/nj-student-says-he-was-kicked-out-of-class-over-trump-banner.html

35. Hans Roscoe Finkelstein, *For Whom the Grammar Bells Toll*, (Chain Publishing), 2019, pp. 6–7.

36. *LGBTQ Resource Center*, "What Are Some Commonly Used Pronouns?" 2021. https://uwm.edu/lgbtrc/qa_faqs/what-are-some-commonly-used-pronouns/

37. These words come from the English playwright George Bernard Shaw, but I like to ascribe them to my father, who fought in Normandy in June of 1944.

38. For years it has been acceptable to have bigoted views toward Christianity and Christians. Schools, from the primary grades on, go out of their way to accommodate Muslims, Hindus, and Jews. However, Christians are fair game when it comes to intolerance. In other words, a student would never present a classroom speech full of rancor for Islam; however, lambasting Christians has become begrudgingly acceptable.

39. *National Speech and Debate League* website, comments thread, September 21, 2020. NSDL.com

Chapter 3

Bizarro

WHEN LIFE MADE SENSE

America's iconic superheroes have left an impact on generations of Americans of all ages. They have watched their superheroes leap tall buildings in a single bound, and swing from structure to structure on a thin strand of sticky spider web. They felt solace in the predictability of their heroes' actions and were united behind their honorable philosophies and goals: "With power comes great responsibility."[1] "Fight for truth, justice, and the American way."[2]

About that last one: fans became suspicious when one of the later theater versions of *Superman* had distorted that famous opening to his episodic adventures by claiming, "Superman! He fights for truth, justice, and . . . *all that stuff.*"[3] That was in 2006. Jingoism had been set up as a straw man and attacked by Hollywood.

One of the oddest characters in the *Superman* series was Bizarro. It isn't clear if Bizarro appeared in the TV series—he probably hadn't—but he is a featured character in some of the spin-offs and has a presence in the comic books, having made 146 appearances. That's a lot of Bizarro!

So just who was this weird character, this superhero that emboldened the citizens of Metropolis to fight against crime—"to fight for truth, justice, and the American way!"?

Bizarro was not a super*hero*. *Superman* fans may have looked forward to exploring the exploits of this Bizarro guy, but as Dan Westin, of *Hollywood Reporter* commented, "Readers loved reading about Bizarro . . . but they were afraid of him."[4] Bizarro, as all readers eventually had figured out during his odd stint in DC Comics, was a "supervillain," an exact antithesis of a superhero.

Bizarro embodied traits the opposite of what readers had grown to know and expect: Superman is handsome, friendly, and a force for good; Bizarro is ugly, unfriendly, and a force for evil. Bizarro's powers are the opposite of Superman's (such as freeze vision as opposed to heat vision, and heat breath rather than freeze breath). And he attempts to kidnap Lois Lane! To Bizarro, kryptonite is good, and can eat it! Of course, kryptonite makes Superman vulnerable; the alien mineral is lethal to the Man of Steel. Bizarro causes crime. Superman fights crime. And the list goes on and on. Bizarro = bad; Superman = good.

Teachers used to be America's real-life superheroes. That was how most children saw them. So were the rest of the education establishment. School counselors were superheroes, too, in some cases creating miracles, motivating children to stay in school and earn their diplomas.

Teachers inspired children they didn't know they had inspired. Maybe most educators never fully realized the extent of the positive influence they had on kids. Everybody worked together—setting aside their differences, often compromising, always sacrificing—because it was in the best interests of the children for them to do so.

Slowly, however, the lands of Superman, Batman, and Spiderman were invaded by an insidious, odorous penetration of characters from Bizarro land. Mere fears and trepidations about Bizarro had transmogrified into an acceptance of the arrival of—if not evil—the most combative, indestructible adversary of all.

DC Comics described Bizarro this way: "Since his hilarious debut in the 1950s, Bizarro has been a character of equal parts humor and confusion. The imperfect duplicate of Superman, the chalk-faced hero lives on the cube-shaped world of Bizarro where everything is the opposite of life on Earth. Beauty is hated, ugliness is revered, and it is a crime to make anything perfect."[5]

Readers that are familiar with Bizarro are reminded how two different people may view the same thing and come away with completely different reactions. One person thinks the thing is good; the other thinks it is bad. The "thing" remains a constant, with two *perceptions* voiding reality.

This paradox does not stop with "good" and "bad." In the new world, with Bizarro having invaded the schools, bad *is* good. What's more: wrong *is* right. Black *is* white. Down *is* up. And old *is* new. Get the picture? Educators' acceptance of "Bizarro" has led America—and will continue to lead America—down the rabbit hole in reading, writing, history, and math.

So, what is Bizarro?

WHAT *USED* TO BE—WHAT *IS*

1. Cafeteria lunches suck.

It used to be . . . Schools went out of their way to make sure that the kids would eat lunch; they provided some time for a little extra nourishment in the way of a snack. Now, schools serve lunches that children will not eat. School officials know the kids won't eat food that doesn't taste good to them; yet, they pour millions of bucks into providing, and then disposing of, the leftover food, which is considerable. What's particularly mystifying is that schools repeat the same food mistakes, again and again. And *again*.

Kids are guided by their palates. In the past, eating foods chucked full of protein and calcium was encouraged by teachers, school officials, and health experts. Today meat products are out. If you like to eat meat, you are ignorant about your health needs, a murderer of animals, and a contributor to climate change, the ultimate demise of the planet.

There shouldn't be a beef with those who disdain animal protein. These kids have peculiar tastes and needs that should be respected. But it's tough now. Things have changed. Most children looked forward to their school lunches. For many it had become the highlight of their day. Not so much anymore—in fact, not at *all* anymore. Bizarro has taken over your kids' diets.

Local school kitchen supervisor, Bonita Miller, said, "Every day we throw out food the children will not eat, no matter how much we encourage them. And it is usually the same food: garbanzo beans, vegetables, salads, milk, and lima beans."[6]

Bizarro is hungry.

2. Civil servants suck.

It used to be . . . Often as a matter of daily routine, schools praised the courage and hard work of police and firefighters. The police, when all else failed, which it usually did, were there to help; firefighters would risk life and limb to carry a baby from a burning building or rescue a cat from a tree.

Now, even firefighters have captured the wrath of some local politicians, along with some of the civilians they serve. During the riots in the summer of 2020, scores of firefighters bravely tended to their duties, as they valiantly served alongside cops and other members of law enforcement; consequently, they, too, faced the wrath of angry mobs.[7]

Every perceptible movement by civil servants is under scrutiny. What was once good (a heroic cop showing up at a domestic dispute to protect the abused and restore calm), has been categorized as a glaring potential for acts of evil by the cops. Boys no longer grow up wanting to be police and firefighters; they now process the possibility of being physically harmed by rioting throngs that would hurt the police and firefighters just for doing their jobs.

The portraits painted by the schools, once glamorous when it came to either of these sought-after professions, are now ugly: "What do we want? Pigs in a blanket! Fry 'em like bacon!"[8] Remember those chants by antipolice protestors, even prior to the Summer of 2020? Most people do. In schools, these sentiments are not uncommon. Antipathy abounds toward any form of law enforcement, even that which used to be considered essential to a school's safety.

NPR's Cheryl Corley claims to have done investigative intelligence on the attitudes of schools toward having police on campuses. Here's what she found: "This [more police and armed security in schools] is largely a failed approach in devoting a significant number of resources, but not getting the outcome in school safety that we are all looking for."[9]

It isn't as though an evolution of events and the passage of time have molded new attitudes toward the police. Regulations regarding policing and the history of behaviors and misbehaviors of cops has maintained a consistent pattern for decades. What changed is the public's *perceptions* of law enforcement. The media transmit sinister portrayals of the police to millions. But not a fair, impartial media. The media of the progressive elites in this country take part in a campaign to demonize law enforcement. Once the princes and saviors of the American people, the police have become incorrigible, barbarians at the gate, an institution beyond repair. *They need to be deleted.*

Bizarro is smiling.

3. The military sucks.

It used to be . . . Americans took unabashed pride in the men and women that wore the uniforms of the United States military. The pounding of their drums to the accompaniment of the "National Anthem," inspired millions for decades.

American schools now portray the military as threatening to various groups of people *inside* U.S. borders. The demonization doesn't stop there. The American military, uncontrolled and barbaric, is a grave threat to the entire world.

ROTC groups, classes, and special recruiting events have been kicked off college campuses. Many high schools refuse to allow recruiters to set foot on their turf. The U.S. military kills people—innocent men and women and babies; that's enough to ban them.

Antagonists point to Vietnam, a war that ended almost fifty years ago; they show their children photographs of napalmed cities in Southeast Asia.

The dastardly deeds and atrocities committed by American war planes speak for themselves. Teachers and their guest "speakers" relay this information to kids—the bombings, the killings, the massacres—and the children eat it up like chocolate candies.

Without a firm knowledge of history, lacking anything approaching a detailed and *contextual* description of these events, kids are prone to understanding what is fed to them, especially when the information comes from their beloved teachers, or outside agencies that are only too eager to send "entertainers" to student assemblies. Suffice to say, propaganda about the military would have been taboo in public schools twenty years ago.

High school history teachers still talk about Lieutenant William Calley and the My Lai Massacre of 1968. Calley was convicted of the premeditated destruction of a village and the murder of over five hundred Vietnamese civilians. Lieutenant Calley was a bad dude, a *very* bad dude, but continually casting aspersions about the callousness and barbarous behavior of U.S. military personnel does not reflect the truth about the *entirety* of this establishment. Highlighting incidents like the one at My Lai gives your children one more reason to hate the institution that protects their lives and freedoms.

School age children grew up to revere soldiers, sailors, marines, and cadets. There may have been a few bad apples—like a few bad apples in the police force—but overall, the military was special; it radiated honor, courage, and dignity.

Sometimes the negative effect on teenagers is tangible. A local high school student, as a part of an argumentative essay assignment, wrote, "I have no desire to fight in meaningless oil wars, risking my life and maybe coming back with PTSD, with my only contribution being to help rich white men get richer. Don't get me wrong, I have respect for our troops and our veterans, but I disagree with America's history of imperialism and see no reason to become a cog in its war machine."[10]

Today the military is replete with its critics. To be in the marines or army highlights a testosterone driven urge to kill. The military drains the economy, diverting money away from important social programs, like combating climate change and instituting socialized medicine.

Some believe that only society's rejects sign up for the military. One theory is that men and women use the armed forces to further their career goals. Another theory: potential criminals and thugs go into the military in order to turn their lives around. Young people see the military as an opportunity to get a college education without having to pay for it. Recently, men and women have taken advantage of active-duty benefits that pay for sex change operations. And the most troubling theory of all: Violent men and women use the military to live out their proclivities for violence and sadistic pleasures.

The progressive culture in this country specializes in taking snapshots in history of places where the armed forces was compelled to use violence to achieve a greater good. They blot out all contexts. And then they might hold up a famous *Newsweek* cover from 1968, showing a terrorized, naked Vietnamese girl fleeing a village that has just been bombed with napalm from American planes. "See that," your children are told, "this cowardly act was done by Americans! We should be ashamed of ourselves!"[11]

Your author's father spent untold hours proudly describing his exploits on the beaches of Normandy: He explained that Europe had been freed of the reigns of Adolph Hitler, because of the selfless courage of *Americans* that had stormed the shores from their Higgins boats into a sea of machine gun fire and artillery explosions. His dad even spoke at his elementary school, telling a classroom of wide-eyed kids of the sacrifices of many of his friends and "brothers." Without the blood and guts of the men at Normandy, those kids in the classroom may have never been born.

But that was *then. Bizarro is now.*

4. Men and women are the same.

It used to be . . . Men were men; women were women. There were clear differences between the two sexes; through the prism of these differences, society could rest assured that men and women cooperated in tandem with each other to go to work, raise families, and live their lives in harmony. Stereotypically, men liked to "spread the seed," while women yearned to make a safe nest for their children. Teachers recognized that boys were more prone to hyperactivity and acts of aggression. Although boys' aggressive tendencies were not always mean-spirited, they tended to act on their high levels of testosterone. Clearly, a difference existed between the sexes. That difference operated to regulate, balance, and codify society.

Schools supported sports for boys *and* sports for girls. Exceptional moments happened, but for the most part, the schools posed the view that boys and girls were happy and confident when they were separate from each other (as in sports, clubs, and various academic activities), and they were also happy and confident when they were joined together (as in sports, clubs, and various academic activities). The rule of thumb: everyone had *his* or *her* own boundaries and levels of tolerance when it came to either separate or co-ed organizations at school.

These days, however, arguing for separate boys and girls—well, *anything*—can get you ostracized from the mainstream of school society faster than Queen Daenerys could order her dragons to parch one of the bad guys on *Game of Thrones*.

As of this writing, some schools have considered opting for unisex bathrooms. This means seven-year-old boys share those bathrooms with seven-year-old girls. President Biden—though he probably isn't aware what he's saying—has endorsed mixed gender bathrooms.[12]

Boys and girls are meant to be combined for some activities; they are not meant to be combined for other activities. And if you ask any sixteen-year-old girl on the planet, female adolescents don't *always* want male adolescents around. They want privacy. They want to talk. They want to exercise without being on display for every goggling teenage boy to study. They want to share secrets; thus, you have organizations like Girl Scouts and dance studios that cater to teenage girls that want to learn ballet.

The same may be said for boys; boys sometimes just want to be boys: they want to hike, wrestle with each other, talk bad-ass, and privately share their sometimes-blunt observations about girls. Sure, no self-respecting father would encourage his son to speak of young ladies in terms that are other than reverent or appropriate. But that's what boys sometimes do; it shouldn't be a federal offense.[13]

When social scientists (whoever and whatever they are) conclude that boys and girls are basically the same, as are grown men and women basically the same, *anything goes*. Which usually means that *nothing* goes. Roles may no longer be assumed, for to assume gender roles is to conclude that one or other of the sexes (or genders, if you prefer), is better than the other, or better suited to something that the other is not. That kind of thinking is now taboo. If you teach it to kids at school, the teachers' union won't like you.

It is no longer fashionable for society to make those sorts of snap judgments or to reach even well-documented conclusions about gender differences or—God forbid—gender superiority in a specific aspect of the culture: mental, emotional, or physical. Even to argue that boys are *sometimes* better at science than girls is to insinuate there are inherent differences in the sexes that translate into variables for determining mental, emotional, and physical prowess.

Ordinarily, this would be the place in the book to list the obvious—and the subtle—differences between males and females. But what a waste of time that would be! America's schools try ridiculously hard to make certain that traditional and religious views of gender are dashed. To any person with even a grain of common sense, those differences are obvious.

Superman, are you there? Bizarro lurks.

5. Racial and cultural divisiveness constitute a societal nirvana.

It used to be . . . Society shunned acts of racism and claims of cultural superiority. From slavery, through the Jim Crowe era, America's history blushed from the embarrassment of abject racism toward Black people, whether they were African-Americans or others with African ancestry that lived in this country. Some American leaders dangled the carrot of "separate but equal" in the faces of Black men and women, but that didn't work out too well; if anything, it perpetuated the notion that white people, many of whom seemed genuinely apologetic for the racism of their ancestors, were putting up a facade.

Fast forward a decade or two: The passage of sweeping civil rights legislation by Congress in 1964 (partly to pay homage to the recently assassinated John F. Kennedy) instigated huge changes in public policy, creating laws against racism, some of which were later enforced in criminal courts, and many of which inspired hefty monetary settlements in the civil judicial system.

Culminating with the election of Barack Obama for two terms (2008–2016), most Americans felt good about their country's levels of tolerance toward minority groups, and both Republicans and Democrats heralded these historic elections as triumphs in race relations. Polls (before George Floyd's death) suggested that a majority of both Blacks and whites in America believed race relations in the United States to be "good" or "better than good."[14]

School children didn't question America's motives when it came to race. Although they understood that racism hadn't completely dissipated, despite the monumental legislation of the early 1960s and the election of a Black President to consecutive terms, most children, including those of color, went on with their lives. They ignored the complexities of politics that were, after all, best left to adults to handle in all their infinite wisdom. Kids attended school, held part-time jobs, and played sports. They competed. Some worked hard. They viewed education as a means to climb the ladder of success.

The crash of the economy in 2008 frightened American kids, but hardly anyone, except notorious left-wing agitators, attributed the economic collapse to anything remotely related to racism. Indeed, in most schools—and from the lips of teachers—children were encouraged to be tolerant and understanding of races, religions, and cultures that were different from their own. Martin Luther King's words had been invoked repeatedly: "I dream of the day . . . that my children may be judged . . . not by the color of their skin, but by the content of their character."[15] And Jewish concentration camp survivor Viktor Frankl projected a similar view about the hysteria of racism in his book, *Man's Search for Meaning*. Frankl's words were profound: "There are . . . but two races of people in the world . . . the decent and the indecent."[16]

Teachers encouraged children to understand that skin color matters *not*; character matters a *lot*.[17]

Times have changed.

The introduction of Critical Race Theory, intersectionality, and antiracism curriculum in the schools, both private and public, has begun a trend of reversing the progress toward a tolerant and rational view of racial issues. The mandatory introduction of the 1619 Project into public education has changed the way teachers talk about America.[18] Their vitriol is obvious. The trending dictum that a whole group of people is bad because of the shade of their skin (and the shade of the skin of their ancestors) is plainly, and overtly, racist.

The underlying philosophy for fighting racism starts with the belief that *a person's skin color does not matter*. Good people have believed this for decades, probably centuries. Even on the surface, the concept that skin shade makes any sort of difference in a person's character or their intrinsic worth as a human being is so incredibly naive and shallow, it is hard to believe that anyone in public life currently subscribes to such dogma, one born out of ignorance. Evil may be a factor as well; for racism in its purest form is evil.

Given these premises, consider the odd words that have become underpinnings to new ideas being taught to school children, as young as age five: Christina Sanchez Martin preaches to her students a rather strange slant on incorrect grammar, ambiguous syntax, and improper spelling: "Standard English is anti-Blackness that is used to diminish Black language of Black students in classrooms is not separate from the rampant and deliberate anti-Black racism and violence inflicted upon Black people in society."[19]

Kids go to school to learn how to write and speak; their teachers and those that demand adherence to formal, traditional uses of language in the context of certain proper situations are condemned as racists.

Teach for America observed, "Many school leaders and educators are looking to go beyond uprooting the white supremacist viewpoints baked into their curriculums. They're also working with students, families, and their communities in a number of ways to reimagine their school policies."[20]

Beyond the curriculum, these views manifest themselves in disciplinary policies, too: Even the best-intended policies can fail to be antiracist or even perpetuate white supremacy culture if educators and school leaders do not critically analyze the "why" behind every policy and practice when implementing them.[21]

If you have begun to feel that "white supremacy" is a given, you are not alone.

As you examine this text, you will learn how these troublesome ideas have woven their way into the curriculum, even into main course offerings, such as English, history, math, science, and the informal course of "attitude." An *attitude* umbrellas everything that is taught, preached, and indoctrinated in the school system. Educators once considered racism to be a bad thing; now, many of them teach and preach it.

Hi, Bizarro.

6. Science is fact, but only if it concludes what we *want* it to conclude.

It used to be . . . When you considered all that was taught in the schools, "science" was safe; as a matter of fact, scientific *fact* had eluded controversy. Science, after all, spoke truth—science *was* the truth! Of course, in the old days—the *really* old days—all kinds of doubters existed. When Newton staggered into proclaiming, "What goes up, must come down," hardly anyone disagreed with that theory.[22] Which is somewhat surprising, because so many people had struggled with this concept before then. If you throw a ball into the air—*up* into the air—that ball will come down. Try to imagine how scientists would have handled the theory of the existence of two dozen different genders, or what they would have said about men having babies!

Anyway, at a given point, science is settled.

Fast forward to now: Science is *not* settled. Science is based in changing theories, extended theories, and hypotheses that often seem to be concocted—not *constructed*—out of the clear blue.

Educators thought it acceptable (though controversial) to teach the theory of evolution in a high school biology class, because that class, presumably, was based in science. Teaching the story of Adam and Eve was rarely acceptable in a public school; Adam and Eve had nothing to do with science, unless you considered the "biology" that was going on between Adam and Eve while they "toiled" together to create Cain and Abel. That wasn't the kind of science school kids studied, unless it had become a novelty in one of the hip sex education courses being taught in the second grade.

The truth of today's science may be at the whim of whoever holds the most powerful political offices. And that's sad. If anything should be totally void of politics, it is science and math (which you *thought* was a kind of objective science); after all, scientific conclusions are reached based on the latest data and experiments and other *objectively conducted research*.

Here's what you have: a few billion people in the world that are being coaxed into believing if they don't give up their way of life, which includes most of their luxuries and modern conveniences (think air travel), they will be *dead* in a few years because of the earth's changing climate. The proof is in the pudding. *The science says so.* Never mind that not *all* science says so. Forget that much of science concludes differently or vehemently contradicts the "infallible" science championed by the most radical climatologists and politicians.

So, for the most part, science is still a fact—but only if it adheres to the party line, and only if it fits the agenda of those that have the goal of wanting to eliminate all carbons (which means dependency upon all oil and gas); the United States would cease to be energy independent and be forced to rely on wind turbines and solar panels. Those who gain power may build up the economy in the way they had wanted it to look in the first place (think Build Back Better), and capitalism be damned! *Some* science is wrong; it is wholly unreliable and even racist—and if not racist, sexist and transphobic!

Nuclear power, an alternative that, according to reputable scientists approaches viability, isn't on the radar screen of wokes. A lack of critical thinking skills, mixed with an abundance of *emotional* thinking, may have diminished a woke's ability to distinguish between nuclear *weapons* and nuclear *power*—or how to recognize safe, doable alternatives for the disposal of nuclear waste.

The science of biology has forever told us that people were born as male or female; in fact, science announced that startling revelation about the animal kingdom, too: most nonhumans were either male or female. Men and women dominate the sexes; they corner the market on genders, too.

Laughably, those who sing the praises of science when it comes to climate change, those who look down their noses at the heathens that don't enthusiastically buy into their view of the glaciers melting (at about the same time that the planet is dangerously cooling down), are also the biggest critics of science, but only when they don't like its conclusions.

For centuries people have accepted ideas that seem very basic; there was no need for scientific experimentation and decades of intensive research to verify them: there are two sexes, two genders. Some people are born with various hormonal and mental anomalies that require therapy to sort out; however, the idea that a man can *feel* like he is a woman and join social and athletic activities that are exclusive to women is ludicrous. Transexual surgeries have become frequent, but, at least, science and medicine have dealt with these issues. Unfortunately, what science and medicine may not be fully able to accommodate is the notion that gender identity simply may be *declared*—sometimes impulsively—without so much as a shred of real science to back up that declaration.

As this book details, American schools have been manipulated by special interest groups that encourage children as young as five to buy into this "science." What's worse is the pressure being put on parents that worry about doing the right thing before they irreparably maim their children. Parents, often without a doctor's consent, feed their kids hormones and medicines that not even a voodoo witch doctor would have concocted for his own kid.

Where's the science there?

Science is good. Science is bad. Follow the science. Don't follow the science. The strangeness of teaching children about the "normality" of picking and choosing their own genders has already come to a school near you.

Bizarro would be proud.

7. Most convicts don't deserve to be in prison.

It used to be . . . When somebody did something bad, society assigned him to a prison cell. If he did something *really* bad, society made him remain in that cell for a long time. *Justice*, as applied to the criminal justice system, carried clear and simple definitions: *justice means if you do something good, you should be rewarded; if you do something bad, you should be punished.* In the past, that is what we taught children. It had nothing to do with karma or magic; it had to do with the desire to live in a society that protected its innocent members, while holding fairness as one of its premium values.

Explosive radical legal movements, especially in some of America's largest cities, have diminished the effectiveness of the criminal justice system. When district attorneys like George Gascon, the Los Angeles carpetbagger that faces recall efforts at the time of this writing, dive into a mission to victimize criminals and demonize victims, things can get hairy on the streets. Between Gavin Newsom and Gascon and a disastrous 2018 ballot initiative, California rolled dangerous felons out of prison faster than fictional theater patrons fled the movie house when the Blob oozed through the auditorium's projection slits.

About crime, here's what is now taught to kids:

- some crimes are ok to do (i.e., shoplifting if you don't swipe more than nine hundred bucks' worth of merchandise)
- the death penalty for murderers is automatically off the table
- your first child molestation is complimentary
- marking up freeway walls, keying random automobiles, and throwing rocks through store windows . . . that's cool
- certain demographics of people may commit more crimes; the blame lies with historical Black slavery and systemic racism
- students can't be reprimanded at school for disobeying a teacher; good old-fashioned infractions like *defiance of authority* are viewed as frivolous
- felons and others booked on lesser charges may get out of jail free—and early

Forget about the concept of *punishment* or even *rehabilitation*. Members of society that see the commission of crimes against individuals as antisocial acts that should be dealt with in a punitive—or a restorative—manner by the judicial system have fallen from grace with certain political groups. Those that support a punitive system are often seen as vengeful, heartless, and callous.

John Porter recounted how he was brought before his school's disciplinary council—called a shared decision-making board—for daring to say that young men of color commit a disproportionate number of crimes. In his explanation, Mr. Porter said, "It was scary. One minute, I was considered one of the best teachers in the entire school district; the next minute, I felt like my job was in jeopardy! Fortunately, their 'case' never got beyond our local site administrators."[23]

Mr. Porter had merely stated a *fact*. He had not uttered a word about the whys and wherefores about the disproportionate amount of prison time served by young Hispanic and African-American males. Bizarrely, using data to support this line of reasoning was taboo. The conclusions the teacher drew were not in accordance with the popular narrative in that school; this teacher's words—though *facts*—were enough to threaten his livelihood.

Bad people should be separated from good people, when those bad people, no matter what their race or ethnicity, do bad things. Incarceration exists to protect innocent people from harm, to preserve society. That the system ignites the flames of controversy for wanting to keep the bad guys locked up strikes normal people as odd.

More Bizarro.

8. See no evil; hear no evil.

It used to be . . . Eyewitness evidence ruled the roost in a court of law. This was before DNA, though. Eyewitnesses were usually reliable—not always—and jurors and judges came to expect testimony from people that could claim they "saw it."

If you are watching the news on television, and you see men and women, most of them young, throwing rocks and bottles and bricks, turning over automobiles and lighting them on fire, and bashing the glass from store windows with fire hydrants, there is a good chance you would come away from that experience with the conclusion that those young men and women are committing acts of vandalism and violence.

You would call this a *riot*. You might refer to these people as *thugs* or *arsonists* or *looters*. You would be hoping for intervention from law enforcement, so the damage to property and the physical danger to innocent human beings are minimized. And you would think that everyone else who viewed those events saw the same things you saw and managed to reach similar conclusions.

Nah.

That's not what happens today.

Ordinary citizens, infiltrated by paid agitators and professional rioters and protesters, are not enough to rile up the leaders in charge of keeping the peace. Local level office holders are running scared: on one hand, they cringe at the notion that they might look weak or cowardly in the face of confrontations with hoodlums that burn and loot; on the other hand, they worry that showing any hostility toward lawbreakers can be seen—and labeled—as racism, fascism, xenophobia, white supremacy, or jingoism. Or worst of all, siding with Donald Trump.

Those people in the streets. They are peaceful. They are productive. They are fighting for social justice and hate institutional racism. Their causes are good. *They* are good. What you *think* you see happening is . . . not happening. The protesters are not tearing down; they are building up. They are not hateful of America, your country; they love America, your country—even though they are, right now, burning its flag and bashing statues of Abraham Lincoln.

Should you happen to spot Bizarro on the street holding a *social justice* protest sign, relax. He *belongs* there.

9. Socialism is a panacea for all.

It used to be . . . We taught kids about the exhilaration people felt after putting in a full day's work. People who were employed were paid commensurate to what they produced, and in the process, put food on their table and bought medical insurance for their family. That fantasy was a version of the American Dream. The backbone of America was a capitalistic system that generated tremendous affluence and allowed for most of the citizenry to, at least, subsist. Capitalism was the basis of the "American Dream."

Children in public schools learned about Henry Ford, Oprah Winfrey, and Steve Jobs. They were people to be admired. Yes, their affluence drove others' admiration, but at the same time, they were living, breathing models of inspiration. Their drive, their perseverance, brought them to the top of their professions.

Teachers—most teachers anyway—were thrilled to discuss the lives of successful and decent Americans, and they encouraged children to emulate them. There were millions of wealthy Americans. Not all, of course, but many of these men and women invested their time and money and became rich. Unless they did something illegal or immoral in accumulating their fortunes, they shouldn't be chastised. Johan Norberg of the Cato Institute extolled the numerous virtues of capitalism: "Capitalism has given people both the liberty and the incentive to create, produce, and trade, thereby generating prosperity."[24]

This all-encompassing message generated optimism. It had also raised the dander of cynics, but when it came to protecting the heart of America's institutions, the schools had done their best to thwart that cynicism.

Those that would argue that only the privileged may benefit from America, or peoples' lives are destined to a forgone conclusion, underestimate how efficiently the system works. When your author taught high school, he often touted the capitalistic system and the advantages of working within that system. He told his students that in America there are winners and losers. The winners work hard, take chances, and sacrifice (and yes, sometimes get extremely lucky). But often, the "losers" in a competitive economic system do not have an education; they don't read and study to stay informed. They lack courage and fail to show ambition; they won't invest their mind, body, and soul into seeing their dreams come true.

Of course, many of those that fail do so at no fault of their own; but blaming the system for beating up on the downtrodden and exercising systemic racism is no way to climb the ladders of success.

You can make it here. More so than any other nation in the world, America affords everyone an opportunity to grab themselves a piece of the American Dream. Just speaking economically, if people really want to go the free enterprise route in America, the power of tenacity and commitment presents a true opportunity for success.

That is what we taught then. Now, the schools search for ways to foster an environment of victimhood. We are actively teaching students that they are not on a level playing field; that decades of discrimination and oppression against people of color have deadened their ability to succeed. The deck is already stacked against them before they begin to play their hands. It's not clear how this defeatism is supposed to inspire so-called "marginalized" individuals to rise up and wrestle with their special challenges.

Now politicians are telling young people that they can have it all but must do very little for "it all." They collect unemployment benefits that are at twice the aggregate of the dollar amounts they would have taken home in their paychecks. They long for free college. (Who pays for "free" in this case? They don't seem to care.) And there's more: free medical care, free housing, free money in the form of welfare checks, stimulus checks, and disability checks. The money flows. One kid asked his on-line teacher after the third round of COVID stimulus was mailed out, "This is cool. Can they just keep on printing money?"

Evidently, they can. Why not? The national debt is 180 gazillion bucks, but it doesn't matter, because the printing presses keep rolling. The money falls hot off the iron. "This is cool," the boy remarks. Yeah, maybe, but when he grows up and sneaks a peek at his first paycheck, the shock of noticing how many of his hard-earned dollars were deducted from his paycheck in the form of taxes, may temper his enthusiasm for giving more of his money away. Suddenly, the reality of wasteful, government-run, overly expensive social programs hits home.

Capitalism and individualism inspired American greatness. Now, we tell children that America *could* be great. All we need is equity. Same *outcomes*, no matter what.

Even Bizarro cringes at this one!

10. It doesn't matter how we raise children; it's all *gooood*!

We used to believe . . . Children should be taught about the importance of family. In the "old days," school children came from families that, no matter what their race or culture, were strong and united; often they embraced religion, too. Schools taught children that this was the noble way, the proud way to go. Of course, things often didn't turn out to be perfect, but there was something genuine about *seeking* ideals, especially when it had to do with family.

Kids that came from homes in which their mother and father were married and everyone in the family lived under the same roof tended to do better in life; the data to support this claim is overwhelming.[25] Those that held disdain for the nuclear family usually scoffed at this paradigm, because they were not a part of a nuclear family while they were growing up.

Yes, there were divorces and separations and all sorts of domestic issues with these types of arrangements. But television shows like *Leave it To Beaver* and *Father Knows Best* provided a proper model. Everyone wanted to be like those guys. Even *The Brady Bunch* fell short of the "ideal," but at least all those Brady kids lived with a mom and a dad that loved them, and they all kind of got along.[26]

Mirroring old television shows is not the ultimate way to seek family unity and acceptance; however, the bottom line is clear: *moms and dads matter*. When they *together* raise their children, it matters. Today's America—a segment of it—disses this arrangement. But in the final analysis, *then* was good.

To the extent that the public schools laud the Black Lives Matter movement, the denigration of the nuclear family has been in order. The BLM website condemns the nuclear family. If the condemnation is no longer true at this writing, know that it existed for months, long enough to do damage. Imagine teaching young Black men and women that it is *bad* to be raised in a nuclear family. It is *bad* to raise children with a married mother and father in the same home as their biological children. Imagine telling small boys who are yearning for the presence of their dads that their dads really don't matter. What we really should explore is how the idea of having supportive, connected, and committed families has mutated into an intense disparagement of that kind of arrangement.

Again, we see a chilling example of something *good* that rapidly turned into something *bad*.

Bizarro doesn't even come close to describing this one.

NOTES

1. The oft-repeated line and one of the themes of *Spiderman*, Columbia Pictures, 2002.
2. The famous introduction to the *Superman* television series and most of the *Superman* films, which began with *DC Comics*, July 1938, by writer Jerry Siegel and artist Joe Shuster.
3. *Superman Returns* (Warner Bros), 2006.
4. My mother knew some of the people that worked on the 1950s *The Adventures of Superman* television show. I was only around ten years old, but I remember a friend of my mother making the same comment. I thought it was so cool that someone as ugly and scary as Bizarro could be this popular.
5. This is from a description of fifteen stories about Bizarro: Written by the creator of *Superman*, Jerry Siegel, *Superman: Tales of Bizarro World*, which includes fifteen nonsensical tales of Bizarro's twisted heroics and insane interactions with Bizarro-Lois Lane, Bizarro-Jimmy Olsen, Bizarro-Supergirl, Bizarro-Lex Luthor, and Bizarro-Krypto the Superdog.
6. Ms. Miller (alias) may not have had the stats in front of her: A new World Wildlife Fund report estimates U.S. school food waste totals 530,000 tons per year and costs as much as $9.7 million a day to manage, which breaks down to about 39.2 pounds of food waste and 19.4 gallons of milk thrown out per school day per school.
7. Janelle Foskett, "Firefighters Attacked, Apparatus Damaged During Civil Unrest," *Fire Rescue 1*, June 2, 2020. https://www.firerescue1.com/firefighter-safety/articles/firefighters-attacked-apparatus-damaged-during-civil-unrest-9AfaNiScSHVXhNTC/
8. When I first saw the marchers echo these ugly, cop-hating slogans, I could not believe my eyes and ears. Of course, they *couldn't* be saying those things! But they said them, and those horrendous words became a part of a national movement that comes to schools and speaks to middle graders.
9. Cheryl Corley, "Do Police Officers In Schools Really Make Them Safer?" *NPR*, March 28, 2018, "Special Series: Justice Collaborative." https://www.npr.org/2018/03/08/591753884/do-police-officers-in-schools-really-make-them-safer
10. One of your author's former students, his name has been withheld. The essay was memorable and reminded me that kids in school need to learn about things that affect *them*. Theory is nice, but theory often lacks entertainment value.
11. "Story Behind The The Terror of War: Nick Ut's Napalm Girl," *About Photography*. Check out this picture and imagine telling little school kids that America did this, without any context or explanation. https://aboutphotography.blog/blog/the-terror-of-war-nick-uts-napalm-girl-1972
12. Does anyone really think that a healthy, clear-headed Joe Biden from thirty years ago would have been thrilled about allowing boys and girls to share the same school bathrooms?

13. Distinctions need to be made between what is appropriate public speech, and what is appropriate private speech, and appropriate speech while at school.

14. "Blacks Upbeat about Black Progress, Prospects," *Pew Research Center*, January 20, 2010. https://www.pewresearch.org/social-trends/2010/01/12/blacks-upbeat-about-black-progress-prospects/. This came at about two years into President Obama's first term.

15. Dr. Martin Luther King delivered his famous speech during the March on Washington on August 28, 1963.

16. Viktor E. Frankl, *Man's Search for Meaning*, (Beacon Press), 1946.

17. Like most other decent human beings, decent human beings who were also teachers believed in this concept.

18. Naomi Riley, "'The 1619 Project' Enters American Classrooms," *Education Next*, Vol. 20, No. 4. https://www.educationnext.org/1619-project-enters-american-classrooms-adding-new-sizzle-slavery-significant-cost/

19. April Baker-Bell, *Linguistic Justice: Black Language, Literacy, Identity, and Pedagogy*, (Taylor & Francis) 2020, Chapter 1.

20. Jessica Fregni and Laura Zing, "Shaping An Anti-Racist School Culture," *One Day*, September 11, 2020. https://www.teachforamerica.org/one-day/top-issues/shaping-an-anti-racist-school-culture

21. Lagra Newman, "Examining The Why Behind Every Policy And Practice," *One Day*, September 11, 2020. https://www.teachforamerica.org/one-day/top-issues/shaping-an-anti-racist-school-culture

22. Except for the folks that believed in the existence of about twelve different genders, they would have disagreed with Newton.

23. Mr. Porter is not this dude's real name. His name has been changed here for obvious reasons.

24. Johan Norberg, *Johan Norberg Quotes.* https://quotefancy.com/quote/1664967/Johan-Norberg-Capitalism-has-given-people-both-the-liberty-and-the-incentive-to-create

25. *FBI Crime Report*, 2001, indicated that 90 percent of those in prison for a violent crime are males; 75 percent of those incarcerated males grew up in a home without the presence of their father (2000).

26. The nuclear family is about giving children a solid foundation for spiritual growth and academic achievement.

Chapter 4

Diversity Wears No Clothes

RETHINKING THE OBVIOUS

Y.A. novelist Jacqueline Woodson said, "Diversity is about all of us, and about us having to figure out how to walk through this world together."[1]

The inspirational website, *Mind Fuel Daily*, capsulized its contributors' thoughts about diversity: "Diversity inspires cultural growth and makes society richer. When a community has people of different backgrounds, beliefs, and skills, each person is able to contribute their unique story and gifts to make a greater whole."[2]

In the fable, "The Emperor Has No Clothes," nobody is courageous enough to confront their bragging king with the truth: He is naked. The crowd lines the street and sings their praises about the emperor's beautiful, luxurious new wardrobe; but, alas, he is not wearing anything at all![3]

Everyone obediently smiles and nods at the mere suggestion of institutional cultural diversity. But is that what everyone is *thinking*? Or is diversity, like the acceptance of the belief that the emperor's clothes are striking and beautiful, akin to the nakedness that no one is courageous enough to point out?

Diversity of *ideas* is, generally, a good thing. To the extent that *diversity* means, "a collective sample of different,"[4] diversity is helpful for binding together a wide range of thoughts and suggestions, from which sound reasoning may be accomplished to solve problems. At times those solutions are reached based on *majority* consensus, in which there is an actual counting of the *quantity* of opinions; other times, inferences may be drawn based on a *blended* consensus, with which compromises are reached. No matter which way you go, the overall concept is the same: Differing *multitudes* lead to a sounder, wiser result, in which all group members have a stake in the consensus.

It is not difficult to understand the reasoning behind the benefits of *diversity of ideas*. Yet, for Americans—many of them highly educated and normally considered to be extremely smart—the understanding of why or how or *if* racial and cultural diversity is a plus for society is still in its embryonic stages. You wouldn't know that, though. The default position is to slobber all over anyone that pontificates about the magnificence of diversity or, even better, figures out innovative ways to implement diversity programs.

Mr. Stans, a young dynamic teacher, posed the following question to his high school public speaking class: *Which should be more highly sought after by universities and private sector corporations:* diversity *or* excellence?

Mr. Stans can still hear the gasps from his class of twenty-five bright teenagers, most of whom have made it a special point in their schooling to dissect controversial social issues. They were nary to steer away from this philosophical question, right?

Wrong.

You would have thought Mr. Stans had just asked them whether they would prefer to spit on the Old Testament or the American flag! (Never mind: Sadly, hardly anyone cares anymore about either of these formerly sacrosanct symbols.) The distress among students from his mere posing of the diversity dilemma, Mr. Stans recounted, was palpable.

Have you forgotten the question? Most of you probably didn't think twice about the question. You may not have cared what high school kids thought about this. But for students that had been weaned on public education since they had barely learned to walk, the teacher's question had prompted more than just a few double takes.

Which should be more highly sought by universities and private sector corporations: diversity or excellence?

A quick knee-jerk reaction to this question is that it is insulting to *contrast* these two concepts—excellence and diversity. *Come on, man*! *Do diversity and excellence have to be mutually exclusive*? Of course, they don't. It's best if they're not. Which leads to this question: Diversity comes with sociological benefits and psychological positives that make it a laudable goal, but is that goal worth achieving if—in *some* cases—excellence has been sacrificed?

Here's the famous analogy—and it's famous only because it's indicative of those proposing an unwavering, diversity-slanted argument that many can't answer: If a team that plays in the National Basketball Association is made up of 90 percent Black players, and this team wins the championship (not an unusual scenario), the team doesn't need to defend the excellence of their play. It's obvious. Their excellence has been rewarded. Diversity, however, shrinks in its lack of relevance when analyzing the success of this team. No diversity here. They're already good. They don't need more white players or

Asian players or Latino players to win games. They have already risen to the top of the mountain.

Should civil rights groups, Black activists, and woke politicians complain about a lack of white representation in the NBA? Would NBA owners settle for a quota system—a mandate that requires, for example, 35 percent white players on each team's roster? Maybe devise a rule that demands each team has an openly gay or transgender player? You could reduce this concept down to its lowest common denominator, and ask that sexual preference, race, and culture be broken down according to the amount of playing time each group has during a game.

Then comes this: Would such a rule undermine the excellence that is currently inherent in this sport?

Diversity.
Equity.
Inclusion.

That's what everyone wants, right? For our schools, for our communities, for our institutions at large? Right?

Now you would have diversity in the National Basketball Association! It would be *required*.

The NBA would personify inclusion. Totally. It would go out of its way to force teams to hire men and women—obviously off the court—that have unfortunate illnesses, diseases, and seriously debilitating handicaps. Again, they could not possibly require an *equitable* performance on the court: No one can control outcomes. The only way—and this is a stretch—outcomes could be managed would be to mandate those outcomes, using superficial dictates to specify an exact number of points, or baskets, for each player. And that might even be broken down by race or gender or sexual preference.

You have captured equity in the NBA. Remember, this denotes *equity* of actual results, not about providing opportunity. You want more white men that can't jump to play in the NBA, you will probably have to *put* them there. Equal *opportunity* would never cut it here. Some men, maybe white men—not to sound racist about white people—don't play basketball as well as others, no matter how much opportunity you give them. So, upset the apple cart—or whatever—and *require* that white men be on the roster and even receive the same amount of playing time and, of course, compensation, as the team's Black players.[5]

Sometimes you must simply *choose* between excellence and diversity, because against all the best wishes of do-gooders, well-wishers, and dedicated wokes, haphazard attempts to create a culturally or racially diverse, superficial environment sometimes loses its efficiency and efficacy.

The Airline Pilots' Descent

Secretary Kristen Clarke, a recent appointee by President Biden to head the Civil Rights Division of the federal government, weighed in on a recent decision that compelled the airlines industry to factor *the color of an applicants' skin* as a primary concern for hiring new recruits to fly airplanes.

In essence, Cook admitted that job performance should be among the top considerations for deciding who should fly passenger airliners across oceans. And that was a bold confession on her part; however—and this is where it gets good—she went on to qualify her statement by saying that the *diversity* of those ultimately hired is equal to job performance in importance.[6]

She then lectured reporters, accusing them of not really understanding the dynamics of diversity and how precious it is to the people of this country.[7]

Ok. Got it. Kind of.

Just why is having a multitude of skin colors present (inclusive) so important in job practices that hold in their hands the lives of millions of men, women, and children? You might have missed her explanation. So did your humble author.

If you have ever boarded a commercial airplane, chances were good that one of the men or women flying the plane greeted you at the door. You may have seen inside the cockpit a buff, handsomely dressed Black man (or individual of any race) with stripes covering his shirt. He may have been smiling and looking happy and confident. You had an innate sense that you were in good hands for the next however many hours.

Now, with the popular diversity emphasis, you don't really know if that Black man you met as your pilot, the man that holds in his hands your life, and the life of your children, was selected for his position because he is among the most qualified, or because he is Black. *Of course, this man and the others flying this plane were selected based on their competency*!

But not necessarily. And that is enough of a reason to jettison the diversity plan in favor of a policy that hires the best and the brightest, like the airlines used to. If any company, private or government, discriminates against a Black man, a woman, or a Native American, the racists responsible would experience the full wrath of the laws the federal government passed in the 1960s. These are laws that rioters and looters and statue destroyers never talk about. All the federal government must do is *enforce* those laws. They are already on the books.

The *best* men and women, the most qualified, should be flying people 30,000 feet in the sky. That's nothing more, or nothing less, than common sense. This reliance on the best and the brightest may turn out to be practically *all* Black men, like in the NBA!

Oh, yeah, don't mention *common sense* while discussing the people and institutions that educate America's kids, especially with the wokes now exerting more influence in the nation's schools.

The Military Up in Arms

Guidance counselors have worked with our kids for centuries. An effective guidance counselor can make a huge difference in a school. Not everyone is going to college (Shh!), and not everyone continues their education on a vocational path, although the vocational school has returned to being a good fit for many high school graduates.[8]

It used to be that military recruiters liked to hang out on high school and college campuses. Yes, it is no secret that the recent past has been unkind to ROTC students or the military, in general (as were 1960s cultures unsupportive of ROTC programs); however, as the pathway to obtaining a solid education became more accessible, more doable (and participation purely voluntary), an increasing number of young people turned to the military for a viable post public school option.

Unfortunately, politics reared its ugly head. Trump was elected, and the military, for which Trump voiced a high regard, suddenly plummeted in popularity. And the military turned against Trump.[9] Rigid stereotypes had reemerged. Some educators and much of the mainstream media portrayed the military as a gum-chewing, gun shooting, finely disciplined group of mostly conservative white men that used poor grammar, except for highly decorated officers; they were, of course, *old*, conservative men that would make the traditional followers of the right-wing John Birch Society look like a bunch of Abby Hoffmans.[10]

What college professors remained mum about, mainstream media lied about, was the inner workings of the military, the intelligence gathering agencies, and the federal crime investigative bureaus, all of which were changing from within. They had become—less rigid, less traditional, and less conservative.

It is no secret that despite the overwhelming popularity of Donald Trump among the *rank-and-file* military men and women, among the upper brass of those same branches, President Trump was not looked upon as the Messiah. The upshot of this (no pun intended) is the inner leadership has become more progressive; some of those leaders have been described as *woke*.[11]

Journalist Seth Cropsey observed, "It has become increasingly apparent that the military, under Presidential pressure, has turned to the radical and bizarre ends of the antiracism camp for guidance in a national discussion of race.... We must recognize the difficult position of military officers and their boss, Defense Secretary Lloyd Austin: The Biden administration's directives have placed them squarely in the midst of an increasingly noxious, nihilistic culture war."[12]

At the orders of the Biden administration—and maybe *many* other sources—the American military brass has made it a point to prioritize diversity in its advancement of officers and recruitment policies. The Army, Navy, Marine Corps, and Air Force, those courageous units of fighters that protect our country and preserve our freedom, are, according to Secretary Austin, made stronger through the diversity policies that had suddenly come into vogue.

Ross Edwards, whose father fought in the Second Wave at Normandy, said, "When my dad was released from his boat and waded to the shores with machine gun bullets flying over his head, he had many things on his mind. But in the telling of those events, he never mentioned to me that he was a little dismayed that there were not enough Black men on the mission."[13]

Or, for that matter, Mr. Edwards, homosexual men, women, or transsexuals. The empirical truth was that the mission at Normandy turned out extraordinarily well, despite the lack of cultural and racial diversity in the American assault. Maybe it was kind of like the NBA, but in reverse. Enough top-notch men could get the job done, and there was apparently no need to tamper with quota formulas.

When ROTC comes into a high school, they don't mention much about diversity to perspective recruits. They may say in passing something about the different branches of the military being diverse and representative of America, but they don't spend an inordinate amount of time promoting diversity. New recruiters are apt at not revealing the most recent sociopolitical tendencies. Veteran recruiters hardly go out to recruit anymore. If anything, their forced participation in live recruiting seminars and special events flattens their enthusiasm for diversity. Throw in a bunch of old people and see how quickly the diversity party candles burn out.

Tucker Carlson of Fox News has lamented on more than one occasion how the new diversity goals of the military have turned into real head scratchers.[14] How does having equitable numbers of Blacks and Asians and Native Americans and Latinos and women and Muslims and Jews and transsexuals and homosexuals and nonlibidoist asexuals make America safer? Or better? Or stronger?

Is America now to be respected or feared by our foreign adversaries because of its most recent diversity changes in the military? Are there Communist Chinese citizens suddenly writing their government officials and imploring them to change their diversity policies to enlist an increasing number of Pansexuals into the People's Liberation Army?

America's military leaders—obviously, not all—have suddenly developed an itch to scratch. It's the diversity itch. Normally, during a classroom discussion about the relative benefits of diversity verses excellence, students are perplexed that the question is asked in the first place. Feeling good about a club or a workplace is not the paramount reason that people choose others for their qualifications of responsibility. They want results. They look to the bottom line which, in the case of the United States military, is the best and most protective fighting force in history, whose main responsibility—above all—is to protect their country.

Does a diversity *priority* achieve this goal?

The military's Department of Diversity reported on January 25, 2021, "The diverse makeup of the armed forces is one of its greatest assets. When service members of different races, ethnicities, religions, sexual orientations, and other identities unite for a common mission, the result is a stronger and more effective force."[15]

Army General Mark Miller made this comment to a Harvard ROTC class: "Opportunity in our military must be reflective of the diverse talent in order for us to remain strong."[16] Try explaining the logic of these statements to students that can *think*. Good luck. One student near the back of a classroom turned to another and whispered, "The Chinese are laughing at us."[17]

Those enterprising individuals that own a business know the many variables that determine whether they turn a profit or a loss. If at any juncture disaster strikes, their business may be gone for good. Too many incompetents? Not enough varieties of skin colors?

When you invest in a business, you take chances. Your risk analysis speaks volumes for what type of employer you are. You are entitled to a "feel good" hiring policy, because the risks and benefits to your business are all about your choices, especially those choices that determine a boom or a bust outcome. If a sociological reason or a personal moral code motivates you to consider hiring more men and women of color, you have a justifiable position, no matter what choice you make. *It is your business*!

Look at the military as a business. They protect America. "Hiring" practices should reflect policies in action that move toward that goal. If *that* business folds, so does the United States.

Teachers and Tribes

When you staff a school, or teach students, the rules for hiring are different. You are not trying to make money. It isn't a business decision; it is an education decision. You are required to establish and maintain the best learning environment possible for your students and your staff. And though it isn't about business, the ends you are striving for may be of more value than any amount of money.

Does a diverse classroom, based on a criterion of skin color, help kids to learn better?

The answer is *yes* and *no*. If teachers continue to preach the tribe mentality, children will succumb to that mentality. When you really think about it, the concept is a bizarre one. Wokes emphasize that skin color matters. A Black student in an all-white classroom is automatically doomed to failure. Mix in a few more Black kids, and that student would excel. But the evidence does not support that theory. What the data *do* confirm is that underachieving students, while working with achieving students, tend to do better in almost any school subject.

The intangibility of the variables disqualifies the theory that skin color matters. Skin color is not a variable. Why would it be? How does that make any sense? Perhaps, socioeconomic conditions play a part in learning. But the color of one's skin does not. If it did, you would not find students on both ends of the economic spectrum from every race and culture.

Jay P. Greene and Catherine Shock, of the University of Arkansas Department of Education Reform, concur. They state, "A good education requires balance. Students should learn to appreciate a variety of cultures, sure, but they also need to know how to add, subtract, multiply, and divide. Judging from the courses that the nation's leading education colleges offer, however, balance isn't a goal. The schools place far more emphasis on the political and social ends of education than on the fundamentals of learning."[18]

As with most progressives, the woke tendency in education is to appeal to kids' feelings, instead of their brains. Rahim Reed, a University of California at Davis administrator, boasted, "To be an academic institution of excellence, you must incorporate diversity into the core mission. What we are trying to do is build a sense of community here, to build a more inclusive community. Diversity without inclusion leaves something out."[19] *Inclusion* is now a buzzword for something good, although it is not tangible, provable, or even academically advisable.

And high school principal, Kenneth Lu, told a student essayist, "When I look around the school and see this group and that group . . . talking . . . getting along . . . I know we have come a long way. It's good to see all the cultures around, even if they don't talk to each other or hang out together that much."[20]

Mr. Lu's warm fuzzy should make you feel good. Whether it's accurate or manages to describe an education institution that attempts to impart actual knowledge, can be a question for a serious debate. And his comment should make you do a double take. Wokes inspire a lot of double takes around America. No matter how much they sing about all their beautiful rainbows, the verdict on whether diversity elevates student achievement is, at best, *out*.

Research Magazine confirmed this in 2006: "Academic research has yielded mixed results on the benefits of multiculturalism and diversity."[21] In other words—let's sit back, sigh, and then take a deep breath—the academic achievements linked specifically to diversity don't exactly make a compelling argument for stacking the cultural mix. This is not to say that striving for diversity in the schools impinges on academic excellence; the evidence of a beneficial effect on learning, however, isn't there.

Be honest about this: You can argue until Al Gore's Arctic glaciers melt away that diversity offers positive social influences on kids; however, test scores will stay where they are, until students and teachers approach learning as if they were sitting in a rigorous academic environment, rather than participating in another "feel good" sociological experiment.

Diversity encourages children to band together with commonalities that have absolutely no relationship to issues of character. Those who argue that cultural attractions have natural ties to goodness and positive ideals are mistaken, misguided, or misinformed. They have ignored what most kids have learned over the past fifty years because of, ironically, that pesky Civil Rights legislation passed during the early 1960s: *that the most important cohesion of human beings pertains to issues of character and virtue—not to skin color or family lineage.*

Obviously, some diversity is good. It's the premise for integration. It's America: a diverse, integrated society working for one common goal, the success of the United States of America. Through the workings of American culture, which is a conglomeration of all cultures that have come here, settled here, and claimed a stake here in the American dream, the United States beacons as a force for justice and goodness in the world.

American teachers, when unimpeded by their unions and political action committees, understand this; they strain to do the right thing. In their efforts to stay on a politically correct path, they steer clear of anything even close to sounding bigoted—racist, sexist, prejudice, homophobic, anti-Indian, anti-Semitic, anti-left-handed, or anti-whatever—and tremble from even the remotest possibility of not seeming cool and open-minded about race talk.

Can you guess what either Viktor Frankl or Martin Luther King would have thought about the call to blend students at all costs, often according to precise mathematical formulas, into mixed racial groups?

All would all agree that discrimination and racism are wrong, but what do you call it when a school district administrator says to another high official, "Well, Carl, we got us only about 12 percent white kids at Caesar Chavez High School. We gotta' add some whites over there. And while we're at it, we need some more Asians over there, too. So, how do you suggest we gonna' do that?"

Dennis Prager hinted a solution while speaking before your author's high school English classes. "What I care most about you is your *individual* identity—not your *group* identity [italics added]. . . . What I want most of all is for you to see yourselves as individuals, not as members of a group."[22]

Dr. King and Dr. Frankl both held the belief that people are not appendages; they aren't attached to skin color. They boast of their individual achievements and mourn their personal failings. A white child sitting in a classroom in the Bronx should be able to look over at a Black child in the same classroom without entertaining preconceived notions about the private views and values of that classmate; after all, people are *individuals*. They have hearts and souls and brains and dreams and ideas and hopes and loves and hates and fears. Their skin color is separate from any of those things. These are *human* qualities. And their lives have nothing to do with the sins of their fathers.

NOTES

1. *Brainy Quotes*, "Jacqueline Woodson Quotes," August 8, 2021. https://www.brainyquote.com/quotes/jacqueline_woodson_633497

2. *Mind Fuel Daily*, August 10, 2021. https://www.mindfueldaily.com

3. Mattimore Cronin, "Parable: The Emperor Has No Clothes," August 16, 2019, Origin: Hans Christian Andersen (1837). https://medium.com/@mattimore/parable-the-emperor-has-no-clothes-ace63fef6eb8

4. Diversity: "a collective sample of different"—is an acceptable definition from any standard dictionary.

5. This would never be attempted, of course; but let's play a little game: Take a few minutes and conceive of a way this "equity" practice might be successfully implemented. And then think about how popular the move would be in the NBA and among basketball fans.

6. Tucker Carlson, "Pilot Ability No Longer Matters To United Airlines, Skin Color Does," *Real Clear Politics*, April 8, 2021, posted by Tyler Stone. https://www.realclearpolitics.com/video/2021/04/08tucker_carlson_pilot_ability_no_longer_matters_to_united_airline_skin_color_does.html

7. ibid.

8. Anne Dennon, "The Value of Trade Schools in Today's Economy," *Best Colleges*, April 29, 2020. https://www.bestcolleges.com/blog/the-value-of-trade-schools/

9. James Staviridis, "Here's Why Trump Has Lost So Much Support In the Active Duty Military."

10. Abby Hoffman, initially convicted of inciting violence during a Vietnam War protest, was, arguably, the most left-leaning revolutionary of the 1960s protest movements; at least, he is often depicted that way.

11. Mike Gonzales and Dakota Wood, "The Woke Takeover Of The US Military Endangers Us All," *The New York Post*, May 23, 2021. https://nypost.com/2021/05/23/the-woke-takeover-of-the-us-military-endangers-us-all/

12. Seth Cropsey and Harry Halem, "Now Is The Time To Think About The Character Of Our Armed Forces," *Hudson Center*, March 20, 2021. https://www.hudson.org/research/16744-now-is-the-time-to-think-about-the-character-of-our-armed-forces

13. Ross Edwards is not his real name; he was very close to me. He liked repeating stories about his heroics at Normandy; I couldn't blame him for that. Before he died, he must have related the same stories at least two dozen times. There wasn't a racist bone in Ross's body, but he never complained about a lack of diversity in the military on D-Day.

14. Tucker Carlson is a brave man. Sometimes I worry for his safety.

15. Department of Diversity, "How The Military Supports Diversity And Inclusion," *Military On Source*, January 25, 2021. https://www.militaryonesource.mil/military-life-cycle/friends-extended-family/military-diversity-and-inclusion/

16. General Mark Milley, "Top US General Mark Milley Urges Greater Racial Diversity In Military," *The Economic Times*, March 6, 2021. https://economictimes.indiatimes.com/news/defence/top-us-general-mark-milley-urges-greater-racial-diversity-in-military/articleshow/82429351.cms?from=mdr

17. Seth Cropsey, "China's Military Prepares For War, While America's Military Goes 'Woke'" *The Hill*, July 7, 2021. This article explains why this fictitious kid was pointing out China's hilarity about recent dictates of the American military. https://thehill.com/opinion/national-security/561796-chinas-military-prepares-for-war-while-americas-military-goes-woke

18. Jay P. Greene and Catherine Shock, "Adding Up to Failure," *City Journal*, Winter 2008. https://www.city-journal.org/html/adding-failure-13072.html?

19. Dave Jones, "Rahim Reed Retires From The Community He Helped Build," *UCDavis*, July 19, 2021.

20. Bruce J. Gevirtzman, *Audacious Cures for America's Ailing Schools*, p. 267 Rowman & Littlefield (2011).

21. Sookhan Ho, "Are You Multiculturally Mindful?" *Virginia Tech Research Magazine*, Winter 2006, Vol. 1, p. 1.

22. Prager emphasized "e Pluribus Unum." These Latin words are on American money. It means "From many—one," *not* from one—many. There's a huge difference.

Chapter 5

The Math Doesn't Add Up

NOT A MATTER OF OPINION

In the widely acclaimed television series *Breaking Bad*, former high school chemistry teacher turned kingpin meth manufacturer, Walter White, produces a product so valuable and special that that any self-respecting drug cartel south of the border wants it, and every druggie in New Mexico craves it. The meth that Mr. White creates is perfect. Quality is what sets his dope apart from the rest; in fact, its perfection can't be emulated by anyone else. Mr. White uses his superior knowledge of chemistry and his genius in dealing with mathematical equations to create the perfect product.[1]

In the woke world of formulas, equations, and numbers, correctness hardly matters. Accuracy is an afterthought. The wokes have a different view of math: it is racist. Laurie Rubel, Brooklyn College Professor of Math Education, offered her words of wisdom on Twitter, writing that the $2 + 2 = 4$ equation "reeks of white supremacist patriarchy."[2] Sadly, she wasn't joking.

USA Today ran a headline on December 7, 2021, asking (with a straight face) a burning question: "Is Math Racist?" As the original headline began to trend on Twitter, the newspaper changed the wording to "Is Math Education Racist?"[3] *USA Today* implied, though subtly, that math curriculum is prejudicial toward minority children, because the way it is taught is beyond the reach of children of color.

"Math isn't racist . . . but the 'educators' who think it needs to be changed and made easier because some black kids struggle with it . . . *are*,"[4] *Washington Times* columnist Tim Young countered.

As your author was typing this chapter, his son happened to be sitting next to him, playing his simulated baseball game on his computer. One reason the boy loves baseball with unbridled passion is that baseball—especially in recent years—has been all about numbers. He loves *numbers*. Baseball and numbers go together. At the time of this writing, your author's son was about to embark upon his college career in a very competitive University of California. His excellence in mathematics had led to his acceptance there.

Why does he like math so much? "Well, math is unambiguous and straight forward. The answer is either right or wrong. I like that. I am that type of guy, simple—right to the point."[5]

Some students are right brain. They revel in the creative and artistic. They like the subjectivity of the universe; they thrive while dealing with open-ended questions and baffling concepts. Even words thrill these people; words have meaning, but very often the meanings are symbolic or metaphorical. There is no exactness; clarity is not high on the list of priorities for right-brain people.

For left-brain kids, the opposite is true. These youngsters see the world in terms of order. They like cause and effect, sequencing—one, two, three. If uncertainty exists in the solutions, they are fish out of water while answering questions or solving problems. For left-brainers, subjectivity challenges sanity. All options are independently connected to a right and a wrong, a black and a white. If they don't readily arrive at the correct answer, they still know that the correct answer is out there. They embark on a mission to find it. Objective truth is the only kind of truth; otherwise, "truth" becomes a matter of opinion, and opinion cannot be truth. Truth is fact. One and one equals two is *fact*. It is not opinion.

People can possess a mixture of right and left-brain dominance, but it is the mostly left-brain students that wholly embrace mathematics. They find careers as accountants, pharmacists, space engineers, and scientists. They glow as the beckons of hope for America's future. Critical to sustaining national prominence on the world's stage is mathematics: science and medicine, space and engineering, computers and technology. These sublets of advanced math hold special importance. America's competition with other countries is fierce.

When Premier Nikita Khrushchev, while pounding his shoe on a table at the United Nations General Assembly in 1961, threatened the United States with, "We will bury you!"[6] he was not referring to a military victory. He was talking about an economic victory, to be the undertaker of capitalism. Americans then took stock of their waning efforts to keep up with the Soviet Union in science and mathematics. After the Russians had launched a man into space orbit with Sputnik in 1959, the race was on for economic, political, and military superiority.

Even then, U.S. schools were doing poorly with math. American students—still do—sucked at math. Erin Richards wrote in *USA Today* on February 28, 2020, "American students struggle in math. The latest results of an international exam given to teenagers ranked the USA ninth in reading and 31st in math literacy out of 79 countries and economies. America has a smaller-than-average share of top-performing math students, and scores have essentially been flat for two decades."[7]

America's students' math scores have changed in recent years: They have become exponentially *worse*. Not only is this country lagging more than ever in its ability to maintain pace in math, but it is also falling behind at a time when it is urgent to get *ahead*.

Communist China doesn't care about how many skin colors sit in positions of economic authority, or how many cultures contribute to the research, development, and production of important complex items (such as medicines and software technologies); China cares only that the job gets done, that the mission is accomplished. This is also true for India, but at least India is not in direct competition with the United States to be the number one world power, or so they say.

Other nations (not only China) understand that math is of unwavering significance. If you are smart enough, you can figure out the answer. But you have to be smart enough. Rendering your *opinion* for an answer to an equation is silly. It makes you look like you don't belong anywhere near a math problem, let alone in the same room with world-renown scientists, technicians, doctors, and researchers. The solution to the equation doesn't change with deference to the race of the man or woman trying to solve it. Most people understand this; those that do not are probably products of the public schools.

It used to be that math communicated in a universal language. America's schools spoke that language. Schools around the world spoke that language. It was hard to imagine a different language. In videos of teachers in Korea tutoring little children, the teachers and kids often use a language with which most Americans have no familiarity. When everyone mentions *numbers* and works in different formats to manipulate those numbers, all those watching the process catch on.[8]

If a math slide problem contained the number 5, and a + sign connected that 5 to another 5, followed by a = sign, no language they spoke could have distorted the answer. The number 10 was expected; number 10 then flashed on the slide. People can use words to communicate with weird symbols or literary elements, but the *numbers* they use represent—and will *always* represent—the same entities, in the identical manner as before.[9]

Politicians, unions, and special interest groups are currently trying to change the language of mathematics, and the outlook is bleak for students that have, until now, excelled in their math studies. Some kids have complained that their schools have changed their approaches to math studies so often, their heads are swimming with numbers and senseless symbols.

DUMB AT MATH? YOU MUST BE BLACK

So-called experts tell us that math is racist. They don't seem to care about how buffoonish they may be perceived by the public. The politicians, unions, and special interest groups have their henchmen out there, making the boldest and, as a result, most ridiculous statements that have been uttered about woke influences on a changing curriculum. *Math is racist*. Understanding the reasoning behind such an allegation is somewhat entertaining.

Maybe all the worry about public perception is well-founded. It's hard to appear separated from an agenda when you stand by the axiom—the *nature* of "axioms" is probably racist, too—that math should be presented through *nonobjective* pedagogies. And to believe math is objective is to accept the edicts and principles of white supremacy.

Hold on. This gets weirder. The Bizarro policies and beliefs that have shaped curriculum and have been marching on autopilot into the schools for several years now, contain no rules; they have little conception of the rational; they actively—though sometimes subtly—reject truth. Anything is possible in the world of Bizarro. Anything. Those long-time, established boundaries for understanding mathematics aren't immune to manipulation, distortion, and craziness.

You would think that after hearing of the following change in the math curriculum in Virginia's public schools, you had heard it all wrong; surely the *opposite* is true! Come on, man! "The Virginia Department of Education (VDOE) is moving to eliminate all accelerated math options prior to 11th grade, preventing higher-achieving students from advancing ahead of others in the school system."[10]

What?

Why would they do this? Doesn't the nixing of advanced math courses penalize higher-achieving kids? Doesn't it figure children who have demonstrated keen math skills, even as early as first grade, should be elevated to higher levels of learning, not kept stagnant or dropped down a notch? After all, America's kids are, well, dumb, when it comes to math. When teachers come across young people who can excel in this critical subject, shouldn't they go out of their way to support them? These children are the leaders of tomorrow in space exploration, medical research, and computer technology. These three areas will determine which countries dominate the world, and which nations fall into passive compliance, under the control of superior nations.

Wokes believe that the students assigned to learn remedial math wind up feeling bad about themselves. Educators uncovered this attitude years ago when they distributed students into *reading* groups; it was called *tracking*. If you found yourself in the "dummies' track," you were probably treated like a dummy by others and reacted accordingly. Maybe other students, fearing *they* might wind up in the dummies' group too, made fun of you. All this may have convinced you that you *were* a dummy![11]

The positive response by educators—not parents—to this modality of teaching led the way to even more homogeneous cooperative grouping. Tracking was supposed to be a secret, but all participating students knew who the "dummies" were. This did little for the "dummies'" self-esteem or, for that matter, the self-esteem of the "dummies'" parents.

But the construct of higher-level classes within a single subject matter was different. Students enrolled in those classes—or their teachers recruited them—because they had *earned* their way there. Once they had passed geometry, they were allowed to register for Algebra II, trigonometry, and calculus. The tier system afforded kids the benefit of striving for personal goals, passing Advanced Placement exams in their quest for college, and moving to the front of the line when it came time for submitting a job application for a position in which they had to be *smart*.

This sort of philosophy, one in which quality is recognized, excellence rewarded, is currently under fire. It is being attacked. And you'll never guess *why*. Ok, maybe you will guess *why*. A policy of recognizing excellence is racist. It fails to achieve equity. By roadblocking the ability of brighter children to march through a tougher, more advanced curriculum, you achieve (by way of warped thinking) equity. *Everyone* is even. The merciless meritocracy loses.

Children have been stigmatized. Minority kids are told they're too stupid to do math; furthermore, they're being relegated to the slow group from the get-go. Baffling. These boys and girls are identified as excelling in athletics, theater, dance, art, and music. They are respected for being able to opine on almost any subject in the universe. But when it comes to figuring out the correct mixture of life-saving additives to stuff into a medicine capsule, many patronizing, condescending educators consider Blacks incapable.

THE UNIVERSAL "REMEDY" OF EQUITY

The combinations of those life-saving additives must be precise. Accurate formulas for making medicines work are not a matter of opinion. The chips are on the table when you work in the medical field. There is no room for error. You don't iron out discrepancies in a discussion. That's a tough concept for some people to grasp. For whatever reason, wokes, want to interject emotion into everything, even working with pharmaceuticals.

It does not come down to whether certain racial groups can do the math; it *does* come down to whether certain *individuals* can do the math. Math has nothing to do with race or religion or sexual preference or culture. Either you can calculate the formula, or you can't. This seems straightforward; math proficiency requires extraordinarily hard work, intense desire, and hours and hours of study and remediation for most students to succeed. Finding math solutions should be void of opinion.[12]

Evidently, teachers like Lori Meyers don't like the notion of hard work and hours of study. "Unfair. Racist." Meyers suggests, "With California schools consistently performing below average in math on both the CAASPP [California Assessment of Student Performance and Progress] and on our Nation's Report Card, it is especially important that the State Board of Education provides us educators with resources that [don't] demean teachers and single out one race for blame."[13]

Meyers' group sent a letter to state leaders with a request to reconsider the Equitable Math program, which is included multiple times as a reference in the state's draft framework.[14] Apparently, California's endgame is not to do a better job of teaching math to *all* students; it is to achieve sensitivity for diversity, while making certain that equitable *outcomes* occur. Using that logic, if high scoring math students are pulled down to become "even" with low-scoring math students, equity is achieved; the mission is accomplished.

Equitable is a reference to outcomes, not opportunities. The goal is for everyone to score the same in math: ***The goal is for everyone to score the same in math.*** It's not, *we should try to raise test scores*; OR *we should raise the level of math achievement overall, not with respect to one ethnic group;* OR *here are ways to help our students achieve their goals in math, whether they are finishing high school, going to college, or working in Dad's accounting office.*

Why do kids have to score the *same*? Isn't it more important that they *all* score better? The "same" could mean they all score badly. The same, yes. But *badly*, the same.

One thing that challenges equity is, as Meyers refers to it, "divisive content that will impede us from accomplishing these important goals in math instruction."[15]

Enter the Oregon Department of Education and its *Pathway to Equitable Math Instruction* tool kit where "math equity" can be achieved by "visibilizing the toxic characteristics of *white supremacy culture with respect to math.*" (italics added) Two "toxic characteristics" include: (1) focusing on the "right" answer; and (2) independent (individual) practice valued over teamwork or collaboration.[16]

Did you catch that? White supremacy is impeding match scores in the schools. White supremacists bring a culture of *focusing on the right answer* and, heaven forbid, *valuing working as an individual*, as opposed to, say, a member of an underachieving *group*.

You can't make this stuff up!

RACIST AUTONOMY

The people that support the notion of "divisive content," in the math curriculum are not, except for leaders of the teachers' unions, educators. They are political and sociological cronies; They emerge from colleges and universities, where educators have been implementing—at least, discussing—this nonsense for several decades. Driven by their woke agendas, these people have discovered that the squeaky wheel gets the oil.

You would think educators know better than to believe that math, based on its inherent objectivity, is racist. On the surface, none of this would seem to make any sense. One must dig deeply to identify systemic racism in the schools, based on math content. Even educators are confused. A few individuals are talking about racist math; hardly anybody seems to know exactly what that *means*.

Interim Upper School Math Department head, Tom James, said, "There's a hunger for how math can be used to make the world a more equitable place, how it can be used to understand racism and other dynamics of oppression, and how it can be used . . . as a tool for social justice."[17]

One noteworthy behavior is the way in which teachers are attempting to shape classroom culture. While collaboration is common in other disciplines, James suggested students sometimes approach math with a strong focus on personal, rather than collective understandings, a mindset that is prevalent in dominant culture.[18] The "new math" teachers emphasize collaboration. Individualism, relying on your own cognitive and computation skills, they claim, discriminates against group culture. Math is not just what you can get out of it for yourself. In the "new math," born of antiracist pedagogies, teachers focus on *collaboration* skills.[19]

Of course, collaboration skills are nothing new to education. If the entire *group* works the problem, and they wind up with the "wrong" answer, then it is a collaborative misunderstanding and not pinned on a single individual. What's different now, however, is that the collaborative group is diverse. It is not a race-labeled wrong answer; the heterogeneous mathematicians botched it together.[20]

Progressive educators are working to humanize mathematics—bring it alive—by having students read stories about the professional journeys of mathematicians across group identifiers. Some of those educators claim that they're not tokenizing mathematicians of color. They have cited female mathematicians and LGBTQ mathematicians, too. While China is forging ahead in every aspect with disease research and technology, the United States remains proud that their budding mathematicians learn from scientists that comprise a nice sampling of ten different genders.[21]

Without a doubt, those multiple genders should come up with the correct answer to a common problem. If they are unable to do so, they would not be doing math. Your author is not particularly familiar with the ten different genders in the study, but he does know a man from a woman (most of the time), and it is an absolute certainty that when a man counts ten donuts, and a woman counts ten donuts, they would both conclude there is a cumulative of twenty donuts.

Still, the progressive "improvements" in math continue. Ongoing efforts include additional shaping of the curriculum, as well as further exploration about how math is taught, how work is graded, and how to achieve proportional representation across course levels. The goal of this work is to create an inclusive and supportive learning environment so that all students will be equally engaged in the study of mathematics.[22] Note here the term *equally engaged*. This is not the same as having an equal *opportunity* to be engaged.

Equity does not mean opportunity; it *means* the outcomes will be distributed in equal proportions among races, cultures, genders, religions, and who knows what else. Proportional sameness is the bottom line. It doesn't matter if students arrived at the right answers or the wrong answers; it matters that they arrived at the answers together as a beautiful diverse mix of skin colors and genders. Before anyone starts squawking about the irrelevancy of this phenomenon, one must remember that all subject matters should be used as tools of antiracism. If that is not one of the outcomes—antiracism—then the subject itself is racist.

Are you shaking your head yet?

Holding minority students to a black and white, wrong and right mode of learning is racist, especially when much of the time their answers are wrong. Only privileged children have the luxury of treading through the mud of math, only to eventually rest in the purity of truth, which means that one plus one equals two.

Is there a way to interject *opinion* into this formula? In other words, after the student comes up with the answer *five*, is it possible for her to argue that she is right about that answer? The way a teacher might respond is something like, "Close, Bobbie. Very close! Figuring out that two plus two is *five* is moving in the right direction! Very good!"

Some teachers award partial credit to students for showing *process*, but that isn't good enough for woke educators. The theory of racist math rests with the belief that mathematics is a tool of white oppression, inherently biased against Blacks. Black kids shouldn't be expected to master the precision of math; they should be celebrated for just talking around it, gamely approximating the answers.[23] To level the playing field, Black children should be held to a different competency level, an alternative expectation, a lower standard. Mathematical *approximations*, as opposed to correct answers, is the goal.

Just ask those who are trying to help.

JENNIFER'S CAR, JUAN'S GUN

For years, educators have complained about standardized math tests. Their contention is that word problems present a cultural bias. If you start a question with, "*Jennifer bought a new car and put a down payment of a thousand dollars*" you are reaching into a world that doesn't exist for a lot of poor kids. The assumption is that poor kids would not be able to afford a new car; they would never *consider* buying a new car. Because of their life experience limitations, they would not know about "down payments," either.

The confusion between class bias and racial bias is alarming. Adult educators should know better. The pandering to minority groups, and the condescension toward them, displays a bigoted view toward some groups of people. There are lots of white people who are too poor to shell out dough for a new car. Many Black people *can* spend money on a new car. The limited assumption that pale skin people have money to spend, and dark skin people do not is, in fact, a form of bigotry.

Besides, what does it matter if word problems discuss racial associations and cultural norms? If a white boy, Tommy, is working on a math problem concerning how much money he must spend on a gift for his friend's *quinceañera*, is Tommy unable to answer, because the exam posed a question about a holiday outside his own culture? Of course not. Adults don't give kids enough credit for being able see through this garbage. Kids instinctively know that attempts to insert culture into the wording of thought problems have no bearing on the answers.

Mathematician and author, James Lindsay commented, "Feats of engineering like space travel and rocketry utterly depend upon accepting stable meanings of mathematical statements like 2+2=4 as objectively true, not mere accidents of culture."[24] Which is a statement and belief consistent with common sense, although common sense was thrown out the window a while ago. A strong argument can be made that common sense in public education never existed in the first place. Woke infiltration of the schools accentuates that belief.

According to John Benson, an award-winning long-time mathematics educator, "Mathematics is the only place where there is absolute proof that something is true."[25] In mathematics, everyone must first agree to certain assumptions within the system. Since we all start with the same assumptions and follow the same rules, inferences don't need to be drawn, leaps in logic don't need to be made.[26]

Critics don't really care about such logic. They move on to other powder kegs; they need to get something started. It's not satisfactory that math, the most basic and time-tested of school subjects, has escaped unscathed from their antiracist propaganda. So, they are enraged by "racist" math questions from standardized tests that look like this:

> *Marvin steals Juan's skateboard. As Marvin skates away at 15 mph, Juan loads his 357 Magnum. If Juan takes 20 seconds to load his piece, how far away will Marvin be before he gets whacked by Juan?*

Or this one:

> *Tyrone knocked-up four girls in the gang. There are 20 girls in the gang. What is the exact percentage of the girls that Tyrone knocked-up?*[27]

It is an interesting dichotomy: On the one hand, the presumption is if student test-takers more closely identify with the questions, they are more prone to getting the right answers; on the other hand, the exam creators have committed a serious sin by stumbling upon (or intentionally creating) cultural stereotypes that lots of folks find inappropriate or blatantly offensive.

The easiest solution is to stop worrying about creating *any* stereotypes, positive or negative. To be successful at doing this, test creators—and those that spur them on—need to be in concurrence with the idea that *cultural identification with the content of a math test has no positive impact on students' results*.

Whether it is about Juan committing a gun crime, or Tyrone deciding which scholarship offer to accept to a prestigious university, the test itself is rife with *objective* answers that do not change based on the student's ability, or inability, to figure out that after you count to ten, the next number is eleven.

Wokes promise that their antiracist solutions will advance America's students in leaps and bounds on the world's math stage. They claim their ideas are aimed at enhancing student learning. They recommend that you teach math via "storytelling circles," incorporating dance, music, song, call and response, and "other cultural ways" of communicating.[28] Their priority is to establish diversity among math teachers, test problems, and course selections; optimum diversity is attained by measuring the criteria of race, gender, and cultural class. They want "close answers" to pass for correct answers; to demand absolute correctness is a form of racism.

There: that raises levels of student achievement!

Jason Rantz wrote that teachers' unions are pushing the envelope. Unions argue that white supremacy culture shows up in the classroom when teachers "treat mistakes in problems by equating them with wrongness" because it "reinforces the ideas of perfectionism [that students shouldn't make mistakes] and paternalism [teachers or other authorities can and should correct mistakes]."[29]

If this is true—and what a *stretch* it is—why is it to be universally condemned? There are those who advocate perfectionism; there are those who disagree with striving for perfectionism. No matter, why is one view launched into a sky of devils and heathens? Why is authority a form of paternalism? And *why is paternalism always wrong*? Sometimes a man knows a better way; sometimes a woman does. Often an *older* person, a father, may have gained enough wisdom during his long lifetime to pass along a mature judgment on issues that haunt us, that challenge us. Is it wrong for us *sometimes* to believe that father knows best? Paternal wisdom has been dumped upon.

Instead, the advocates of this new woke philosophy are more concerned with a weirdly perceived racism than they are with the development of adequately developed skills in American children. Equipping students so they gain the ability to compete in a changing world, in which math concepts become more and more sophisticated and complex, should be a paramount goal of all educators, even wokes. But it is not. Their main goal is to combat the racism of white people. They drive the classroom as their vehicle to achieving that end.

NOTES

1. Mr. White is not the prototype television teacher hero. But we still root for him. He is brilliant in his practical knowledge of chemistry and physics. He is also a bad-ass.

2. M.K. Sprinkle, "Racist Mathematics Or 'Racism Propounded As Antiracism'?" *The Baltimore Sun*, March 13, 2021. https://www.baltimoresun.com/maryland/carroll/opinion/cc-op-sprinkle-031321-20210313-m2lg4tomcndolfj5kebf6asike-story.html

3. *USA Today*, "Is Math Racist?" December 7, 2021, via Lindsay Kornick, Fox News, December 9, 2021. https://www.foxnews.com/media/usa-today-mocked-asking-is-math-racist

4. ibid. Tim Young, *Washington Times*.

5. When he was about four years old, I had introduced baseball to him in the form of little plastic balls he could bat around the house. After he swung and missed a few times, I told him, "Keep your eye on the ball." He picked up a ball and pressed it up to his eye. He wasn't kidding.

6. *Exploring History*, "'We Will Bury You'—How A Mistranslation Almost Started WW3," July 14, 2020. https://medium.com/exploring-history/we-will-bury-you-how-a-mistranslation-almost-started-ww3-4a285162e2b9

7. Erin Richards, "Math Scores Stink In America," *USA Today*, February 28, 2020, par. 1. https://www.usatoday.com/story/news/education/2020/02/28/math-scores-high-school-lessons-freakonomics-pisa-algebra-geometry/4835742002/

8. Students often bolt awake when they hear an easy problem. They know the answer. *Everybody* does.

9. By the time you read this, Virginia's policy of dumbing down math classes may have changed. Sweeping changes, as the result of the November 2021 election, could be responsible. We'll see.

10. Sam Dorman, "Virginia Moving To Eliminate All Accelerated Math Courses Before 11th Grade As Part Of Equity-Focused Plan," Fox News, April 22, 2021. https://www.foxnews.com/us/virginia-accelerated-math-courses-equity

11. But you weren't a "math dummy" because of your skin color. I am white, Italian American—and as dumb as they come in math. I can add fractions, but only if the bottom numbers are the same.

12. I may be out of line here, but it seems to me if you provide the wrong answer, for example, to a literature question, there may be a *little* stigma; after all, if you identify Steinbeck's works as esoteric and stuffy, the teacher may disagree with you. You have a stake in it; it is your opinion. If you try to calculate the time it would take for you to fly to Mars and back, and you get it wrong, no big deal. No offense. You have no personal stake in your calculation.

13. Lori Meyers, "California Promotes 'Dismantling Racism In Mathematics' Guidance In Draft For Statewide Framework," Fox News, April 14, 2021. https://www.foxnews.com/us/california-racism-math-framework

14. As of this writing, they have not approved the dumping of accelerated math. That could change at any time, Virginia could decide to water the bill down, accruing the same deadening affect. We'll see what happens under their new governor. But school districts in other states are making the same kinds of poor decisions with gifted students' programs.

15. ibid.

16. Authors not specified, *A Pathway to Equitable Math Instruction*, "Dismantling Racism in Mathematics Instruction," May, 2021. equitable math.org. What?!?! This booklet must be read to be believed. I feel sorry for all kids, now that I have become somewhat familiar with this manifesto about white supremacy in *math*.

17. Tom James, "Spotlight: Building an Anti-Racist Math Curriculum," *Impact*, December 10, 2020. https://www.packer.edu/about/diversity/anti-racism/impact-detail-page/~board/impact-newsletter/post/impact-spotlight-building-an-anti-racist-math-curriculum

18. ibid.

19. Presumably, a more diverse collaboration would reach a more diverse right answer to the problem, which would then diversify the numbers that would benefit from the exercise—or whatever.

20. Authors not specified, *A Pathway to Equitable Math Instruction*, "Dismantling Racism in Mathematics Instruction," May, 2021. equitable math.org. I extrapolated their conclusion that collaborative wrong answers are better than individual wrong answers, though, for the life of me, I do not understand why this is true.

21. Tom James, "Spotlight: Building an Anti-Racist Math Curriculum," *Impact*, December 10, 2020. https://www.packer.edu/about/diversity/anti-racism/impact-detail-page/~board/impact-newsletter/post/impact-spotlight-building-an-anti-racist-math-curriculum

22. Austin Kelly, "5 Ways To Build Equity In Your Math Lessons," *We Are Teachers*, August 5, 2019. https://www.weareteachers.com/equity-math/

23. M.K. Sprinkle, "Racist Mathematics Or 'Racism Propounded as Antiracism'?"*Carroll County Times*, March 13, 2021. https://www.baltimoresun.com/maryland/carroll/opinion/cc-op-sprinkle-031321-20210313-m2lg4tomcndolfj5kebf6asike-story.html

24. Emma Colton, "Math Professor Claims Equation 2+2=4 'Reeks Of White Supremacist Patriarchy,'" *Washington Examiner*, August 10, 2020. https://www.washingtonexaminer.com/news/math-professor-claims-equation-2-2-4-reeks-of-white-supremacist-patriarchy

25. Zachary Herrmann, "Finding What's True," *Harvard Graduate School of Education*, May 17, 2020. https://www.gse.harvard.edu/uk/blog/finding-whats-true

26. ibid.

27. These are not actual standardized test questions. But in order to make a point, these parodies are brought to CBC.CA by contributor Billy Brooks, November 26, 2021. https://br.ifunny.co/picture/when-regular-math-is-too-difficult-so-you-introduce-africentric-7W3630Wd8

28. ibid. They also call for the curtailing of order in the classroom; *order* and *routine* reek of white supremacy. When teachers demand that students raise their hands before they are called upon to give an answer, it is suggestive of a patriarchy.

29. Jason Rantz, "Melinda Gates Foundation Bankrolls 'Math Is Racist' Lunacy," *The Jason Rantz* Show, 770 KTTH, February 19, 2021.

Chapter 6

The War on Boys Massacre

A PSYCHOLOGY OF FAILURE

Sociologist and author Christina Hoff Sommers wrote in 2000, "This we think we know: American schools favor boys and grind down girls. The truth is the very opposite. By virtually every measure, girls are thriving in school; it is boys who are the second sex."[1]

The U.S. Department of Education concluded, "A review of the facts shows boys, not girls, on the weak side of an education gender gap."[2]

Sociologists call the phenomenon, "A war on boys [in America]." This war is the unlikeliest of all wars. Perhaps, in response to a perceived institutional sexism, and, perhaps, in response to the undying assumption that America is being dominated by an unrelenting, undying hierarchy of perpetuated paternalism, America's institutions have called for, and exercised, an all-out war on men and boys.

This book deals with education institutions, the places where young people and their teachers hang out; it is an examination of the effects of the new progressive teachings in those institutions. In accordance with their goals, woke educators, bossy politicians, and school boards have partially succeeded in affecting parity in the schools.

What does this "war on boys" have to do with parity?

The answers may leave you disgusted.

A generation ago, young people were able to make various assumptions about their futures that, for the most part, turned out to be their reality. If you were promised by your parents and teachers from a very young age that you will be rich—because you were smart or talented or good looking—you had a greater chance of *becoming* rich. Your reality often molded to your circumstances, not only through your own actions but through the reactions of others towards you.

On the flip side, if you were told that you were destined for poverty or unhappiness or an early grave, you were more likely to wind up poor or unhappy or prematurely dead. Your race is holding you back. Your parents are holding you back. Your gender is holding you back. *You will be held back*! You will find a way to fail, either by an inherent deficiency in your motivation, or because of the ways others treat you, based on what *they* perceived of your potential.[3]

So much has already been said by brilliant writers and educators, who have written books, published journals, and conducted seminars about self-inflicted failure. The negativity comes from *somewhere*. And it can be relentless.

YOUNG MALES AT THE CROSSROADS

Unfairness in the education system speaks volumes in the disturbing manner it treats *boys*. Yes, you heard this correctly. It may sound quite different from what you have been led to believe—or thought you already knew.

In the 1950s, and well into the 1960s, if you were a boy and about to enter high school, you knew you had challenges ahead and ominous barriers to hurdle. You were also aware of numerous life options immediately available to you, many of which—to be perfectly honest—because you were a male.

You chose your own path. You would either . . .

> . . . graduate high school and go to work at a menial job for a little while. You might decide to help your family with their finances. Or your family might help *you*, until your head becomes fully screwed on, and you have an ample chance to explore the limitlessness of your future.

OR . . .

> . . . graduate high school and immediately land a job in the full-time labor force. With this job, you would make enough money to support a wife, children, and even buy a modest home—at least, qualify for a mortgage. The notion that a boy just coming out of high school could get a forty-hour a week job and earn enough money to support a small family is unheard of today. (The racial barriers and inequities to securing these jobs began to disintegrate with the adoption of Civil Rights legislation in 1964.)[4]

OR . . .

> . . . graduate high school and attend a four-year college or university. This option would help you to win favor with women and bring a promise of financial security for the rest of your life. A two-year college was also an option, but you could

land a spot in a four-year university, almost as easily as a two-year college, so why go the route of a junior or community college if you didn't have to? Money issues constituted a challenge, but a university usually wound up being affordable for those who yearned to attend one.

OR . . .

. . . enlist in the United States military. Military education in those days was not as all-encompassing or sophisticated as it would later become, but that option stood in the open and was ripe for the taking.

Knowing these options, American boys attended high school with a degree of certainty. Males in those days had to deal with the social ills that have plagued all generations of young Americans—gangs, poverty, maligned masculinity, and family concerns that inhibited them from meeting their goals. Those happened, too.

No matter which option they wound up pursuing, life would be, at the very least, neatly packaged for boys (or so it seemed).[5] This was more than could be said for girls, who struggled with the sexism they faced during their public-school lives and from society, in general. Girls had to contend with the stereotypical belief that young ladies should not have a career—or attend a college.

Many of the girls that enrolled in college did so because they were looking to meet a college boy. Despite the truth about high school graduates being able to find decent jobs with which they could start a family, college men presented a more attractive option for young women than high school grads. Families that were looking out for their daughters' welfare endorsed their daughter's quest to marry a college guy. And they did so with enthusiasm.

All in all, young men were in a much better place, until . . . they *weren't*.

The War in Vietnam played havoc with the lives of young American males during the 1960s. Suddenly, the option of going into the military and getting a free education didn't look so attractive. It was one thing to enlist in the Air Force and learn how to fly airplanes; it was another thing to *be drafted* into the Air Force and forced to jump from those airplanes into enemy rice fields, where machine gun bullets blazed over their heads and artillery rockets exploded just a few feet from where they were hiding.

During the War in Vietnam, the once scared military, the heroes of Normandy and Iwo Jima, were labeled "baby killers." They took their places as the rejected, unsavory minority, unqualified to apply for college deferments or unworthy of landing a high security government job.

Vietnam changed America in ways that dozens of books and movies and thousands of articles have highlighted. Most of those changes were cataclysmic. The manifestations of a life of uncertainty, as opposed to the certainty that existed before it, caused turmoil in American society; and the outgrowth of that destruction and confusion, came at the expense of male adolescents.

Young Black and Hispanic Americans were drafted into the war first. They were less likely to attend college. They were also less able to afford nifty attorneys to find ways for them to evade conscription. Young men, once they had finished basic training, were faced with the ambiguity of what would happen to them next—where they would be assigned, where they would be stationed, where they would be destined to spill their blood.

Sons of the well-to-do, despite the pronounced and highly regarded objectivity of the United States military, were relegated to safer and saner futures. The brass assigned them to cushy on-base jobs or directly into an education specialty. These young men had greater access to officer training programs. Sometimes the military omitted the economically privileged from their plans altogether.[6]

In 1965, deferments for *married* men were cancelled. Though the college deferment remained, male students were expected to maintain full-time status (at least 12 credits a semester) and at a 2.0 (middle C) Grade Point Average. If they did not, they became susceptible to receiving an induction notice. This put an enormous amount of pressure on college professors, who had power over life and death, incentivizing a young man's willingness to cheat on exams.

After all had been said and done, life for boys in the late 1960s held little certainty. What made it even uglier: when men returned from the war—*if* they returned—the economy looked bleaker than it did when they had shipped off to combat. The economic perks of a nation that had once settled into a post–World War II standard of living had vanished.

A WAR ON BOYS BEGINS

American men—those in high school or younger—looked around at the world and questioned why so much had changed. The wonderment of having purpose in life, sustained goals, and clearly outlined guidelines to success, had dissipated.

Men in America had concluded . . .

- Women don't need me to provide for them anymore. They are providing for themselves. (Or are being provided for by a myriad of Great Society welfare programs.)

- Women don't need me to shield them anymore. It is insulting to a woman that I should stand up for her, open a door for her, or protect her from an unwanted advance. Women take karate now, you know.
- Women don't need me to make babies anymore. They can make babies in a lot of different ways, *some of them without a man.*
- Women don't need me to marry them anymore. There is a variety of genders from which women may now choose a spouse; many women don't wish to marry *anyone.*
- Women don't need me to please them sexually anymore. With so many sexually delightful options, what woman really needs a *man* to stroke her?

What once had served as reliable indicators of consistency and success in male-female relationships has evaporated. A man's self-worth is sometimes defined by what he means to a woman. If he loses a sense of that purpose, he may surrender his self-worth.

Three boys, seniors in high school, chimed in on this subject. The boys play on the varsity baseball team, and they all have a sense of self-respect: [7]

DANNY: I used to think about the time I got to be a senior, I would know what I wanted to do with my life. But here I am, a senior, and I have no idea what I want to do now. I don't have the grades for a good college, and I have no job prospects. My dad used to tell me that he would teach me his trade (an electrician), but he died two years ago, and I lost interest in that. My big concern now is how I am going to make money after I graduate. I don't want to live with my mom and sister for the rest of my life.

GRACIANO: My life has been all about baseball. And my girlfriend. Well, my girlfriend dumped me around Christmastime, and then the baseball season was cut short because of the pandemic. I tried to fix these things. I got on a team that played out of state (in Nevada), but a couple of months later, Nevada closed their (youth) baseball too. Then I asked my girlfriend if we could get back together; she told me no, not a chance. That seemed strange to me, an answer like that, so I pressed her to tell me why, and she said that she likes girls now. Here I am, about to graduate high school, hardly any friends, no baseball, no girlfriend, and I have no idea what I am going to do in the future.

NICO: I am probably going to live with my parents for a while; that is, my mom and my stepdad. It looks like I might be headed for the navy. He (my stepdad) keeps threatening to throw me out of the house now that I'm eighteen unless I contribute to our finances. The economy is just beginning to turn around, but I don't see a good job for me. My stepdad said that he would help pay for community college if I got a job and chipped in. My sister is going to Cal State. She's doing great. She's always had the best grades. In two years, she will have a college degree, and I'll be working at Taco Bell.

Awkward for boys is when girls outperform them, especially academically. The last anecdotal example highlights the embarrassment some boys feel when their female siblings do better than they do. But more than anecdotal, consider how society has slanted against boys, especially in the education arena. Across the country, boys have never been in more trouble: They earn 70 percent of the D's and F's that teachers dole out. They make up two-thirds of students labeled "learning disabled." They are the culprits in a whopping 9 of 10 alcohol and drug violations, and the suspected perpetrators in 4 out of 5 crimes that end up in juvenile court. They account for 80 percent of high school dropouts and attention deficit disorder diagnoses.[8] Read those statistics again. And some of you thought girls were doing *worse* than boys?

The sirens of panic and despair among the male population are sounding louder and longer. Consider . . .

1. Teachers communicate better with girls. Most people do not think this is the case; however, after forty-some years as a classroom teacher, your author knows of the superior interaction capabilities of girls. And so does any other educator that claims to do even a modicum of introspection.
2. Girls constitute over two-thirds of college students headed toward undergraduate degrees, and three-fourths of students headed toward postgraduate degrees.
3. Girls have surpassed boys in math and science scores, once the cornerstone of bragging rights for boys.
4. Girls earn most of the academic scholarships.
5. Girls are more likely to be awarded as "scholar-athletes" than are boys.
6. Teachers more often refer boys for discipline related issues.
7. Boys are far more likely to wind up incarcerated in the criminal justice system.
8. Girls are involved in much higher numbers than are boys in speech, drama, academic decathlon, model United Nations, and other high achieving extracurricular activities.
9. Girls spend more time volunteering for, and contributing to, charities.
10. Girls are more likely than boys to wind up with careers in the medical field as technicians and pharmacists. More than half the students in medical school are females.

Although it has not been measured or surveyed in a formal arena, several pieces of data have shown boys tend to be more politically conservative (if they are political at all) than girls. This, too, is a mixed bag, as girls are more likely than boys to vote or to become social activists. Until 1980, men voted in higher numbers than women.[9] For some reason—perhaps, a multitude of reasons—today's young men have disengaged from the political process. They have grown cynical and despairing.

There are several reasons for this turn-around in America. What used to be termed, "The Battle Between the Sexes," while discussing different sociological phenomena regarding gender differences, now appears as a successfully implemented war on boys.

Thirty years ago, women's lib groups, civil rights advocates, and educators in search of fairness, looked inward; conditioned by a rapidly changing society and the vulnerability of young men, they noticed a few "facts." *And panicked*:

1. Girls lag behind boys in public education. (*That was never the case. Girls did not focus on math and science, but they still scored better grades in school.*)
2. American paternalism has assigned girls to lesser societal roles. (*That's an opinion. Some people still believe that raising your own children in a safe family environment is a "lesser societal role." Go figure.*)
3. Legal barriers seem to perpetuate gender stereotypes and sexism.
4. Males dominate as recipients of college degrees.
5. Males dominate as lawyers, doctors, and scientists.
6. Men's and boys' sports rule the roost on amateur and professional circuits.
7. Women make less money for equal work. (*That is complicated, and not totally true. Children in American schools are still being harangued with this notion; it is now a lie.*)
8. Women are expected to be subjugated to nesting and child rearing. (*Subjugated? That's the word they wanted to use?*)
9. The federal government is dominated by male politicians and judges. (*It was. And women voted for those guys!*)
10. Service careers (police, fire-fighters, paramedics) are composed of mostly men. (There were physiological reasons for this. Again, it's changed, where it has been safe to change.)

So, something had to be done . . .

Society pulled the switch, ignited the fire, unloaded a cannon . . .

It started with the schools. It always starts with the schools. Get in; get out. Make it seem quick and easy, and before you know it, you will reach your sociological Eden.

TOXIC TEACHING

Today, adolescent males, plagued by their lack of self-worth, are sitting in ninth grade classrooms. They are figuring out their purpose in life, and where they are going to be in ten years—or even *next* year. They are pondering why not even one girl has asked them to the Sadie Hawkins Dance, or why the new acne cream they bought online hasn't started to work. They listen to their teacher drone on about "toxic masculinity," and how boys are violent and aggressive and mean and bigoted, *just because they are boys*. Various news outlets and books have blamed a new concept, "toxic masculinity,"[10] for rape, murder, mass shootings, gang violence, online trolling, domestic abuse, climate change, and the 2016 election of Donald Trump. And they do so with a serious face.

They teach that boys, simply by being of their male gender, exude *bad*. Sociologist Raewyn Conner observed, "When the term *toxic masculinity* refers to the assertion of masculine privilege or men's power, it is making a worthwhile point. There are well-known gender patterns in violent and abusive behavior."[11] In other words, Timmy, you are a boy; therefore, you are bad . . . unless you get it (your boyhood?) under control.

Children hear this bunk from men and women in positions of authority, and they *listen* to it. In one ninth grade classroom in Texas, the teacher typed up—*and handed out*—copies of the ten most poisonous traits of toxic Masculinity.[12] Your author could not resist a brief commentary on each.

Being stoic. It's not altogether clear why outwardly displaying your vulnerabilities is such a terrific characteristic. Even if stoicism is a masculine trait, it is not obvious why it is *toxic*.

Being promiscuous. Women are not sometimes promiscuous? *Teacher, my mama has three boyfriends my dad doesn't know about.* Most men do not praise promiscuity in other men. If anything, infidelity is a sign of someone being a jerk, and good men despise other men that are jerks.

Championing heterosexuality as the norm. That could be a religious position. But a gender *poison*? Hmm . . . don't a lot of women prefer heterosexuality to be the norm? Maybe they are bigoted. But *that* trait is not unique to men.

Violence. This may have something to do with hormones. It was probably a good thing that men stepped up and didn't regret their high testosterone levels from 1941 to 1945, while Hitler was hanging around. The violent acts of decent, courageous men saved the world.

Dominance. Studies have shown that a good man—not a louse—will do most anything to please his woman. The same studies indicate that men allow women to have the final say in arguments, if these women are not espousing ideas that are illegal, immoral, or unsafe and unhealthy. Some women prefer their men to be in control—though not abusive. They like men that are strong in that way.

Sexual aggression. The same idea: the difference between a decent person and a jerk comes into play. Again, so do hormones. No morally rational person excuses rape or sexual abuse or crassness. But if a man comes on to a woman, please explain why that is always poison.

Not displaying emotion. Yes, it is true: Emotion *is* a feminine characteristic. But guys do a lot of blubbering, especially while they are watching baseball movies.

Not being a feminist. Do you know *anyone* that seriously thinks if a man believes in equal rights for women, he is weak, frail, and not masculine? Seriously. *Come on, man*!

Risk taking. Danielle says that boys who take risks, such as mountain climbing or riding fast on motorcycles, are sexy. Sorry, Danielle, these scary boys have been contaminated with toxic masculinity; what turns you on about a guy needs to change!

Not engaging in household chores or caregiving. Men who clean their dishes, wash their clothes, and take care of their children rarely brag about it. But large numbers of men have been domesticated; they help with these things. Normal people believe these are good men, kind and considerate and loving; there's nothing wrong with them. Some men refuse to participate in these traditionally female behaviors. They seem selfish, too. And they probably are. But *toxic*?

Imagine hearing from your teachers that the things you thought were good and special about you—because you were a boy—were suddenly contorted and twisted and manipulated into sounding *bad*.

Psychotherapist Diane Barth wrote, "Men are not so clear about what it means to be a good guy. We're in a moment where what it means to be a man is shifting—and to some [boys] it feels like there are a lot of mixed messages floating around. . . . There's a very unclear set of expectations as to how a man should behave."[13]

THE CASUALTIES OF WAR

American boys claim behavioral characteristics that may not be ideal for bragging material. Lately, boys have been noticed for their high rates of suicide. In the past, girls managed to try to kill themselves at higher rates than boys. As of now, boys more often succeed at offing themselves.

The Conversation offered data on the mental health crisis of male suicide. "There is an important sex and gender gap in deaths by suicide: about two or three boys to one girl."[14] Girls talk about suicide more often than boys. They surely think more often about killing themselves. But the ultimate winners, eliminating themselves at a higher rate than their gender counterparts, are *boys*.

The suicide rates for every age group and gender mix went up during the height of the pandemic, but boys are more serious about offing themselves. Teenage boys, especially without sports and person-to-person male contact, could not recognize themselves in the mirror and saw no light at the end of the dark tunnel; suicide was their only means of "success." Boys are better at killing themselves.

Doctors have examined the usual culprits of despair, loneliness, and isolation, and have applied them to young males between twelve and twenty-two, those much more likely to commit suicide than are girls in the same age range. A few reasons for the predilection of boys to commit suicide stood out: First, boys often use more violent means, making medical intervention difficult. Second, traditional gender roles (be *tough*) discourage boys from sharing their thoughts and seeking out help. And third, boys have heard for decades that they are in some cruel way a microcosm for all that is wrong with the world.[15]

And so . . .

It used to be that American boys were the pride and joy of their families. They would carry on the surname. They would set a precedent of college enrollment for their families of future generations. Because the coveted professional careers were dominated by boys, males born into the family ignited inspiration, hope for the future of that family. Boys had displayed more potential for becoming doctors, lawyers, professors, and CEOs.

That has changed.

Being a boy today is harder than ever.

For a boy to sit in a classroom, he must endure; most teachers don't care about the inherent differences in learning modalities (Boys must move around; they are kinetic learners.) of boys and girls. Boys catch the double-whammy: impatience of their teachers, and disrespect from a society that irrationally believes it can change what makes boys tick. Add to this the mistaken notion that girls lag behind boys in education, some still believe that the *girls* have a lot of catching up to do!

As so much that has happened in America, society has tried to right wrongs at the expense of generations of people that had less, little, or absolutely *nothing* to do with inflicting those wrongs on others. Instead of stepping back and assessing their impulsive bigotry, countless progressive educators have doubled down on fighting this war. Accusing a six-year-old of being a sexual predator underscores the depravity of educators that have engaged in social engineering, while throwing critical thinking and decency out the window.

NOTES

1. Christina Hoff Sommers, "The War Against Boys," *The Atlantic*, May 2000 Issue, par. 1. https://www.theatlantic.com/magazine/archive/2000/05/the-war-against-boys/304659/
2. ibid., par. 5
3. Psychologists call this a *self-fulfilling prophesy*. Only, in this case, the prophesy is fueled by the accompaniment of victimhood psychobabble.
4. The "privilege" of whiteness began to dissipate with the '64 civil rights legislation.
5. This is a gross oversimplification. The *options* boys had were clear, straightforward; however, some of those options did not appear promising: going to Vietnam, marrying as a teenager, working in sectors of the labor force that offered little attraction, such as coal mining deep under the earth.
6. Favoritism toward the children of the famous and wealthy was not universal. Unlucky rich kids were sent to Vietnam, too, and some of them did not make it back.
7. These comments are compilations of discussions with young men. They did not write out their contributions, nor were they solicited or recorded.
8. Anna Mulrine, "Are Boys the Weaker Sex?" *U.S. News & World Report*, July 30, 2001, 131(4), 40–48.
9. Laurin-Whitney Gottbrath, "US Vote 2020: Why Women Decide Elections," *Al Jazeera*, November 1, 2020. https://www.aljazeera.com/news/2020/11/1/us-vote-2020-why-women-decide-elections
10. *Toxic masculinity* is a symptom (and an invention) of woke psychology.
11. Michael Salter, "The Problem With A Fight Against Toxic Masculinity," *The Atlantic*, February 19, 2019. https://www.theatlantic.com/health/archive/2019/02/toxic-masculinity-history/583411/
12. Ms. Perez, a pseudonym, had learned these traits from her graduate studies at the University of Texas. She then edited them, based on her own experiences with men. I'd like to know her *original* perceptions of men!
13. F. Diane Barth, "Why Are Some Men So Terrible?" *Think*, July 28, 2018. https://www.nbcnews.com/think/opinion/why-are-men-so-terrible-what-can-we-do-about-ncna895306
14. *The Conversation*, "Teen Suicide Prevention During COVID-19," January 28, 2021. https://theconversation.com/teen-suicide-prevention-during-covid-19-how-parents-and-kids-can-have-honest-and-safe-conversations-152485
15. These ideas are a compilation suggested by a multitude of sources.

Chapter 7

Me-Too for Kids

KIDDIE PORN IN VIRGINIA

At the beginning of 2018, Rachel Simmons, contributing writer for the Huffington Post, made an intriguing comment, although many had originally thought her words were a part of a late-night comedy sketch: "A few weeks ago, a Girl Scouts message advising parents not to force girls to hug relatives at Thanksgiving went viral. To tell your child that she owes someone a hug either just because she hasn't seen this person in a while, or because they gave her a gift can set the stage for her questioning whether she *owes* another person any type of physical affection."[1]

First glance: *What*!?!

Second look: Well, that makes sense. Hugs at Thanksgiving or Christmas shouldn't be thought of as a delivery of a promise or a payback for serving you a nice dinner or buying you a gift.

Final Analysis: *What*!?! Who, even in a confused state of adolescence, looks at Thanksgiving hugs with Grandma as something owed to her for baking nutty chocolate chip cookies or a pumpkin pie with a dash of whipped cream?

This messenger for the Girl Scouts of America is not the only nut-job around. Our schools have become a safe and efficient vehicle for helping to legitimize the Me-Too Movement in America.

It should be abundantly clear that this book *in no way* condemns the courageous efforts of women to combat sexual harassment, assault, rape, or obnoxious male behavior. This text takes a hard look at how the schools are dealing with the escalation of reported assaults and organized movements that have committed to stand strong against sexual harassment.

A major misjudgment by educators has been their rush to introduce age-*inappropriate* materials into the lower grades. Well-intentioned individuals may disagree all day and night about the appropriateness of dealing with issues like sexual harassment and rape with children as young as five or six. But a peek at the chaos in a few elementary schools casts further doubt on the common sense of educators in charge of your kids for large chunks of the day.

Taking advantage of their expanded flexibility in deviating from state standards and school curriculum (due to COVID), school districts have expanded their required reading lists. With the coronavirus pandemic underway, schools felt forced to make departures from the norm. Sometimes they didn't have to make those changes; they took advantage of the opportunity to do so.

In Loudon County, Virginia, teachers (allegedly) wanted to "expand their students' horizons" when it came to reading; they expected their students to become more involved with books. To do this, teachers made their book choices especially "interesting"—peculiarly provocative—to their students. And did they push the envelope with *that* idea!

High school freshmen were assigned questionably appropriate books that featured underage sex acts, as well as vivid scenes of domestic abuse. One book depicts a scene in which a man beats a woman, stuffs her in a closet, and continues to beat her when she asks for water.[2] The scenes of sex and violence project an explicit writing style, one that introduces high school students, as young as fourteen, to "more mature" types of literature.

When a parent began reading aloud passages from a couple of books at a regular school board meeting, several people in the room interrupted her several times and told her to stop. By the time she had finished, however, her mission had been accomplished.[3]

The Loudoun County school board released a statement responding to a backlash from the community, "clarifying," that if parents feel a book is not appropriate for their child, they may request an alternate text to be assigned . . . "LCPS recognizes that its students and families come with a host of varying life experiences, values, and sensitivities."[4]

Two books, *Monday's Not Coming*, by Tiffany D. Jackson, and *#MurderTrending* by Gretchen McNeil, dominated the controversy for several weeks. One sentence that a parent read aloud, illuminated how some modern teens communicate: "She sucked my d**k."[5] But when the parent stumbled through the sentence, her failure to enunciate clearly all the letters left nothing to anyone's imagination.

The spokesperson for the school district was right in arguing that everybody has a different life view. It is not required, however, that all life views be shared in a common forum, especially a ninth-grade classroom. Not all teens are equally mature. Some are undeniably *immature*. Most normal adults would not find it advisable for teachers to have kids, no matter what their degree of maturity, read books depicting oral sex and masturbation.

The sudden push for sex-oriented novels, especially for boys and girls, is oddly incongruent with the attention given to the Me-Too movement. Most schools warn little kids to be extra careful about touching each other and to refrain from gestures that may indicate a form of aggression, such as hugging; and by the time these children are budding teenagers, teachers have provided them reading materials that some parents describe as "kiddie porn."

Fortunately, these books are not the norm. There has been a mounting backlash by parents and members of various communities around the country. These and similar books do, however, sporadically pop up in the public schools, and cause a lot of head scratching when they are whispered in the same breath as, "Me-Too," The spirit of these novels tends to contradict the essence of "Me-Too." Girls (or women) offering sexual favors to boys are not exactly the ideal clients for Gloria Allred.

It's worth a brief mention here: the ongoing controversies in Virginia's public schools, including those in Loudoun County, were probably a major contribution to the election upset of incumbent governor Terry McAuliffe by businessman Glenn Youngkin in 2021. Woke education has begun to take its political toll.

MAN-SLUT, MEET BRENT KAVANAUGH

Along with the growing numbers of reported cases of sexual harassment among adults, the current mode of reporting exposes possible instances of sexual harassment among pubescent children. Reporter Rachel Simmons recently concluded, "Sexual harassment is an epidemic in U.S. middle and high schools."[6]

In 2016, at an elementary school in the Jamaican Plains area of Boston, a student was caught on Snapchat distributing a photo of another boy using the bathroom. "Other students at the school often make derogatory comments about one another, using words such as 'man-slut' and 'man-whore,'" says Angela Sahliti, a grade-five English teacher.[7]

Man-slut? Where do elementary school kid learn expressions like this?

Sahliti continues. "The consensus in the public schools is that children have been sexualized and are not behaving themselves. Boys have primal and learned behaviors that have caused many of them, even before puberty, to behave like untamed little animals."[8]

Would Sahliti have referred to a *girl* that had been hypersexualized as an "untamed little animal"?

Rachel Simmons, also a parent, voiced her concern: "Shortly after last year's election, at an elementary school near my home, boys played 'Trump tag' by grabbing at a girl's genitals. A school counselor at a Midwest middle school told me this week about 'Grab Tits Tuesday.' The mother of a ninth-grade girl emailed that boys shouted, 'grab their asses' [and they did] as girls filed out during a fire drill at their upstate New York high school."[9]

Parent groups, along with feminist organizations, fixate on the harassment issue. They claim that harassment is an epidemic in U.S. middle and high schools. In a 2014 study of 1,300 middle school students, University of Florida Professor Dorothy Espelage and colleagues found that one-quarter (of students) had experienced verbal and physical sexual harassment.[10] Another survey by Espelage's team found that 68 percent of high school girls were sexually harassed at least once, compared to 55 percent of boys.[11]

The previous chapter of this book discusses society's war on boys. Schools continue to make changes in their academic curriculum. They challenge boys to question their own desires and feelings and attitudes concerning sexual attraction; they cause them to wonder about even routine information their parents may have passed along to them, or "truths" they have gathered on their own. Girls are, "sugar and spice and everything nice" and boys are, "lizards and snails and puppy dog tails,"[12] which does not exactly express a positive nonbias impression of boys.

When there is an encounter between a boy and a girl, as a matter of routine, the school's authorities are going to believe the girl's rendition of events. Upon accusation, the boy inherits an enormous task. He has no rights. He has no credibility. The Salem Witch Hunts afforded those accused of conspiring with Satan more rights than young males are granted today in the event of a "sexual harassment" accusation at school.

Which, contrary to what may be your instinctive reaction, makes total sense. During the fall of 2018, the entire nation watched Brett Kavanaugh being hounded by venomous politicians. Their sole intent was to block his confirmation to the U.S. Supreme Court. It didn't work, but Judge Kavanaugh was forced to defend his sexual experiences and drinking habits for the past thirty years to vindicate himself against an accuser with about as much credibility as Casey Anthony.

By their demonization of males, wokes imply that a boy's word matters less than a girl's word. We are teaching girls that they can get away with most anything because they are girls. Or, as Senator Hiato of Hawaii said in a video recorded interview, "Always believe a woman's word over that of a man's. Women don't lie."[13]

With those remarks, Senator Hiato did not exactly shine as the brightest bulb in Washington.

THE MYTH OF TOXIC MASCULINITY

Those pushing programs of Me-Too in public schools claim sexual harassment is a symptom of noxious childhood lessons about gender, sex, and power. Female whistleblowers have taken down titans of the entertainment industry, as legions of underage "harassers" have continued to roam playgrounds with impunity.[14]

They will *continue* to harass unless they can be contained at home (which hardly ever happens, according to them), or in the public schools, where all the control lies on the virtuous side of the argument. It's *boys*. Always boys. And it's usually about "toxic masculinity," which, in the last couple of years, has been somewhat refined to mean, "*white* toxic masculinity."

The expectation is a "real man," as sociologist Michael Kimmel says, should "be strong, tough, and never expose [his] feelings." To be a real man is to be hyper competitive, get rich at all costs, and have sex with lots of women. These messages are delivered by members of a boy's inner circle: fathers, uncles, coaches, male friends, and older siblings.[15]

Your author taught high school for almost four decades and college for ten years; he has raised a son into adulthood. He rarely heard anyone in a position of authority talk to boys like that, telling them "what it takes to be man," with those stereotypical characteristics of "be strong, be tough, and never show your feelings."[16]

But that was *then*.

It is true that some fathers, coaches, and buddies have pushed for these types of displays of "masculinity." However, to argue that poisonous behaviors are pervasive and endemic in the culture is to do a disservice to boys; it also does a disservice to educators, who have been handed the responsibility of hunting down and destroying that ambiguous monster, "toxic masculinity."

Classes and workshops for teachers about sexual assault and harassment have popped up across the country. School administrators can't escape a year, even during COVID shutdowns, without attending conferences on the subject.

Teachers must adjust to handling their students' relationships while the kids are on the playground. They counsel children on how to protect themselves (if she is a girl), and how to control themselves (if he is a boy). They are warned of the following: One-quarter of those age eighteen to twenty-four reports having been harassed online, an experience that can happen at any time of the day or night.[17]

The unveiling of vague statistics may have a striking effect on how schools deal with harassment issues. But when educators hear of a case of blatant sexual *assault*, it is like having a nuclear cannon in their harassment artillery bag. Harassment issues pale in comparison to rape charges, but they are nonetheless severe: At one high school in Philadelphia a fourteen-year-old girl pulled out her phone in class to find a Snapchat from a peer asking if she wanted to measure the size of his penis. A therapist shared that a male student texted her fourteen-year-old patient to ask her to perform oral sex on him in the bathroom.[18]

A teacher that reported these cases at a district workshop editorialized. "Clinicians tell me these incidents are commonplace, not rare."[19]

Who determines that these incidents are "commonplace, not rare"? That's important. Anyone can be the victim of something and say, well, you know, it happens all the time. Like, he was run over in the parking lot by a truck that just happened to flip off the freeway. . . . It happens all the time. It's commonplace.

If it is, in *fact*, an ordinary series of events for teenage boys to send text messages promising their female classmates adventures in oral copulation, you have a sad commentary on the state of child-rearing in this country, and refusing Grandma a loving hug at Thanksgiving is not going to do diddly-squat to make things any better for women.

So, classes are born, workshops financed; special interest groups move into schools, and small children are warned of the dangers of touching and getting too close to one another—and how to report being "harassed." Feminist teachers now have weapons in their arsenal, and even though they can't explode bombs in the vicinity of Supreme Court confirmation hearings, they can do a lot to expose the predators, five-year-old boys that are stalking around the monkey bars while frothing at the mouth during recess.

But the wokes see red flags denoting sexual harassment at every turn:

WOKE WARNING #1: Boys must stop trying to reaffirm their masculinity.

And how do boys discontinue affirmations of their masculinity?

By acting hypermasculine around each other and those whom they perceive as weaker. Professor C.J. Pascoe in the book, *Dude, You're a Fag*, wrote, "To affirm their maleness, boys stigmatize sensitive peers as 'gay' or a 'fag,' gossip about girls' bodies, and brag about sexual experiences."[20] Victims may respond to the abuse by modifying their own behavior: Children taunted with homophobic slurs are more determined to prove their masculinity and more likely to perpetrate sexual harassment in the future in order to do it.

REACTION TO WOKE WARNING: It takes one to know one, but in this case, she ain't one. C.J. Pascoe is a *woman*. Which certainly doesn't disqualify her as an authority, but it does, in the minds of at least some, lessen her credibility on this subject. Has this woman nailed what it is like to be a man? Does she understand the needs of men? You must research this to get to the bottom of it. Pascoe's credentials: *Cheri Jo Pascoe is an American sociologist and author. She is currently an associate professor at the University of Oregon. Her research focuses on gender, youth, homophobia, sexuality, and news media.*[21]

Your author's daughter recently took a college course in which Pascoe's work had been assigned as the main textbook for the class. His daughter's reaction to Pascoe by the end of the course: "Cheri Jo hates men. So does my professor."[22]

WOKE WARNING #2: Boys must attain intimacy literacy.

What the—?
 Educate. Educate. *Educate!*
Teach boys how to behave in pubic. Show boys that girls are people, too; in fact, make certain you teach that *all* girls are special. You know, *sugar and spice and everything nice*—no snails or puppy dog's tails allowed.

Boys have stomped on girls; they have dismissed them, taken them for granted. For women, it's a form of reparations. Just as Black people were enslaved and needed to recover from the harms inflicted upon them hundreds of years ago, so, too, have women been held in a sort of gender bondage. And little boys need to start the healing process by making it up to little girls.

REACTION TO WOKE WARNING: The wokes would like to begin this intimacy literacy as early as kindergarten. But why not start in preschool? Heck, why not begin showing boys and girls how to get along in close quarters from the moment delivery room nurses place them in bassinets? *Gotcha!* Here's the reason why: Relationship intimacy *sexualizes children.* Five, six, seven-year-olds know from nothing! Then again, thinking back to those books that schools are requiring for ninth graders, it's easy to see where kids might be picking up some juicy information.

WOKE WARNING #3: Schools must clarify for children just when, and *how*, they are being harassed.

There is a need to clarify "harassment" to the children. Child psychologist Jamie Howard, PhD wrote, "Kids I'm working with will say, 'I was being bullied.' And when they describe what happened, sometimes it was just teasing. Maybe someone was giving them a hard time and it was difficult to deal with. But not every incident of meanness, rejection, or hostility is bullying."[23] For fear of making the mistake of crying wolf, children often remain mum, even during a sexual assault by another child.

The most dismissive children are more likely to perpetrate homophobic bullying. If young people don't take harassment (or bullying) seriously, it stands to reason that they may be less likely to report the provocations as victims or bystanders, and more likely to perpetrate the behaviors.[24]

REACTION TO WOKE WARNING: If children have not yet been sexualized—many haven't before puberty—they are incapable of *sexually* harassing anyone else. Oh, yeah. Those dang boys! They're the meanies again. What may be mistaken for *sexual* is some form of acting out. Boys tend to be more aggressive. They are hormonally driven. But the word *sexually* at five or six, doesn't seem to work. Think about any boy in kindergarten that you know. Visualize him. Does that five-year-old fit the prototype of a sexual villain?

If you tell a five-year-old boy he can't even *unintentionally* rub up against a girl behind him in the lunch line, he won't get it. *But it was an accident*! It doesn't matter. All he understands is that girls are fragile, annoying, and "they get me in trouble." *That* could translate to pent up anger being let out recklessly somewhere down the line. This doesn't excuse the anger; it may explain it, though.

If young kids don't know they are being sexually harassed, explain the actions of the aggressor to them in another way. There is no need to sexualize these kids' lives. You should relish this approach, teachers. It lets you a bit off the hook.

WOKE WARNING #4: Schools must advise elementary school kids about the pleasure of their body parts.

Which is an immediate reason for them to *protect* those precious body parts. That which is pleasurable to small children is automatically more valuable to them. Children treasure the pleasure centers of their bodies; in fact, even if something has not been clearly identified as a "pleasure center," parents and teachers may want to bring the sacredness of their bodies to their attention, a concept children might take a while to absorb. But once they do, it becomes apparent to kids why they should resist sexual harassment.

REACTION TO WOKE WARNING: When teachers discuss body organs in the classroom, that discussion is probably a part of an academic discussion, maybe in a biology class or a health class. It's doubtful that public school teachers are reading to third graders from *Fifty Shades of Grey*. But sometimes teachers get carried away with their own sexual proclivities, and that this may be dicey is an understatement. Teachers must monitor their own language. And carefully.

WOKE WARNING #5: Educators must listen to women and girls: they tell the truth and know what's best.

By implication, don't trust men and boys. Men lie. Women work to discover the truth, finding out about their sexual nature. Men don't ever do that. Men have different roles: little girls have been raped by their fathers, uncles, neighbors. Teenage girls have been wooed by supposed friends of family and by boys with whom they have gone on dates. Women are pressured to respond to the advances of men, and, ironically, they are sometimes left with feelings of rejection if they are not hit upon. It isn't their fault, though. This patriarchal society has conditioned girls to be subservient to boys. Male attention should be expected; unfortunately, that attention is not always the kind she expects—or wants.

Girls are pressured to please others at the sacrifice of their own boundaries and comfort levels. Health and safety courses, along with regular sex education classes, go a long way toward negating these archaic cultural practices. These sex ed classes should begin as early as the first grade (so say the woke experts), and the care and attention paid to the needs of girls and women should increase exponentially.

If society wishes to end a culture suffused with sexual harassment, it should listen to adult women who are courageously speaking out. It must also make room for girls to speak: If society listened, it'd find that many *middle schoolers* are trying to tell others, "Me, too!"

REACTION TO WOKE WARNING: As you are reading this, you must be shaking your head. And, honestly, this stuff has not been made up. Material about the Me-Too movement for first graders is, unfortunately, abundant. There is no need to be "creative" on that front. It's all too real; anything concocted for social impact would be more believable than the real deal, and purposeful "fiction" could not compete with the truth for its incredulity.

The consequences of the implementation of anti-male woke policies and curricula are known. Lauren Camera studied school discipline strategies and procedures and concluded in *U.S. News and World Report, on* June 22, 2016, "One of the big things that jumped out [in a discipline study] was the fact that the same behavior problems in boys and girls were penalized a lot more in boys than girls."[25]

Which hardly shocks anyone. You know, boys will be boys. . . .

She continues, "So, in addition to the fact that boys come to school [on average] having more problems, they also get penalized more for having these behaviors."[26]

As documented earlier in this text: The achievement gaps between young males and females have shown up, and they are enormous. What may be more revealing are the emotional wellness gaps. But, of course, boys don't feel much, and boys don't cry, so for the present, they play the role of society's punching bag.

NOTES

1. Rachel Simmons, "When Middle Schoolers Say #MeToo," HuffPost, December 15, 2017. https://www.huffpost.com/entry/sexual-harassment-in-schools_b_5a32b145e4b00dbbcb5bb530

2. Houston Keene, "Virginia Parents Torch Loudoun County School Board," Fox News, May 12, 2020. https://www.foxnews.com/politics/lcps-torched-parents-critical-race-theory

3. ibid.

4. *Loudon Public Schools*, Newsletter. "Update: LCPS Offers Parents Options In Selection Of Reading Materials," May 19, 2021. https://www.lcps.org/site/default.aspx?PageType=3&DomainID=1&ModuleInstanceID=274904&ViewID=6446EE88-D30C-497E-9316-3F8874B3E108&RenderLoc=0&FlexDataID=404999&PageID=1

5. Kelen McBreen, "Furious Parents Read Vulgar Material Assigned By Public School," *News War*, August 12, 2021. https://www.newswars.com/furious-parents-read-vulgar-material-assigned-by-public-school-she-sucked-my-dck/

6. Mojola Omole, "The Case For Teaching Kids About #MeToo In Elementary School," *Quartz*, January 14, 2018. https://qz.com/1182842/the-metoo-movement-should-begin-in-elementary-school/

7. ibid.

8. ibid.

9. Rachel Simmons, "When Middle Schoolers Say #MeToo," *HuffPost*, December 15, 2017.

10. Dorothy Espelage, "Sexual Harassment Common Among Middle School Children," *Erekalert!* December 9, 2016. https://www.eurekalert.org/news-releases/920812

11. A. Bidwell, "Sexual Harassment Frequent Among Middle School Students," *US News and World Report*. Retrieved from usnews.com/news/articles/2014/04/06/study-sexual-harassment-frequent-among-middle-school-students

12. Why does everyone not laugh at this? I mean, I do.

13. I'm not sure if she put it exactly in those words; she has stated repeatedly that a woman should be believed. Does that not suggest she thinks women don't lie?

14. Rachel Simmons, "When Middle Schoolers Say #MeToo," *HuffPost*, December 15, 2017. https://www.huffpost.com/entry/sexual-harassment-in-schools_b_5a32b145e4b00dbbcb5bb530

15. Michael Kimmel, "When Middle Schoolers Say #MeToo," *HuffPost*, December 15, 2017, par. 3. https://www.huffpost.com/entry/sexual-harassment-in-schools_b5a32b145e4b00dbbcb5bb530

16. Except in joking about the stereotype. I have done that, too: Real men like crunchy peanut butter. Sissies like smooth peanut butter. Who would take that seriously?

17. Monica Anderson, "A Majority Of Teens Have Experienced Some Form Of Cyberbullying," *Pew Research Center*, September 27, 2018. https://www.pewresearch.org/internet/2018/09/27/a-majority-of-teens-have-experienced-some-form-of-cyberbullying/

18. Rachel Simmons, "When Middle Schoolers Say #MeToo," *HuffPost*, December 15, 2017. https://www.huffpost.com/entry/sexual-harassment-in-schools_b_5a32b145e4b00dbbcb5bb530.

19. ibid.

20. C.J. Pascoe, *Dude, You're a Fag: Masculinity and Sexuality in High School*, (University of California Press, 2011).

21. From her University of Oregon web page.

22. My daughter likes men. So does my wife. My wife is a teacher. She would never teach her students that America is being controlled by hypermasculinized, testosterone-driven, heterosexual patriarchs. I don't *think* she would, anyway.

23. Jamie Howard, PhD, "How To Know If Your Child Is Being Bullied," *Child Mind Institute*, August 12, 2021, par. 4. https://childmind.org/article/how-to-know-if-your-child-is-being-bullied/

24. Various Authors, "A Longitudinal Examination Of Homophobic Name-Calling In Middle School: Bullying, Traditional Masculinity, And Sexual Harassment As Predictors," *American Psychological Association*, August 14, 2021. https://psycnet.apa.org/record/2016-62668-001

25. Lauren Camera, "Boys Bear The Brunt Of School Discipline," *U.S. News and World Report*, June 22, 2020. https://www.usnews.com/news/articles/2016-06-22/boys-bear-the-brunt-of-school-discipline

26. ibid.

Chapter 8

Rewriting History

EYEWITNESSES

Sam Wineburg, history professor and Director of the Stanford History Education Group, writes extensively about historical thinking: "The first thing that historical study teaches us is that there is no such thing as free-floating information. Information comes from somewhere."[1]

During earlier times, generations communicated with one-another in a variety of ways; it didn't matter exactly *how*—only that the generations connected. Events were familiar to most of the people, the stories consistent. When an historian examines the occurrences in the context of their time, they rarely expect another historian, one from a different generation, to interpret that context in the exact, same way; thus, there is subjectivity in the validation of history, as well as differences of opinion as to even the *existence* of the events being discussed.

Rabbi Bernard Goldman spoke of "validations" but by placing them in a religious context. He said, "One can choose to believe in God or not to believe in God. Because we never know for *certain* as to God's existence, many choose the side that they feel is better suited to them. *Is there God*? I think there is, mainly because I *want* there to be God. My answer is based on my desire, my *faith*."[2]

The actual *truth* of the matter is that the Rabbi, or any member of the clergy, will not know with certainty the answer to that question—at least, not in this life. The "ways" he may observe the evidence of God's existence, and the many "conclusions" he reaches through those observations, hold the same subjectivity of the conclusions passed on by those who have written history books distributed to fifth graders in the public schools.

What are the motivations of those who wish to paint an historical canvas that conveys for today's children only the ugliness of the United States of

America? Even if some historians have legitimate reasons to question the validity of the reporting and sorting of events of the past, how is it that their conclusions are grounded in venom for a country that has done so much good, and whose people have sacrificed their lives for the freedom of others?

Bypassing fierce challenges and vehement pronouncements by people with set agendas, the recounting of American history has, up until recently, maintained most of its integrity. It is usually not the *existence* of a person or place that is in question; an interpretation of the nuances of how people behaved, and the places they allegedly lived and roamed often determines how history is written.

Dozens of myths have been perpetuated over the years. They are harmless. Stories of American folklore bring people together, help them to share a common bond. They are privy to information about their ancestors that makes them look good, that makes *everyone* look good. The cutthroat behaviors of uncivilized settlers, or decent people struggling to survive are well-documented. Sometimes this nation's dirty laundry must pass inspection; other times it can be ignored or relegated to a place of little or no importance. History is like people. Most people are complex. They are not all good or all bad. Everybody understands that other people also have dirty laundry to hang out; that is why they don't mock them for it.

No one alive now actually saw the Pilgrims touch Plymouth Rock; no one watched the Battle of the Little Big Horn River in the Black Hills of South Dakota, when General Custer and 240 members of the Seventh Calvary were ambushed there. George Washington probably never chopped down a cherry tree; Paul Revere never cried, "The British are coming! The British are coming!"[3]

Eye-witness recounting is not necessarily the best purveyor of truth; it is much less reliable than video recordings. Unfortunately, few witnesses to fifteenth century American history are still around, and the technology of the video recording goes back only so far. Historians rely on other ways of finding out about events of the past and then make extraordinary attempts to draw contextual conclusions about those events.

Historians, as well as teachers and students, rely on documents, what others have written and photographed, to interpret history. Science is not the only discipline that is preoccupied with data. Data matter in history; it's also important to know who gathered it, how, and why.

This is an authentic internet observation: *Eighty percent of people over the age of sixty-five in Boulder, Colorado, have aliens from outer space living inside their bodies.* At a given point—hopefully, right away—one would want to check out the validity of this information. There is a decent chance that this claim about space aliens is false. Further inspection of the website from which this statistic came may indicate that the account was conjured up by a teenage blogger by the name of Ricky Hornsby. And your first hint of the amateurishness of his writing is the twelve grammar and punctuation errors in the first paragraph of his blog.[4]

The *source* of the information triggers suspicion. Ricky Hornsby sounds like the kid who found himself stuffed face-first into trashcans throughout his freshman year of high school, as a part of a hazing ritual. Maybe an unusual preoccupation with bullies damaged his psyche for the rest of his life; he began making things up, twisting stories in ways that his disturbed mind had wanted them to turn out all along. History is more than just factoids; its complexity makes it difficult to learn exactly why something happened the way it did, or even if the event happened at all.

By the time they have finished the third or fourth grade, most school children are introduced to the history and culture of the state in which they live. The fifth grade begins the children's quest to learn United States history. As they merge into middle school, most kids are treated to a fragmented potpourri in world history and geography (social studies). United States history is presented as a full course of study, usually in grades eight and eleven.

Today woke organizations like teachers' unions and political special interest committees think the study of history—particularly *American* history—has mutated into a massive creature with uncontrolled power. They insist that what teachers have been doing in their classrooms for decades has been wrong, and that educators must fix it. They clamor for change: in the methods of teaching history; in the selection of events to be emphasized; in the actual interpretation of those events; and because of those changes in interpretation, a deconstruction of the "truths" reported in the American history curriculum in the schools.

THE EXPLORERS

Adventurous European men, backed by wealthy, powerful leaders, set upon long and ominous excursions that brought together an unprecedented mixture of cultures. It is noteworthy that the purposes of these trips were guided by manifestations of a thirst for adventure, the settling of curiosity, and a quest for an economic advantage for nations whose populace was dying off from starvation or inhibited by gross political and social weaknesses—which included most of the countries in Europe.

Chris Columbus was an explorer, no different from Ferdinand Magellan, Ponce de Leon, Balboa, or a myriad of others. Their motives were a mixture of monetary and religious goals and the perfect stage for self-promotion. American school children absorbed information about these men in their social studies courses, usually bored by the whole process; after all, by the time kids arrived at their eleventh grade year, they had heard their craggy teachers drone on about Christopher Columbus and those other guys for too many hours and with nothing new to report.

In *those* days it was even more difficult for teachers to promote the engagement of history. Before social media, hardly anyone under the age of twenty paid attention to events that were developing around the world. Current events or "the news," as it had been typically termed, remained an abstract, unreal concept for children. Watching soldiers come home in body bags from far-off lands where America fought questionable wars constituted a part of the daily routine for most school kids, but unless they understood how and why those events shaped their own lives, they were apathetic about them.

This mentality had changed during the war in Vietnam (discussed in-depth later), but overall, discussions about "the news" had remained less than thrilling. What *really* altered the landscape of the places where political and social consciences butted heads was the introduction of social media into the lives of young Americans.

If nothing else, American students carried an ambiguous view of the settlers, not knowing a whole lot about any one pioneer, usually forming a positive view of those who had braved the discovery of the New World. Originally, the explorations of the West had spurred a less jaundice view among students than they did decades later, after having been held to closer scrutiny. The real beginnings of American history became a descriptive narrative of the everyday lives of those that tried to survive: the indigenous folks that had already inhabited the so-called "New World," and the new voyagers from Europe—and what were later called Central and South America.

American history during this early stage came over as mundane. Maybe that's how schools intended it to sound—boring, meaningless. Those children learned that Columbus thought he had landed in India, thus the term "West Indies." His agenda wasn't the subjugation of any people of any stripe; it was to find a shortcut to Western Asia.[5]

Enter the revisionist crowd, the progressives, and, lately, the wokes. Most educators claim that they are just trying to teach the facts. History was not *actually* known before recently, they argue. Suddenly, it has become *known*, revealing itself after college professors, politicians, and union leaders did a little prodding and poking around. Educators now blame the explorers for everything that turned out, according to them, morally wrong.[6]

No one bothered to make a video recording of the landing at Plymouth Rock; there is nothing conclusive to document the legitimacy of the events in question, although the old axioms that have to do with "seeing is believing," have recently taken on some strange challenges of their own.[7] American students in our public schools have been treated to the history of cynical eyes.

Woke-affected U.S. History curriculum sports the following "truths":

1. Christopher Columbus did not discover America.

Of course, he didn't. And pointing that out to traditional scholars and naive school kids does not constitute a *gotcha!* moment. Columbus hadn't really discovered America, like they told you about for decades; what turned out to be particularly galling is the frequency by which the Italian explorer had been praised—and for such a long time!

Columbus never set foot in North America. During four separate trips that started with the one in 1492, Columbus landed on various Caribbean islands that are now the Bahamas, as well as the island later called Hispaniola. He also explored the Central and South American coasts.[8]

This information has been available for decades; to be fair, most teachers imparted it accurately. But there were some educators that could not get it right; they just couldn't get over the idea that Christopher Columbus, who sailed the ocean blue in 1492, was not the guy who discovered America. Or others that couldn't get over the idea that a *white* Italian *had*.

2. The explorers were mean and cruel.

You have already heard stories about the Pilgrims breaking bread with the Indigenous, the folklore of which soothing, patriotic tales about Thanksgiving are made. The powers that be, however, now want your children to know the "truth": The early explorers would not have been able to apply for positions on hospitality committees in Jamestown; in other words, those folks that claimed to have sat down in peace with the natives were *mean*.

Wokes argue that those who celebrate Columbus Day believe the genocide of Red/Brown people was a good thing; or, to give these deniers the benefit of the doubt, they know absolutely nothing about history and geography. A day celebrating Christopher Columbus is not only a day celebrating racism; it's also a day commemorating massive land robbery, barbaric slavery, serial rape, systemic torture, and cultural obliteration.[9]

Michael Coard of the *Philadelphia Inquirer* wrote, "The indigenous Red people in the so-called New World are commonly but erroneously called *Indians,* because Columbus mistakenly thought he had arrived in India and, therefore, arrogantly—like Europeans do—imposed a name on them."[10]

Who had recorded these tidbits of information means *everything*. Serious TikTok posts about racist white Europeans are too frequent to take any one post seriously. The real question then becomes, where did this revamped information come from, and how did it get here?

Biography Newsletter took it further: "When Columbus first set foot on Hispaniola, he encountered a population of Indigenous peoples called the Taino. A friendly group, they willingly traded jewelry, animals, and supplies with the sailors. 'They were very well built, with very handsome bodies and very good faces,' Columbus wrote in his diary. 'They do not carry arms. . . . They should be good servants.'"

The Indigenous peoples were soon forced into slavery and punished with the loss of a limb, or death, if they did not collect enough gold (a portion of which Columbus was allowed to keep for himself). Between the European's brutal treatment and their infectious diseases, within decades, the Taino population was decimated.[11]

Western Historian Parter Umbot said, "This is the truth about dear ol' Christopher Columbus. Some school kids seriously mix up Christopher Columbus with the British folk hero Robin Hood! Columbus wasn't that benevolent guy with the toothy grin and the forest hat. White Europeans, own up to this *fact*!"[12]

Beyond the observable, what confounds most serious thinking people, is the lack of motive for this distortion. Maybe it is part of a larger scheme, as in the introduction of CRT to public education, to convince Americans to hate America. How bad of a country is the United States? *So bad, that it idolizes as one of its founders, Christopher Columbus*, a "white man" from Spain that embarked upon a brutal and cruel systemic genocide to gain power and be inscribed for all time in the annals of history.

In October 1929, the Hispanic Council published the report, "Columbus Day, *Si Gracias*," in which the author, Professor Maria Saaverda, painstakingly analyzes the facts about Columbus's contribution to history. Her findings yield positive responses to the "sling as much crap on the wall as you can" allegations about Columbus's intentions and actions during his life, as one of the most notable explorers in history.[13]

Columbus did not foster a genocide.

Columbus did not set foot in the territory that is now the United States during his lifetime; furthermore, as an envoy of the Spanish Crown, it must not be forgotten that since the Catholic Kings, Spanish law considered the native inhabitants of America to have the same rights and obligations as the inhabitants of peninsular Spain.

A *genocide* is the murder of an entire group of people for the purpose of eliminating a whole race. Columbus did not have that purpose in his explorations and gatherings of riches. It makes a dazzling story, though, lays the premise for future accusations of genocide and bigotry and racial purification, set into motion by white men.

Spain was the first country to pass laws protecting the inhabitants of America.

Unlike other countries that colonized the world, Spain promoted a variety of laws to protect the natives of America. It is tantalizing to ignore the positive contributions of the colonists, because anything good or decent about them does not fit the narrative. Of course, America is a horrible country today; just look at the horrible men that began it!

The decline of the native population was mainly caused by the transmission of diseases.

There were, in fact, acts of violence, condemnable and brutal. Sometimes they were punished by Spanish laws; sometimes the kinder and more humane among the explorers would rebel against those who were inhumane and viscous. The existence of brutality in the beginnings of the settlement is not a secret. But the claim that violence was the principal reason for the diminished native population is false. Disease, inadvertently carried across oceans, was the actual culprit for the deaths and suffering of most indigenous peoples.

The cultural mix is the most evident proof of Spain's policies in America.

Unlike other countries whose policies were based on the annihilation of the inhabitants of the conquered territories, the cultural mix between Spaniards and the natives is clear evidence of Spain's philosophy of cultural integration. In fact, between 1551 and 1792, Spain built nearly thirty universities and forty cathedrals in its overseas territories.[14]

The attacks against Christopher Columbus lack historical rigor.

Columbus has become the scapegoat for those that try to rewrite the history of America and the United States, which is why several events that took place several centuries later are erroneously attributed to him.[15] Every breathing school kid has familiarity with the name *Christopher Columbus*. You need someone to blame for all the bad stuff: *there you are*! Wokes may detail events, describe accounts, and determine truths to fit the narratives they have already written. In all candor, they don't *know* much about Columbus and what really happened in 1492. Sorry, but that last sentence bears repeating: They don't *know* much about Columbus and what really happened in 1492.

Those lovely Thanksgiving stories about sharing turkeys and corn with the natives, followed by a peaceful procession toward colonization, are not wholly accurate; neither are the tales of wholesale brutality and "genocide" during colonization. The truth probably lies somewhere in the middle.

THE AMERICAN REVOLUTION

If you ask instructors of American history, they will tell you one of their favorite periods to teach kids is the Revolutionary War. The drama, the intrigue, and the sheer courage among those involved are enough to energize any tedium that may accompany the endless repeating of the same teaching points.

This may be an oversimplification, but it goes something like this: During the period that the colonists wished to break away from their British counterparts, a cast of thousands dominated the scene. Although the issues involved were somewhat complex because of conflicting values, it came down to the good guys verses the bad guys. The good guys, of course, were the colonists, English by birth, and now determined to establish a new government in the New Land, breaking away from the perceived oppression of their brothers.

The bad guys were the representatives of England, a country self-appointed to be guardians of the free nations of Europe. It wasn't that terribly complicated. The British were the oppressors, the newly formed midget colonies, the oppressed.

The war was fought. Over 15,000 men died.[16] The wounds would be lingering and devastating. The colonists had struggled to make it on their own, and a new nation was born, a democratic republic; thus, began the greatest political and social experiment in the history of the world, one in which the results have yet to be thoroughly analyzed.

The benefits of relating history from this period to kids were incalculable. Every teacher had their favorite stories, from *The Boston Tea Party* to *Paul Revere's Ride*. Much like the way they had reacted to the folklore revolving around the explorers and the indigenous peoples of North America, school children cared little about truth; in fact, they never asked for the truth. Kids assumed what teachers taught them *was* true. They were semi-aware of the tendency for jingoism—though they didn't call it that—and they accepted the facts as they were presented.

Why would, especially teachers, have a reason to bend the truth? Or deflate their school's ambiance of patriotism? After all, kids came into the classroom every morning, and the first thing they did was to stand, put their hands over their hearts, and recite the Pledge of Allegiance. The Minutemen were their heroes. These soldiers of the Revolution stood shoulder to shoulder, loaded their muskets, and fired point-blank at the rows of red-clad military men that threatened freedom, who stood just a few feet away, on the other end of their gun barrels. Many of them died on the spot. The causes of the war, children had been taught, were good. To fight and die for freedom was of the highest honor.

Thomas Paine wrote a series of articles in a journal he entitled, *Common Sense*.[17] In his most powerful piece, Paine argues for war against the British. His highest goal was to convince fellow colonists to follow him into battle. He likened an intruder breaking into his home to the British breaking into his country, his last bastion of freedom. A man would fight, Paine said, to protect his house, his family, and his liberty. If you stand eye-to-eye with an intruder, you have a choice: You can fight or run. Only cowards, Paine insists, would flee, abandoning their homes, leaving their wives and children unprotected and their houses deserted. Only cowards would not make the ultimate sacrifice, if necessary, for liberty.

The woke movement has denigrated these and other concepts of patriotism. They tell your children that it is not the *quality* of life that matters, but the *length* of a life. Dalton Trumbo, American Communist and literary hero to wokes, referred to the Revolution metaphorically in his World War I novel, *Johnny Got His Gun*. Trumbo tackles the "freedom at all costs" mantra head-on. For Trumbo, *life* trumps quality of life. He argues, "I would rather work in a coal mine, deep under the earth, with a whip at my back, and eat nothing but crusts of bread and water twenty-four hours a day; I would rather do that than be dead."[18]

If a teacher or parent has engrained into a thirteen-year-old mind *that* concept about life, liberty, living, and dying, it becomes harder for that child to buy into the arguments from Paine about protecting his own house at all costs, even if it might mean his death.

And then there's this:

Alan Gilbert, of *The Daily Beast*, wrote on January 29, 2021, "The central myth of American history teaching is that the American Revolution was fought for the 'life, liberty and pursuit of happiness' of each person. By each, Jefferson meant mainly *white* farmers" (italics added).[19]

The wokes have continued their coyness (without being coy) when it comes to hinting at hidden agendas and rampant racism during every period of American history.

For the Revolutionary War, no one needs to look any further for evidence of white supremacy than the Founding Fathers and their insistence on owning slaves. The British profited from the slave trade, too. Once slaves had become a large part of America, it was clear to anyone with even a blip of common sense that the alignment of free states and slave states was cranking up to be a big deal. Southern states required slaves—so they argued—to work their rural lands. An agrarian society could not—so they contended—manage an economy without servants (or slaves) to work the land. Again: *so, they contended*.

The slave trade was morally unconscionable. At the same time, especially because other nation-states participated in slavery to a greater and more violent extent, the ends seemed to justify the means: having a strong, democratic regime that could withstand the challenges of all enemies, foreign or within, appeared to be the way to go. The competition from abroad had to be addressed, but the process of buying and selling human beings for the purpose of compelling them to work on plantations shouted out at the highest decibels of *evil*.

Today it is irrefutable—to the extent that anything is irrefutable—that close to one hundred percent of Americans, no matter what their race, believe that slavery was gross and immoral. It is a blatant *lie* (sorry, your author hardly ever uses that word) that American history books sweep the issue of slavery under the rug, masking its ugliness or going so far as to deny its historical existence.

The woke reliance on the 1619 project to reveal the truth about slavery is, at least, controversial and, most likely, ludicrous. Those who have a reason— or *want*—to believe that the American Revolution was fought to *preserve* the institution of slavery will continue to do so, no matter what evidence to the contrary is presented to them. But teaching this to American school children serves no purpose. Besides being unfounded, those teachings promote the decay of Americanism and encourage cynicism throughout the education establishment.

America has addressed—and continues to address—slavery. There is legislative restlessness in the form of reparations for African Americans; there are continuing affirmative action and quota programs for employment and higher education. Kids are being taught that America, a country founded on evil, racist policies, has never owned up to its egregious deeds of the past; that African Americans have generationally suffered,[20] and only "equity" programs in all aspects of society may effectively address these missteps. These programs must pay careful attention to disparity in *outcomes* and fix those, no matter who else must suffer along the equity trail.

The Pew Research Center reported in April of 2019, "For the most part, Americans believe slavery continues to have an impact on Black people's status. About six-in-ten U.S. adults say the legacy of slavery affects the position of Black people in American society today, either a great deal (31 percent) or a fair amount (32 percent). Some 36 percent say slavery doesn't have much or anything at all to do with the current situation of Black people."[21]

To the extent that Blacks had begun their American legacy from so far behind, the country, to be *fair*, must look as though it is being *unfair* to others. This unsettling, unappetizing concept may be difficult for many to understand; it is unmistakably a source of controversy.

THE CIVIL WAR

Most Americans have limited knowledge of the Civil War. Knowing some basic facts about this war, and how the "new historians" have distorted those facts and manipulated them over time, would take open-minded individuals a long way toward clarifying the issues that have recently emerged. The schools teach kids, for the most part, the "facts." Wokes have bludgeoned, distorted, and wiped out some of those "facts" for the purpose of making America look like the greediest and most racist country in the history of civilization.

This list of little-known Civil War tidbits reinforces the view that the issues involved in this war, including slavery and succession, are far more complicated than wokes are willing to concede.

You've heard other ideas about that. There are many theories out there. But here's the truth: Southern states led the charge for states' rights. The Tenth Amendment to the Constitution guarantees that all rights not specifically granted to the federal government be given to the states. And the reason that states should have a basic say on local issues is that their agrarian economy depended upon slaves for survival. Was it right? Was it moral? At that point, the issues had little to do with right or moral; they had mostly everything to do with economic survival.

It is true that at one time America was a slave-owning nation; it is also true that this country fought a war in which almost a half million young men were killed for the purpose of *freeing* slaves. Hey, eleventh graders, check your *world* history books and see how many other countries in recorded civilization have done that, *fought a costly, bloody war to free slaves*. Educators, do you point out those monumental sacrifices when you teach the Civil War? And while you're at it, teachers, you may want to remind your students that sweeping civil rights legislation was passed by Congress and signed by President Johnson in 1964. That legislation basically made it illegal to be a racist in America. *The purpose of these laws was to preclude institutional racism.*[22]

Since 1964, most forms of discrimination have been illegal.[23] Other countries have not passed laws like these. Also, history teachers, you may want to make your students aware that it had been mostly white people (politicians and activists) that were the major figures—the movers and shakers—behind the 1964 Civil Rights laws. Without the support of white people, nothing would have been accomplished by that Southern, white President Johnson and his predecessor that got the ball rolling, the other White supremacist, the one with the Irish background, John Fitzgerald Kennedy.

It is not known how many of these intricate observations school children are able to comprehend; however, it is not out of the purview of a school district to instruct its teachers how to characterize references to the Civil War: "All civilians, politicians, and military personnel related to the North will be referred to as *the good guys*. All civilians, politicians, and military personnel related to the South will be referred to as *the bad guys*."[24]

There is no ambiguity there; instead of presenting history *as it happened* and asking students to make up their minds about the characters and events involved, most school boards make clear what *everyone* should be thinking. Once again, the textbooks have oversimplified. The Confederacy didn't have a morally acceptable position on slavery. But they held one on states' rights. And even if you happen to agree with how your school board comes down on these subjects, you should find their dogma problematic, and their insistence that they own the whole truth condescending and scary.

THE VIETNAM WAR

High school students during the 1960s were told that U.S. involvement in Vietnam, essentially started in 1964, was an example of another American "policing action," in which South Vietnam was being aided by the United States to fight against the Communists from the North. American intervention in Vietnam was primarily a holding policy. The North Vietnamese, aided by Communist China, had designs on conquering the South, helped initially by France and later by the United States.

By 1974, ten years after the war began, the U.S. had invested the lives of over 55,000 young men and hundreds of billions of dollars. The Communists were still in the North; in fact, the dimensions of the war had expanded into Cambodia. The media in the United States gave mixed reviews of the policy, but most of the liberal media of the time (not nearly as radical as today), *backed U.S. policy* and, at the same time, rained sympathy with the antiwar protestors and politicians that also had a dim view of the conflict.

When President Nixon was reelected in 1972, it was largely a response by voters to allow him to keep his promise to bring an "honorable" end to the war, an assurance he had given during his 1968 campaign for president against Hubert Humphrey. Later, in his 1972 reelection bid against challenger George McGovern, President Nixon called for, regarding Vietnam, "Peace with honor."

Those that taught high school students in the 1970s had been children of the 1960s. Many of them had escaped induction into the military by taking advantage of college deferments, or by outright defiance of government orders after having been formally drafted. The positions young people held were based on their fondness for self-survival. Nobody wanted to go to Vietnam and later be shipped home in a pine box.

Public-school teachers wore their politics like badges of honor. It turned out to be an interesting quagmire. On the one hand, these teachers, authority figures and the shapers of youth, did not want to portray America, their country, in a bad light (after all, many of these teachers' parents had bravely served during World War II)! On the other hand, they didn't wish to sacrifice their idealism. Their self-preservation and other self-serving objections to the war aside, many teachers that came out of colleges and universities during the 60s and 70s grappled with holding on to long-time ideals that their parents had taught them—about freedom, sacrifice, patriotism, altruism, and courage.

Interestingly, teachers could coyly, and safely, juxtapose positions here: By arguing that it had been a patriotic duty to keep the U.S. out of the war, they could, at the same time, act upon their idealism, and call their antiwar position a statement of their patriotism.

Basically, Vietnam demonstrated a courageous United States standing up to the threat of Communism around the world. By stopping the threat of Communism (called *the domino effect*) America modeled, in the eyes of some, a certain kind of toughness; yet, compassion also beamed its light, as America attempted to rescue innocent men, women, and children from tyranny and oppression.

But, alas, though the U.S.'s intentions were good, Vietnam was not the place to have made this stand, and the losses to America by pursuing a policy of engagement did not turn out to justify any gains.

Despite the complexities of events surrounding the War in Vietnam, wokes teach kids that America is an imperialistic country. The war in Vietnam is raised as a model of America's barbaric, militaristic foreign policy. Ewe Bott wrote in the *Globalist* in May of 2019, "To light the world on fire . . . America does not need to cross any borders. America's military supremacy and economic power are sufficient to serve as incendiary devices, once that they fall into the hands of a madman and willing accomplices."[25]

Rather than emphasizing the benevolence and sacrifices of the United States when it comes to aiding others, some textbooks disparage America at every turn. Very few are asking that the schools paint rosy, inaccurate pictures of America and teach kids false accounts of the policies this country has practiced over the years; however, accounting for the truth about all the good America has done in the last 200 years would offer more balance in the classroom.

It is mind-boggling how excited people can get as they bathe in the satisfaction they feel while bashing their country. One wonders if they would feel the same way by speaking up about how awful their own families are. Would that kind of hurtful criticism bring them to the throes of ecstasy, too?

Roy Wehrie summed up academia's position on Vietnam in an editorial for the *Illinois Times* in 2017: "The U.S. decision to stay in Vietnam and to send more troops represented a moral failure. . . . The U.S. had become the crutch of the South Vietnamese military. Yet knowing this, and even though they believed that we could not win, LBJ and Nixon and McNamara sent in thousands of American men to be killed."[26] Teachers might easily dismiss Vietnam as a glaring foreign policy mistake; instead, woke educators prefer to portray the quagmire of this war as an *intentional* evil.

A few high school teachers on *Quoua* confessed their attitudes about the Vietnam War. One said, "[Few] Americans know that the American *invasion* was responsible for the deaths of an estimated 2.5 million Vietnamese, who were either fighting for their country's freedom or in the way of American bombs"[27] (italics added). Note the teacher's cynical tone and use of pejorative terms like *invaders* and *in the way of American bombs*.

Further focus on the narrowmindedness of teachers' approaches came in this comment from Al Nolf, former senior chief of the United States Navy: "Today, if [Vietnam] is discussed at all, a 15-minute liberal/PC overview is provided that discusses politics and bears no resemblance to the actual event. No mention is made of honor, dedication, commitment, sacrifice, government interference, or the mistreatment of soldiers who returned home."[28]

At one time, Americans boasted of holding values like these.

Maybe it's time for the schools to ignore this issue altogether. Bringing Vietnam into the conversation as an example of American genocide or imperialism doesn't serve anyone well. What's the point, if not to malign this country? That the war was ugly and awful and unjustified is a given, not America's finest moment. But beyond that, anything said by teachers about aiding and abetting a continuing, nation-wide imperialistic conspiracy by America is a lie, or the result of such historical ignorance, it is frightening. Johnson and Nixon were not Hitler. Your children should hear the facts, without prejudice.

9/11

After foreign terrorists had flown two commercial airplanes into the World Trade Center and crashed another into the Pentagon, and still another aircraft into the Pennsylvania terrain on September 11, 2001, America changed.

The three thousand-plus Americans that were murdered on that day were only part of the story; the long-term consequences were greater than death and destruction. The political and cultural changes in the world—most specifically, in the American way of life—and the social upheavals around the globe resulted in this attack being labeled by *Time* as "the most important happening of the past two hundred years"[29]—maybe longer.

On September 12, 2001, Richard Decker told his high school students, "There are millions of people in the world that want you *dead*. They do not want your money; they do not want your freedom; they want your *lives*. Why? Because you are Americans, and you share the responsibility for the assimilation and the proliferation of Western values—about materialism, women, and pleasure-seeking indulgences that they do not understand, much less agree with. So, they want to kill you. And the only thing protecting you today from being *dead* is the existence of the mighty military of the United States of America. You live in a country that will protect you from people like they are, and they can't stand the thought of that."[30]

That was quite a while ago. Fast forward twenty years. There are no national guidelines that each state is required to follow for teaching what happened on 9/11 in New York City and Washington, D.C., and above Somerset County, Pennsylvania; lessons vary, depending on the state, the school district, and the teacher.

A 2017 analysis of state high school social studies academic standards in the fifty states and the District of Columbia noted that twenty-six states specifically cited the 9/11 attacks, nine listed terrorism or the war on terror, and sixteen failed to mention the 9/11 assault on America or *any* terrorism related examples at all.

Your author substituted for a high school history teacher who left as a lesson plan a video that attempted to prove (to your children) that the buildings that fell on 9/11 did so because they were sabotaged by agents of the U.S. Government, mainly President Bush. America—not foreign terrorists—murdered four thousand Americans.

Maybe this teacher just wanted to spruce things up! "You have an audience that's easily bored," says Don Ritchie, co-author of the 2018 edition of McGraw-Hill's *United States History & Geography*. "When I talk to students, they complain they get bored with history."[31]

Teachers streamline the moral lessons of 9/11 to meet their own ethical or moral tastes. Evidently, the moral barometers of 9/11 work *subjectively*. The outrage from what occurred on that day is generated by opinion. Who better to pronounce the emotional costs of this attack on the United States than Representative Ilhan Omar of Minnesota, who voiced these cringe-worthy words: "September 11 . . . Isn't that . . . wasn't that when some people did something to . . . some people?"[32]

Who could have articulated the horrors of 9/11 more eloquently than Congresswoman Omar?

Seriously.

THE RESURRECTION OF AN "INSURRECTION"

Sari Beth Rosenberg offered this perspective about teaching the events of January 6, 2021: "As a teacher, it is crucial that I address the January 6 insurrection with my students. . . . January 6 was a direct assault on American democracy. . . . It was an unsuccessful coup. *There are no two sides to what happened*" (italics added).[33]

So much for presenting history with a fair-minded perspective.

Not everyone thinks the "insurrection" should be approached by classroom teachers—at least, not yet.

Reporters Katie Meyer and Emily Rizzo of *PBS* promote an example of exercising patience. In an email sent to social studies teachers and school principals in the Pennridge School District, administrator Keith Veverka, who supervises social studies classes, wrote, "If students ask about the insurrection, teachers should simply state that the investigation is ongoing and as historians we must wait until there is some distance from the event for us to accurately interpret it."[34]

Others disagree with the wait-and-see approach. Louisiana Teacher of the Year (2020) Chris Dier has a candid opinion: "Students deserve teachers who can empower them to learn from such a profound national crisis, who can help process the reality before us. I, for one, will not shy away from this conversation. My students and I will have these tough conversations today, tomorrow, and the next day after that."[35]

Obviously, educators must eventually broach what happened at the Capitol. As of this writing, the events of January 6 are fresh in most people's minds. One teacher commented that January 6 was America's Hiroshima.[36] Even among educators, the spectacle of that day is open to interpretation. While discussing this topic with school kids, teachers should, *at the very least*, consider offering their students a few *facts*:

1. January 6, 2001, was not that long ago. Investigations are ongoing. It isn't "a wrap."
2. As of this writing (January 11, 2022) *no charges of insurrection* have been levied against anyone.
3. Those that "stormed" the Capitol that day did not carry guns. No firearms charges have been filed.
4. One person died from gunfire. A Capitol policeman, one with a history of instability, shot and killed Ashli Babbit, a 35-year-old military veteran. Babbit was unarmed and had no prior interaction of any kind with her killer. No one disputes these facts.

5. Four others that died that day did so from natural causes or physical ailments not linked to the violence at the scene. One cop, allegedly attacked and beaten with a fire hydrant, was not. He died of a stroke.
6. Clear video footage exists showing law enforcement calmly opening the Capitol gates and allowing protesters to enter the premises.
7. Vice-President Harris and several others have publicly compared the events of January 6 to Pearl Harbor and 9/11.
8. Several dozen hours of potentially available video recordings have been hidden from the public by media and government authorities.
9. Dozens of those arrested (and none of them for insurrection) are still in jails and other types of confinement and are awaiting—without bail—their trials.
10. Out of possibly 100,000 people on or near the Capitol grounds that day, two thousand individuals moved toward the buildings, and less than four hundred entered the buildings—or around .004 percent of the "insurrectionists."[37]

This protest, or riot, is a part of history now. When it's finally clear what occurred on January 6, 2021, point out to kids the sanctity of the buildings that house the government of the United States, proper conducts of protest of perceived election injustices, and the actual potential for a coup or insurrection or government overthrow.

Be *fair*.

TEARING DOWN HISTORY

Regardless of how people accept or deny various events, history happened. How it happened and why it happened is up for grabs, and that is where sabers have crossed. A baffled child watches TV as a statue of Abraham Lincoln topples to the ground, and he is confused; after all, Lincoln was the good guy with that—what was it—? *Emancipation Proclamation* thing. Right? Didn't Lincoln free slaves? Wasn't he the president that headed the Union, the "good guys" during the Civil War? Kids don't get it. Some adults don't get it either.

Here are nine *facts* about the erasing of history. The destruction of statues and monuments serves a dual purpose: it removes these former icons from America's historical culture; and it transfers their hero status to one of a villainous racist, a condition that "ordinary" people can't know about, tolerate, or understand, unless, according to the wokes, others join them in their attempts to portray America as a nation of abject hate and white supremacy.

1. In many cities, statues of Abolitionists (those that petitioned *against* slavery) have been destroyed or knocked down. (Makes you kind of wonder about the historical literacy of those doing the destruction.)
2. A statue of Col. Hans Christian Heg, who campaigned against slavery and was killed leading his regiment against Confederate troops at the Battle of Chickamauga in 1863, was torn down by protesters in Madison, Wisconsin. These same geniuses went after Lady Forward, a symbol of women's suffrage movements.[38] (You no longer should wonder about their historical literacy.)
3. A monument to George Washington, erected in the 1920s, was ripped down in Portland, Oregon. (Partly because of actions like this, Portland has become the loony bin capital of the West; this prestige no longer goes to Berkeley.)
4. Vandals in North Carolina showed their ignorance of history when they set fire to a statue of General Lee, but it wasn't the Robert E. Lee of the Southern Confederacy. They targeted a statue of World War II Major Gen. William C. Lee, who campaigned for the creation of a U.S. Army airborne division and helped plan the invasion of Normandy.[39] (Case closed on the I.Q. of the statue wreckers.)
5. Several statue destroyers suggested replacing the Columbus statue with another famous Italian American, House Speaker Nancy Pelosi, evidently believing that Pelosi is still living after 400 years.[40] (Sounds like a *MAD Magazine* feature sketch, no?)
6. The statue destruction is often done at night by roving vandals or sanctioned by extremist groups or bullies. Most of the prime targets—the statues of Confederate leaders—have been torn down or defaced at night. (Night provides better cover for these cowards, who often use hammers, fire extinguishers, screw drivers, and baseball bats to drive their points home. Very nice people.)
7. By October 2020, over a hundred Confederate symbols had been "removed, relocated or renamed," as the Huffington Pos*t* reported it, based on data from the Southern Poverty Law Center.[41] (Your author thinks the vandals may have gotten some of their targets wrong. It is easy to be mistaken in the dead of night, while in a hurry, and without any knowledge of history past a fourth-grade education.)
8. Jason Mosely, a local painting contractor, has this view of the statues and paintings that have been destroyed: "We just want to preserve history is all we want to do. You can't really go by what that statue says. The Confederacy doesn't mean that slaves were part of it. That's just a period of time is all it is."[42] (It's ugly sometimes; it isn't ugly sometimes. But warts and all, our history is . . . what it is.)

9. A high school teacher and two others were arrested after they allegedly vandalized a statue of Christopher Columbus. All three suspects were charged with the desecration of a grave/monument and conspiracy.[43] (This teacher is representative of how many more like him? They want *this* guy to teach history to your kids!?!)

For more information on this subject, here is a website that lists dozens of statues and monuments that have been torn down or destroyed during the past two years: https://thehill.com/homenews/state-watch/502492-list-statues-toppled-vandalized-removed-protests.[44]

If the wokes want your children to think that America is the most horrible place on earth, they will have a fight on their hands. Levelheaded educators want to work with a balanced curriculum. History professor at Kentucky State University, Wilfred Reilly, said on a television interview show, "We don't mind a 'warts and all' portrayal of American history. What we object to is a *warts only* portrayal." [45]

NOTES

1. Sam Wineburg, "Why Historical Thinking Is Not About History," *Sam Wineburg's Keynote Address*, 2015. http://on.aaslh.org/Wineburg2015

2. No rabbi that I know would want his name in print, associated with that expressed view.

3. I would like to think he did. Paul Revere is the quintessence of my childhood reverence for American patriots.

4. Ricky Hornsby is a pseudonym. *Rogers* Hornsby, on the other hand, was a shortstop.

5. *The Columbus Dispatch* (Staff Writer), "Statue Decision Is Insulting To Me As Columbus State Alum," June 23, 2020, editorial page, par. 3.

6. At least, it used to be easier—the later the events—to accuse others of racism. Now, accusations may be flung as early as *seconds* after someone says or does something racially suspicious.

7. If you watched a city burning on your television during the summer of 2020, and then heard the "news" commentator refer to what you were watching as a "peaceful protest," you probably lost some confidence in "seeing is believing."

8. Valerie Strauss, Christopher Columbus: "3 Things You Thought He Did That He Didn't," *The Washington Post*, October 14, 2013. https://www.washingtonpost.com/news/answer-sheet/wp/2013/10/14/christopher-columbus-3-things-you-think-he-did-that-he-didnt/

9. Michael Coard, "Anyone Celebrating Columbus Day Is Racist, Ignorant, or Both," *The Philadelphia Tribune*, October 12, 2020, Op-Ed, par. 2. https://www.phillytrib.com/commentary/michaelcoard/

coard-anyone-celebrating-columbus-day-is-racist-ignorant-or-both/article_5efc4464-05c5-5130-9f55-4fa87889e2d9.html

10. ibid., par. 9. Not to stereotype Europeans or to sound racist or anything . . . but it is noteworthy that Mr. Coard couldn't help but eke out a little racism of his own: i.e., "arrogantly—like Europeans do."

11. Michael Price, "European Diseases Left A Genetic Mark On Native Americans," *AAAS,* November 15, 2016. https://www.sciencemag.org/news/2016/11/european-diseases-left-genetic-mark-native-americans

12. Parter Umbot, "The Explorer In The Silly Hat," Peter Houston, *KABC 790*, July, 1999. The date of this interview with Mr. Umbot is an approximation.

13. Maria Saavedria, "5 Reasons To Defend Christopher Columbus," *The Hispanic Council*, October 2019. https://www.hispaniccouncil.org/5-reasons-to-defend-christopher-columbus-today/

14. ibid.

15. ibid.

16. These are the combined deaths of the Union and the Confederacy.

17. Thomas Paine, "The Crisis Number One," *Common Sense*, January 10, 1776, located at SE corner of S 3rd St. & Thomas Paine Place (Chancellor St), Philadelphia.

18. Dalton Trumbo, *Johnny Got His Gun*, J.B. Lippincott (1939), p. 49.

19. Michael Hardt, "Jefferson and Democracy," *American Quarterly*, (John Hopkins University Press) Volume 59, No. 1, pp. 41–78, March 2007.

20. Ta-Nehisi Coates, "The Case for Reparations," *The Atlantic*, June 2014. https://www.theatlantic.com/magazine/archive/2014/06/the-case-for-reparations/361631/

21. Juliana Menasce Horwitz, "Race in America 2019," *Pew Research Center*, April 9, 2019. https://www.pewresearch.org/social-trends/2019/04/09/race-in-america-2019/

22. This valuable, inspiring information needs to be a part of any course in which teachers inform students about America's racist past.

23. Thomson Reuters, "Racial Discrimination," *FindLaw*, 2021. https://www.findlaw.com/civilrights/discrimination/racial-discrimination.html

24. This has not yet been formalized.

25. Ewe Bolt, "The New Age Of American Imperialism," *The Globalist*, May 11, 2018. https://www.theglobalist.com/united-states-donald-trump-iran-nuclear-deal-imperialism/

26. Roy Wehrie, "What Went Wrong In Vietnam?" *Illinois Times*, New and Opinion, October 19, 2017.

27. Jeremy Keller, "Is The War In Vietnam Properly Taught In American Schools?" *Quora*, December 12, 2019. https://www.quora.com/Is-the-Vietnam-War-properly-taught-in-American-schools

28. Al Nolf, "Is The War In Vietnam Properly Taught In American Schools?" *Quora*, December 19, 2019. https://www.quora.com/Is-the-Vietnam-War-properly-taught-in-American-schools

29. Has anyone heard if *Time* later compared the significance of the January 6, "Resurrection" to the significance of the 9/11attacks? Some pundits (or nitwits) have done that!

30. Mr. Decker is a pseudonym. Upon reflection, this may have been what I told *my* classes the day after the attack.

31. Don Richie, "9/11 Is History Now," *Time*, (History/Education), September 10, 2019. https://time.com/5672103/9-11-history-curriculum/

32. Amanda Seitz, "Image Distorts Rep. Omar's 9/11 Remarks," *AP News*, September 11, 2019. https://apnews.com/article/archive-fact-checking-7354840002

33. Sari Beth Rosenberg, "How I'm Teaching My Students About The January 6 Insurrection . . . " *Parent*, January 6, 2022. https://www.parents.com/kids/education/how-im-teaching-my-students-about-the-january-6-insurrection-on-the-capitol/

34. Katie Meyer and Emily Rizzo, "Don't Discuss The January 6 Insurrection With Students," *PBS, BBC World Service*, January 5, 2022. https://whyy.org/articles/dont-discuss-the-jan-6-insurrection-with-students-a-bucks-school-district-tells-teachers/

35. Chris Dier, "My Students Still Have Questions About The Capitol Riot" *Education Week*, January 5, 2022. https://www.edweek.org/teaching-learning/opinion-my-students-still-have-questions-about-the-capitol-riot-they-deserve-honest-answers/2022/01

36. This may not be a fair comparison. Over 80,000 Japanese were killed in Hiroshima. Five people died either shortly before, during, or following the Capitol riot: one was shot by Capitol Police, another died of a drug overdose, and three died of natural causes.

37. These numbers have not yet been formalized.

38. Teryl Franklin, "Who Was Hans Heg, Whose Statue Was Torn Down In Madison?" *Wisconsin State Journal*, September 27, 2020. https://madison.com/wsj/news/local/who-was-hans-heg-whose-statue-was-torn-down-in-madison-heres-why-the-civil/article_4fbfaa15-f1c6-5c4a-b609-a4cab462b448.html

39. Ryan Prior, "Vandals In North Carolina Set Fire To Gen. Lee Statue, But Not The Confederate One," *CNN*, February 21, 2019. https://www.cnn.com/2019/02/21/us/general-lee-statue-north-carolina-trnd/index.html

40. Amy Hollyfield, "Who Should Replace Christopher Columbus Statue At Coit Tower?" *ABC 7*, June 22, 2020. https://abc7news.com/san-francisco-christopher-columbus-statue-removed-sf-coit-tower-replacement/6260070/

41. Christopher Mathias, "Over 100 Confederate Symbols Removed Or Renamed Since George Floyd Killing," HuffPost, October 14, 2020. https://www.huffpost.com/entry/100-confederate-symbols-removed-since-george-floyd_n_5f86255cc5b681f7da1c9d04

42. John Burnett, "Confederate Statues Coming Down Around Us But Not Everywhere," *NPR*, October 20, 2020. https://www.npr.org/2020/10/06/919193176/confederate-statues-come-down-around-u-s-but-not-everywhere

43. ibid.

44. Paste this website in your browser and scan the many examples of the results of blunt-minded ignorance.

45. Wilfred Reilly, Kentucky State University, "The Tucker Carlson Show," Fox News, November 26, 2021.

Chapter 9

Speak Only What I Want to Hear

FREE SPEECH DILEMMA

That anyone would ever have to write a book condemning the infringement of free speech rights is disturbing; in fact, this topic may be the most alarming of all the subjects covered in this text. The curtailing of free speech may have surpassed the dehumanization of white people in the "it's distressing" department. Both are troubling, for sure, but the denying, and subsequent rapid deterioration, of free speech rights in the United States, the last bastion of hope for freedom and democracy in the world, has been the most disconcerting development of all.

This situation illuminates quite a confusing dichotomy, especially for children who are learning about their country, their Constitution, and those "abstract ideals" men and women have died to protect.

In various contexts, parents may talk with their kids about freedom of speech; presumably, they reference the Bill of Rights and proudly point out to their children that they live in the greatest democracy in the history of civilization. They may mention the dangers of challenging the sanctity of the Constitution, and they embolden their children to share with their friends their appreciation of the First Amendment. After a short pontification about the despotic countries of the world and how their government's inhibiting of freedom has injured the people, parents puff out their chests and renew their vows of pride in their country.

Okay, maybe not all parents follow these dicta; but *teachers* used to, and the public took it for granted.

So, to that dilemma: In front of their own kids and students, parents and teachers passionately support freedom of speech, but they may deny speech when that speech involves ideas that they don't like.

KID: *Daddy, Trump is a racist pig.*

DADDY: *No name-calling in this house, kid! Go to your room!*

STUDENT: *There was a lot to admire about Fidel Castro.*[1]

TEACHER: *I can't believe you just said that! I am writing a discipline referral!*

Perhaps, there is a less impulsive, more mature approach to this. Just sayin':

DADDY: *Here, kid, are better, less accusatory ways of referring to our President; in the long run, more careful word choices may help you to influence others with your views.*

TEACHER: *We should discuss the pain, death, and destruction caused by Fidel Castro, and why it might not be a wise idea to be publicly praising this man.*

Parents can handle this situation however they wish. Curtailing free speech at home is within their purview. It's their house. At the schools, most teachers (not their union leaders) stress tolerance while dealing with controversial ideas, encouraging their students to listen to the "other side."

For decades in the state of California, eighth grade students, to advance to the ninth grade, were required to take a comprehensive exam on the Constitution of the United States. A score of 70 percent was passing, and passing this exam was mandatory. A student could not advance to high school without doing so. In addition to the test, eighth graders had to complete a detailed written project on the Constitution. The state's educators obsessed with school children familiarizing themselves with the Constitution, the Bill of Rights, and, especially, the First Amendment. What could be more important, more democratic, more *American* than that?

The answers to those questions may have given parents pause about public school teachers and, especially, teachers' unions. *Just how far should we go to indoctrinate these kids with the view that America is, overall, a decent place?*

Perish the thought!

As a condition of employment, teachers must sign a loyalty oath.[2] Needless to say, American students no longer must pass a test on the Constitution or the Bill of Rights or learn any other concept that makes America sound *good*.

A teacher friend of your author recently asked his eighth graders to memorize a few lines from the Declaration of Independence, and he later caught some flak from his principal. The principal firmly, but politely, chastised the teacher for assigning this patriotic document to his students, and the rest of their conversation went something like this:

PRINCIPAL: *You know, it's just one of those things. Some parents are too sensitive.*

TEACHER: *I get it that some parents are idiots. I don't get why* you are *being such an idiot. For the life of me, I don't understand how you could kowtow to a parent that objects to the students learning about the Declaration of Independence! It's mind-boggling!*

PRINCIPAL: *Thomas Jefferson owned slaves.*

TEACHER: *I'm listening.*

PRINCIPAL: *Well, when he wrote about "life, liberty, and the pursuit of happiness," he was referring only to white people.*

TEACHER: *Gee, then I guess I'm the idiot!*

PRINCIPAL: *You don't see the problem here?*

TEACHER: *I see a man that inspired one of the most important documents in history, declaring that it doesn't[3] matter what color you are; you have a God-given right to live, to be free, and to follow your dreams. Why a parent—and in this case* you—*would want to kill the wide-eyed admiration of our children and taint their view of their country is way beyond my capacity to understand you.*

PRINCIPAL: *Huh?*

TAMPERING WITH THE COMMON SENSE OF CHILDREN

College students are being duped; that's apparent. Look at what's happening at all levels of public education *before* college. The university is a place where one may *expect* the politically correct floodgates to open, controlling what is allowed and not allowed in terms of speech. Scary, writing that last sentence, but it needed to be said. What's absent in today's depressing academic climate is some clarity on free speech, and a discussion of controversial issues that should be brought to the children's attention.

Perhaps, educators handled this better in bygone years.

In the past, teachers hadn't brought attention to the delicacies involved in interpreting the Constitution. Educators took for granted what they taught their students about government and the documents that held the nation together. Children and their parents trusted educators to help them assimilate into a society in which their rights were heeded.

In the past, teachers made it clear to children that the schools would support their "unalienable rights," including their freedom to speak out. But Constitutional rights do not, in general, follow kids to school. The legal concept of *in loco parentis* is usually applicable. The school acts as proxy ("in the place of the parent") from the time children leave home, until they return home from school; this means, the same rights parents may give their own children (privacy, language use, etc.) the school, as a proxy for the parent, may allow or disallow.

Some parents search their kids' bedrooms without their permission; the school their children attend may forcibly open their lockers and utilize drug sniffing dogs on their bodies. These intrusive acts of a school are usually legal and have been interpreted as Constitutional by the courts; however, these same restrictions would not apply to adults. Kids' rights are different. Many individuals, including legal scholars, see this as a head scratching, seemingly illogical and hypocritical dichotomy.

In the past, free speech has been viewed as sacrosanct; however, during specific circumstances, especially those in which many Americans may vehemently disagree with the speaker (or writer), or in which many people find the presenters' ideas to be highly offensive—even disgusting or vulgar—the protected rights of free speech may, indeed, be tampered with.

One of the most publicized examples of this occurred when members of the National Socialist Party petitioned for parade permits to march in American suburbs. Everybody is for the freedom to parade ("no matter what the purpose or how disgusting the theme of the parade"), until it dawns on them that the marchers are Nazis! Quick changes of heart often occur on the spot.

In the past, colleges and universities, a favorite venue for left-wing speakers, also provided—albeit reluctantly—a haven for ultraconservative speakers. Although dissenters often condemned pending presentations, the conservative speakers were allowed to orate. Security forces were hired, and protesters kept at bay. Crowds tried to shut down conservative speeches. It was not a matter of their disdaining the speaker; it was not a matter of trying to control the speaker's information flow and ideas; it was not a matter of having their say and then *leaving* the venue in protest of the speaker's words. It was a matter of, "*I don't like what you have to say; therefore, you may not say it.*"

The Free Speech Movement at Berkeley in the 1960s had provided a blueprint for the liberty of self-expression. Generally, colleges and universities were a bastion for freedom of speech, even though classrooms were controlled by the radical professors that hung out there. God help you if you happened to disagree with your professors!

In the past, if you—even accidentally—offended someone in the classroom with your comments, the teacher mediated the situation. Sometimes an eighth-grade boy would say something stupid to an eighth-grade girl, and she would not take kindly to his comments. The teacher would have instructed those students to deal with their problems. It's called *growing up*. However, if the teacher—in some cases, the school site administrator—judged the child's comments to be *intentionally* malicious, a form of discipline was handed down from the top of a school's power hierarchy; this could have meant anything from a verbal reprimand of the student to a five-day suspension from school.

Educators believed that with free speech came responsibility, but sometimes children would err in their earnest attempts to express themselves or blow off steam. Although most kids meant nothing harmful or hurtful, dumb stuff often came out between their lips anyway. One might wonder *who* gets to interpret *officially* the offensive potency of the deadly spoken words. In those days, setting oneself up to be the judge and jury on speech issues was frowned upon.

Legally—and this is painful for fragile wokes to hear—*you don't have the right* not *to be offended.* Get it? You *do* have the right to offend someone else, though.

In the past, students thought that their right to express themselves in both oral and written discourse was precious. Students were made aware by their parents and teachers that people had *died* so others might freely air their views. There had been no delineation between speech that was offensive, as opposed to speech that was "*highly*" offensive." There was no separation between speech that most people thought inappropriate in the context of a given situation, and speech that was considered "hate speech."

The term *hate speech* did not exist. Most people sensed that using ugly, offensive words should be avoided, and if the border of "too ugly and offensive" had been crossed, a good reprimand was in order. No one *seriously* thought about imprisoning or shooting men and women that exposed their racism in their words. Few argued in favor of making certain words or ideas illegal. They elected *not* to define or specify which words should be publicly targeted as too offensive for public discourse. Americans considered how the censoring of *others* and their words today could mean the censoring of *me* and *my* words tomorrow.

In the past, school-age children sensed that "free speech" existed in America; it was beautiful and special. They were cautioned that free speech was not pure or absolute. Teachers taught older children about the Supreme Court Decision (Schenck vs. the United States) that defined possible limitations on free speech (creating a "clear and present danger," such as "crying *fire* in a crowded theater").

The absurdity of defining *words* as constituting violence, or racist epitaphs as indicative of the Court's references to "creating a clear and present danger," rarely surfaced. Kids of all sizes and shapes and colors knew they were blessed to be living in the freest nation in the world, and logic and common sense relative to the Bill of Rights *must* prevail if America were going to maintain that privilege.

In the past, even though the concept was confusing to them, students could understand the difference between free speech (as in the public forum), as opposed to "free" speech in the privacy of one's own home or business. Some of the kids that worked at McDonald's (and other places where kids worked) found themselves frustrated at not being able to talk back to irritating customers or not being able to wear T-shirts with images of their favorite cannabis leaves spread across the front.

Today, grown adults may not be allowed by their employers to proselytize their passionate religious views or express their strong political opinions. When they complain because their free speech rights have been violated, it takes only one rational person to remind them that they are at work. As a result, they must follow their boss's rules; those rules may disregard their own perceived free speech rights. Most children get this; we rarely give them credit for doing so. It's usually their parents that become adamant about allowing their kid to wear a T-shirt with a picture of aborted fetuses, inscribed, *Kill 'em all and let God sort it out*.

When Colin Kaepernick knelt his body in protest of police brutality during the national anthem, students may have had a hard time distinguishing between what the football player viewed as his free speech rights during the game, and the fact that the game was being played in the backyard of San Francisco 49ers' owners that didn't *want* him to kneel. At the time, the National Football League looked upon that kneeling with disdain, too.

Kaepernick and others could protest America all they wanted, *while they weren't at work.* The football team and the NFL were the bosses. The owners' rules while their employees were on the job would triumph.

Those were the traditional methods of approaching the explanations of free speech in America. Different teachers had varying views on what constituted the First Amendment and how to interpret it. While they were not all in agreement, most educators believed that free speech is a precious gift that the forefathers left for generations that followed to use and possibly abuse. The significance of free speech to the uniqueness of the United States of America was never in doubt. It's demarcation from the crappiest nations in the world incited pride in the citizens of this country, as well as an enhanced feeling of gratitude, sometimes bordering on amazement, for having been born here.

Times have changed. These changes—you decide just how unfortunate they are or not—are reflected in the following ten observations about the woke influence in America's schools when it comes to issues of free speech. Formerly sound ideas have been distorted; respected individuals have been cancelled, and admired works of art and literature have been censored.

THE WOKES AND THE FIRST AMENDMENT

1. The Constitution is on fire!

And not in a good way, as in, "Our American Constitution is *hot!*"

The premise of this sacred document, that individual rights are natural and granted by God, *and government may not take them away*, has slipped into regression. It is now *rights flow from government*; leaders will let you know which rights you still have and may be allowed to exercise. This had been the case even before the arrival of the coronavirus, but since the mandated vaccines and masks and lockdowns, people have resorted to groveling to "get their rights back," even rights that had never been formally limited or withdrawn.

Now, however, consider the strangest of all predicaments: The Constitution of the United States, the backbone of democracy, is a racist, outmoded document that protects the rights of only straight white men. Despite its inclusive wording, the Bill of Rights did not apply to all Americans—and it would not—for more than 130 years (if even by *then*). At the time of its ratification, the "people" referenced in the amendments were understood to be land-owning white men only, many of them slave masters. Blacks were granted equal protection under the law in 1868, but this was purely on paper. Women could not vote in all states before 1920, and Native Americans did not achieve full citizenship until 1924.[4]

Women were not granted the right to vote until 1919! In many states, Black people had to produce identification cards to vote; no Constitutional protections for them! Racists may hide behind this document and behave as though everybody benefits from it, regardless of the color of their skin. Imagine that! The insidious anti-Black spectrum of the Constitution cloaks its own evil.

Catch any sarcasm there?

America *was* institutionally racist (no sarcasm there). It took time for the Constitution to evolve; it took time for Americans to evolve. But few countries—maybe none—set on a fiercer course of action *away* from historical racism. School kids don't even know what the Constitution is, or what it stands for, but they revel in their disdain for the slave owning forefathers that came up with it.

2. Equality for all, no matter what their ages, is smart and cool.

It is no longer vogue to distinguish between those who have matured throughout their lives, become educated, gone through several relationships, and become learned and wise . . . with those who are sixteen-years-old. In fact, a movement by the House of Representatives in 2020 to grant the vote to sixteen-year-olds almost gained serious momentum. It shouldn't be a shock that certain special interest groups believe children should be afforded the same rights as adults.

Your author found out the hard way about equal rights for school children. When he asked to purchase a Coca-Cola from the faculty lunchroom server, she told him . . . Ah, this conversation should be recounted in in detail:

YOUR AUTHOR: *I'd like a Coke, please.*

LUNCHROOM LADY: *Sorry, no Cokes.*

YOUR AUTHOR: *Aww . . . no Cokes today?*

LUNCHROOM LADY: *Nope. No Cokes today—no Cokes ever.*

YOUR AUTHOR: *What?*

LUNCHROOM LADY: *Sorry, Bruce, the district says that we can't serve sugar drinks to kids anymore.*

YOUR AUTHOR: *I know. But I'm not a kid. I'm fifty years old!*

LUNCHROOM LADY: *Right. But they told us that we couldn't serve something to the teachers and deny it to the students. You're all equal now.*

YOUR AUTHOR: *Does that mean no more preordered special lunches for the faculty?*

LUNCHROOM LADY: *I'm afraid that's exactly what it means.*[5]

Never mind that children are immature and irresponsible; their brains are not fully formed. And their propensity for impulsivity often lands them in a heap of trouble. At least, everyone had achieved equity.

And if the school district had been worried about *equity*, they could have had preordered special lunches for the students; instead of *taking away* from the teachers, they could have *added* the kids. You can achieve equity that way, too.

3. Freedom of Speech is reserved for only those that do not offend me.

Freedom of Speech matters.
 Or does it?
 Consider comments from people who should know better. This is what some teachers (certainly not all) convey to kids in school. You be the judge.
 You have the right to speak up . . .

- unless I strongly disagree with you

Speak Only What I Want to Hear   131

- unless you are offensive to people of color
- unless you tell jokes about racial, cultural, or sexual minorities
- unless you support traditional and religious family values
- unless you are against abortion rights
- unless you support the nuclear family
- unless you denounce Black Lives Matter
- unless you argue that *all* lives matter
- unless you question the rights of LGBTQ community
- unless you are pro law enforcement
- unless you like Trump
- unless you doubt the science of climate change
- unless you argue against open borders or in favor of a tougher immigration policy
- unless you question the legitimacy of the 2020 election
- unless you question the science of nonbinary genders
- unless you argue that women should stay home to raise their children
- unless you suggest that all voters must show a photo I.D.
- unless you hold that children should be raised by a man *and* a woman
- unless you disagree that transgender men should be allowed to compete in women's sports
- unless you call America the greatest county in the world
- unless you imply the coronavirus was created in a Chinese lab
- unless you argue the fallibilities of public mask-wearing
- unless you deny there was a "resurrection" on January 6, 2021
- unless you say something in opposition to coronavirus vaccine mandates

4. When you get to college, take your professors' views on social and political issues to heart.

You will hear a mixture of views; the arguments, from a variety of teachers, will be diverse. (*That* is a crock of you-know-what.)

Notice how your professors have managed to bring into even math and chemistry classes their hatred for Trump, and their debasement of the Republican Party. Internationalism prevails. America is no longer an entity unto itself; it is not a sovereign nation anymore. Patriotism is a form of nationalism. Nationalism is a form of fascism. The Nazis were fascists. If you are a nationalist, as was President Trump, you are a fascist. In fact, you are a Nazi.

Challenging this type of logic in a college environment takes some guts. Your principal may order you to sit in the corner of the room and force you to face a wall, adorned by a picture of John Wilkes Booth.

The modern free speech model for the *public school*: get ready to speak up, speak out, and speak often. But remember, your college professors are always right, unless they produce weird, funky, quirky diatribes that cause them to appear loving of their country, trusting of its institutions, or skeptical of Dr. Fauci.

5. Formal institutions, public and private—especially public—have a new responsibility.

This responsibility goes beyond academia the highfalutin philosophical goals they espouse.

To allow offensive and uninformed speakers to share their "information" at colleges, universities, churches, and public schools is to disdain the very fabric of what America is all about. While it may be true that all sides of an issue should be heard—that is not the case 100 percent of the time. There are rare situations in which a public speaker or journalist is so deplorable, so conservative, allowing that individual a platform to push those ideas is a dereliction of duty by those who set up the occasion. (Please remember this is verbal irony.) Sometimes real adults need to step forward. You would not allow Nazis to parade through a neighborhood composed of mostly Jewish concentration camp survivors, would you? Come on, man!

In Skokie, Illinois, in 1979, that is precisely what happened. Granting a parade permit to such a despicable group, whose sole intent was to hurt Jews and to cause pain by invoking awful memories, seemed extraordinarily cruel. However, the Supreme Court found in favor of the Nazis and ordered Skokie to grant the Nazis their parade permit.[6]

Citing the framers' intent of the First Amendment, the Court argued that the Nazis were disgusting,[7] but even "disgusting" speech is protected by the First Amendment. And what about violence? The Court affirmed a lower court's initial reversal of the decision by arguing that if violence did, indeed, ensue, it would be the fault of those that came to watch the parade and threw rocks and bottles at the Nazis. Thus, the Nazis had the right to parade. The spectators had the responsibility to allow them that parade.

What usually follows is perpetrators of anti–free speech movements define key words to their liking. They can't argue that a particular *word* would incite acts of violence, so they simply make the *word* the violence. If a particular word, by its mere utterance, is considered violence, then anyone using that word on the street would, technically, have used violence.

Remember when your eighth-grade teacher proudly quoted a patriot you didn't care about, but the words sounded a little inspiring: "I may not agree with what you say, but I will defend unto the death your right to say it."?[8]

That's disappeared. Gone.

Free speech has been diluted by sociopathic radicals.

6. Not even my employer has the right to zip up my mouth.

Funny how this kind of thinking was unanimously rejected for decades by both large corporations and the people that worked at those places. The distinction between your pulpit in public (your time), and your employer's imperial palace (your boss's time) was quite clear. And everyone accepted it. Even kids that worked at Disneyland understood that they had to swap their tattoos of snakes, dragons, and naked ladies for face shots of Micky Mouse. Disneyland allowed no face or body decor. Their supervisors forbade it.

Of course, you could always choose to work somewhere else, which Disneyland was eager to let you know every chance that they had.

Disneyland presents a conundrum that young people struggle with, as they decide how much of their personal freedom they are willing to sacrifice for the sake of obtaining and keeping a job. The same holds true for professional athletes. On Monday mornings, teachers lead discussions about "right-wing," football team owners and fascist politicians that argued against allowing multimillion-dollar athletes whine on the field about racist America.

This became a head scratcher. The NFL offered no statement or blanket policy on disrupting the "Star-Spangled Banner" with fist pumps and knee bends. Many held out hope that this form of protest and its America bashing would fade out. However, the kneeling, and all that accompanied it, remained for a small portion of the diminutive 2020 Major League Baseball season, as well. As of this writing, the flag troublemakers—at least, at baseball games—have fizzled out. The Summer Olympics created a whole new host of challenges that needed to be worked out, as did the inaugural of the 2021 season of the National Football League.

Baseball earns the distinction of committing the biggest blunder of all when it comes to free speech and cancelling ideas they didn't like.

Because of controversy surrounding a new law mandating certain guidelines for Georgia voters, including presenting a picture I.D. at the polls, Major League Baseball chose to move its annual classic, the All-Star game, from Atlanta, Georgia, to Denver, Colorado. Baseball was protesting. Or maybe Commissioner, Rob Manfred, was protesting. Just exactly *what*—did it really matter? They were *protesting*. The upshot was that hundreds of millions of dollars in business revenues waiting to be invested by baseball fans in the city of Atlanta were never realized. Inner-city neighborhoods, composed almost exclusively of minority shop owners, restaurant entrepreneurs, and hotel enterprises were set back truckloads of cash.

STUDENT: *So, Mr. Richards, just what was MLB so upset about, to the point of moving its big game to another city and losing all that money?*

TEACHER: *Racism.*

STUDENT: *In Atlanta?*

TEACHER: *In the state of Georgia.*

STUDENT: *What was the racism about?*

TEACHER: *Voting. Black people would be having their votes suppressed.*

STUDENT: *How?*

TEACHER: *All people would be forced to produce their drivers' license or another form of identification when they went to the polls to vote.*

STUDENT: *So, their votes are suppressed? How?*

TEACHER: *Black people don't know how to get a drivers' license.*

TRUSTING THE AMERICAN PEOPLE

Government and civics classes are changing. Advanced Placement exams for college bound juniors and seniors are still highly successful moneymaking ploys. Most schools offer government classes, of course—even require them for graduation—but the emphasis on *American* government is waning. Knowing about other countries' forms of government is important for students, but to the tune of *half* their senior year in high school (with American government occupying only the other half)? Come on, man!

Understanding the despotic nature of communism, socialism, fascism, and somewhere in-between is crucial to an appreciation of American democracy. Unless teachers are willing to say that America is not perfect, but other countries are more flawed, your kids' appreciation for America will remain dormant. They may heed the words of Ryan Fazio, who wrote in the *New York Post* on July 3, 2021, "The character of America is always striving to be 'more perfect,' and we must continue to do so today. What separates America in human history is not its sins, but its virtues."[9]

Remember, that was a quotation from a journalist for the *New York Post*, not a public school teacher or one of their union leaders. Teachers can do a better job of boosting America's excellence in the eyes of their students.[10]

Americans will not stand for gross injustices. They will not tolerate an arm of the government poisoning children with the calculated propaganda of woke idiocy. The key to having that amount of trust in the American people is to make sure that the people receive, unimpeded, relevant information; they must know what's going on in the schools, and who's coming after their children with woke absurdities. You should be deadly afraid to shut other people up, or to allow them to shut you up.

BIG TECH'S CENSORSHIP

Big tech is at it again, and if any part of this nation and what helps to make it tick has greater influence on your children than Google, Apple, Microsoft, Facebook, Twitter, TikTok, Instagram, YouTube, and T-Mobile, someone needs to point that out. Your author would like to know.

Google

Google and other search engines censor speech by subtle means. They simply provide more and better access to articles, books, and videos on their search engines—and quicker accessibility—to those sources they would *like* for you to utilize.

Suppose a sixth grader is writing a report about Joe Biden; he types the name of the president in the search box on Google or Bing or Bong or whatever, and information by the boatload about Biden instantly pops up on the screen. What trained eyes may notice is that *favorable* articles about Biden will run their course first—sometimes for pages and pages of screen—before Google may downshift a bit into more unfavorable material. For example, if you are researching Biden and climate change, you may first meet an article called, "Biden Moves Forward on Climate Strategy: Works to Discourage Dirty Energy."[11]

If you click on page *seven* of your screen, you will see something like this (finally): "Biden Ousts 17,000 From Jobs: Cuts Keystone Pipeline." The *Wall Street Journal* would have printed that article. Its presence on Google is ubiquitous, but students won't be able to find it. By the time they had scrolled through all those other articles and pages and eventually arrived at the negative story about the Keystone Pipeline, they would have absorbed so much bias reporting—journalists licking the old man's boots—they would figure President Biden to be the most brilliant overseer of U.S. energy concerns of all time.

Bill Mahr, a comedian that used to be funnier, and less socially responsible than he is now, pointed out that children can't get information off social media, if the tyrants of social media don't want them to get it. The debate about the origins of COVID is a chilling example. Mahr said, "Facebook banned any post for four months about COVID coming from a lab. Of course, now, even the Biden administration is looking into this."[12]

Maher said during a panel discussion, "Google—a *Wall Street Journal* reporter asked the head of Google's health division—noticed that they don't do autofill searches for 'coronavirus lab leak' the way they do for any other question, and the guy said, 'Well, we want to make sure that the search isn't leading people down pathways that are not authoritative information.'"[13]

Mahr despises the self-anointed experts that "don't know shit."[14] Their political agendas have "substituted for their cortex," he says.

Good for Bill Mahr!

Twitter

Twitter has banned or suspended President Trump and other conservative politicians, along with some writers of note. After the Capitol protests on January 6, 2021, more than 70,000 suspensions occurred. Add to those around 30,000 other deleted or suspended Twitter accounts (for content infractions) by the middle of October 2020.[15]

Facebook

Despite reoccurring attempts to salvage their Facebook accounts, the Zuckerberg-led troops have managed to censor thousands of posts and ban users from the social media platform. If their monitors do not like your post or comments to other posters, Facebook may remove you and/or your words for violating their policies. Sometimes your post will disappear, as though it has packed up and run out into cyberspace, never to be heard from again.

YouTube

Social media sites that claim they do not censor material are sometimes the biggest culprits when it comes to the outright *banning* of speech. YouTube is among the most notorious offenders. Teenagers may argue that YouTube offers a fair and balanced approach to social media, but most of these children have no idea what happens in the offices of YouTube, not to mention that they have no idea what "fair and balanced" means. Most kids know only what they see; they are ignorant about the dozens of conservative videos that have never graced the screens run by YouTube.

Dennis Prager has cried foul for years over YouTube's "arbitrary" censoring of material, especially his own work, a successful enterprise called Prager University. Prager quickly realized the censorship policy of YouTube was anything but arbitrary. Their targets were conservatives.[16]

One peculiar decision by YouTube was to prevent several scientists and medical scholars from being heard. Jack Papke, of Stanford, led a round table discussion about the efficacy of masks and social distancing during the pandemic. Surrounding him were the following group members: radiologist and former White House adviser Scott Atlas, Harvard University biostatistician Martin Kulldorff, Oxford University epidemiologist Sunetra Gupta, and Stanford Medical School economist Jay Bhattacharya.[17]

Ron DeSantis, the governor of Florida, headed the panel. He was the guy that made the other states' governors look like mental midgets when he opened businesses and schools and downplayed mask and vaccine mandates in his state. As of this writing, the economy of Florida has remained consistently strong in the absence of lockdowns, closures, and phony COVID death reports.

YouTube wound up *cancelling* the group, with this declaimer: "This content does not meet our standards and may present false or inaccurate information."[18] This boob from YouTube thinks that he is more of an expert in science than the health and medical director at Stanford, and the other distinguished scientists. Her flagrant disrespect for a free flow of information is poor role modeling for your children and disconcerting for the rest of us.

Seemingly unconstitutional, YouTube's efforts to censor those they don't agree with are perfectly legal. "Legal" does not necessarily equate to moral or right. In fact, when legal *is* the same as moral or right, it is often a coincidence. The brass at YouTube have created a private social media platform and established rules and regulations to follow by the people that utilize that platform. Teachers assign YouTube videos to their students all the time. How many of those students are up in arms about having a tough time locating (the banished) Prager University?

They're like the bosses at McDonald's that tell their employees they can't wear red MAGA hats while working the drive-thru windows. There is no free speech, per se. The flow of words is regulated by those that would impose their own views, definitions, and interpretations on speech. Everybody that applies for a job there (or at Disneyland, where the restrictions on self-expression are even tighter), understands the policy about not wearing hats and is willing to abide by those requirements. They don't have to like it or agree with it, but they go along with it—or don't take the job.

YouTube is the same. If you decide to platform on YouTube, you unmistakably understand that your video may not make it all the way through the process of production and presentation. You are probably a bit hazy about the definitions of "acceptable content" or "misleading information," or about the criteria for deciding what is "appropriate material." But you eventually buy into the system. You don't have to accept the job at McDonald's, and you don't have to play your video on YouTube. You abide by the rules, because they are either the only game in town, or they happen to be the game you want to play the most.

The upshot is that you may be *censored.* Censorship is alive and well in the United States of America. Social media sites, though privately run and controlled by a relatively small number of men and women of one political bent, have taken over the public domain.

Technically, the sites are privately controlled; realistically, these social media platforms have a *public* flavor. In fact, in most cases, these platforms are called *public platforms.* They are one of the few exceptions in which a *public* anything is controlled by a private entity, and, therefore, may bask in the luxury of private privileges that provide a de facto asylum for those attempting to abridge the Constitution. Site officials make it sound as though they are helping to weld together the steel pipes of free enterprise.

If you think children can in any shape, manner, or form understand any of these complicated, nuanced ideas, you are probably living on another planet with those children. All that kids know is, *Hey, I can pretty much say what I want to on the internet, and you can, too. Anybody can . . . except Trump.*

Did you hear about Mr. Rocha?[19] He read from *To Kill a Mockingbird* to one of his Honors-English classes. He thought nothing of it, until his principal summoned him to her office. She told Mr. Rocha that one of the parents of his students had complained that he, Mr. Rocha, was a racist. He had used the N-word. Mr. Rocha explained to his administrator that Harper Lee uses that word several times in her novel to make her point about the *ugliness* of the word. This word was not the teacher's; it was used by the author in one of the most acclaimed books of all time for its social commentary *against* racism.

It didn't matter. Mr. Rocha was reprimanded. The principal apologized to the parent, and the book was eventually pulled from the school district's recommended reading list. Rather than combat the shortsightedness that is censorship, school officials buckled. For a change, the school was right. But they caved in anyway.

This incident taught children if you use certain words, you are a bad person, even if you are quoting someone *else,* one of the great American authors, whose book had been universally praised for helping society in its journey to *fight* bigotry. Forget logic (there is none); ignore hypocrisy (the wokes drown in it). In today's climate, certain no-no's and taboos drag a person into a swamp and serve them up to alligators.

Your author's daughter at the time of this writing is in her third year at a four-year college. She just said to me, "I think it's cool that you're writing a book about this stuff, because most people are afraid to speak up, to state the obvious. I am. Some of the things other students are saying in class are *so* wrong. I disagree with some of my professors. But I'm afraid to say anything."[20]

She isn't alone.

NOTES

1. In choosing to use someone uniquely disgusting as the example, I skipped over Hitler, who is always chosen as an illustration of the essence of evil.

2. *Dictionary of American History*, "Teachers' Loyalty Oath," August 9, 2021. "I solemnly swear or affirm that I will support the Constitution of the State of ___ and of the United States of America and the laws of the State of ___ and of the United States."

3. Skokie, Illinois—1979.

4. Susan Cianci Salvatore (preparer), "Civil Rights in America: Racial Voting Rights," *National Park Service, Office of the Interior*, 2009. https://www.nps.gov/subjects/tellingallamericansstories/upload/CivilRights_VotingRights.pdf

5. It makes perfect sense that the Coca-Cola incident should not be considered a big deal. I got the feeling, however, that I was even *then* being judged as a privileged, white, paternalistic old guy . . . who thought he deserved special rights over children, which is what I *did* think—at least the "old guy" part.

6. David Goldberger, "The Skokie Case: How I Came To Represent The Free Speech Rights Of Nazis," *The American Civil Liberties Union*, March 2, 2020. https://www.aclu.org/issues/free-speech/rights-protesters/skokie-case-how-i-came-represent-free-speech-rights-nazis

7. "Offensive" may have been a legal term they used.

8. The remark is often attributed to Voltaire but that's not who originated it. The quotation is the work of his biographer, Evelyn Beatrice Hall.

9. Ryan Fazio, "Young Americans Need To Appreciate The Good Fortune They Take For Granted," *The New York Post*, July 3, 2021 (opinion section).

10. Michael Turner, "Why We Should Teach Students Patriotism At School," *Whereyat*, August 10, 2021. https://whereyat.com/why-we-should-teach-students-patriotism-at-school

11. I made up that topic head, but it sounds like something a search engine would reveal early. By the way, please test this out: Pick any politically charged topic; quickly determine how Google would come down on the subject and notice the partiality by which the subjects have been prioritized by the search engine.

12. Bill Mahr, "Bill Maher WHACKS Google, Facebook for Banning All Lab-Leak Questioning," *TalkFest*, June 21, 2021. https://talknest.com/2021/06/bill-maher-whacks-google-facebook-for-banning-all-lab-leak-questioning/

13. Allana Akhtar, "Google Prioritizes 'Authoritative' Results To avoid Leading Users To Misinformation," *Insider*, Jun 10, 2021. https://www.businessinsider.com/google-does-not-auto-complete-searches-wuhan-lab-leak-theory-2021-6. This is the original source to which Mr. Mahr was referring.

14. Bill Mahr, "Bill Maher WHACKS Google, Facebook for Banning All Lab-Leak Questioning," *TalkFest*, June 21, 2021. https://talknest.com/2021/06/bill-maher-whacks-google-facebook-for-banning-all-lab-leak-questioning/

15. Sean Noone, "Twitter Suspends 70,000 Accounts Following US Capitol Riot," *WKBN27*, January 11, 2021. https://www.wkbn.com/news/national-world/twitter-suspends-70000-accounts-following-us-capitol-riot/

16. Valerie Richardson, "PragerU Fights YouTube over 'Censoring' of Conservative Videos."

17. Meryl Cornfield, "YouTube Pulls Video of DeSantis Panel Discussion Urging No Masks For Children," *The Washington Post*, April 9, 2021. https://www.washingtonpost.com/technology/2021/04/09/desantis-youtube-coronavirus/

18. It's good to know that a few mush heads on the cancel squad at YouTube sites possess more knowledge about science than the impressive group of scientists and doctors gathered for this discussion panel.

19. Mr. Rocha is another pseudonym. I used the names of educators I know personally—but only with their permission.

20. My daughter told me that her professors seemed fair and balanced in their classroom presentations. But she felt in a tiny minority among her classmates, flabbergasted by their woke ideas, often boxed in, too intimidated to speak up.

Chapter 10

Political Correctness, a Laughing Matter

HOWLS MEAN MORE THAN CHUCKLES

Political correctness usually manages to bring a few chuckles and halfhearted laughs to whatever scene it happens upon. Even if a person is in tune with the sensitivities of the individual being protected through careful choices of language, political correctness, at its silly best, can be highly entertaining.

America's schools, as a rule, pander to the loudest voices of dissent, not the most reasonable voices or the most beneficial to the nation. The people that strain the limits of tolerance are also the people that speak the loudest; they echo throughout the land with their dubious interpretations of other people's speech. They impose their own strange, unorthodox judgments on others, and behave as though the limits and standards they have set are agreed upon by all.

America's schools don't debunk these behaviors; they tend to support them, for fear of being attacked for their intolerance, lack of compassion, or prejudice.

Merriam-Webster defines political correctness: "conforming to a belief that language and practices which could offend political or social sensibilities (as in matters of sex or race) should be eliminated."[1]

Political correctness may be divided into two parts: words and actions. Whereas words may be classified as politically correct *speech*, actions, the way people treat others, is politically correct *behavior*.[2] The language of political correctness can be (and often is) very funny. Those who are offended by seemingly harmless words don't agree; they fail to see any humor in whatever the situation. These people are usually seen as hairpin sensitive, offended by almost anything. However, the manipulation of words to avoid offense is so, well, *inane*, it becomes a breath of fresh air in and around academia whenever someone pushes back against the politically correct inertia that hardly anyone else wants to touch.

Though usually benign, the impact of political correctness influences society and is sometimes the lens through which the public views the school system. Politically correct educators appear condescending and pandering. Looking at the broader picture, politically correct behaviors, along with politically correct words and expressions, are a *howl*!

Definition of *howl*: a long, loud, doleful cry uttered by an animal such as a dog or wolf.[3] In the slang usage of *howl*, the word describes a *loud derisive laugh*, usually aimed at woke ideas and at woke educators that propagate those woke ideas.

Politically Correct *Behaviors*

HOWL #1

In October 2014, a school district in Nebraska circulated a handout that suggested teachers avoid "gendered" expressions, such as "boys and girls," in case they may alienate transgender students. The instructions, issued by the Lincoln Public Schools system, recommended using gender-neutral expressions such as, "Hey, campers," or something as nonspecific as "purple penguins" when telling kids to sit down on the rug for circle time.[4]

"Purple Penguins?" The school officials think the children are dumber than they truly are!

HOWL #2

In Frisco, Texas, the colors red and green were banned from the school's winter party, and the children were not allowed to make references to Christmas or other religious holidays. One teacher wanted to add an elf on the shelf in her classroom but decided against it in case she "got in trouble." Earlier in the season, a few teachers in the school had complained about the generic examples of the trees being referred to with the ambiguous identity of "a holiday tree." Most students, teachers, and parents wanted to call it a "Christmas Tree."[5]

Evidently, the principal at this school had doubled down on her initial Scrooge-ness; the "holiday tree" remained, which, for all intents and purposes, cancelled out any probability of referencing that or any other tree as a *Chanukah Bush*.

HOWL #3

In Youngstown, a lesbian couple adopted a child two days after she had been born. Knowing full well that the child was a little blond-haired *girl*, they initially refused to confirm the gender of the child when communicating with their friends and family. Every person that saw the child recognized a female when they saw her, but the mysterious behavior of the parents continued. They homeschooled their child for a couple of years, and when they enrolled the kid in second grade, the administrators of the school sanctioned their decision to wait for a while before "fully announcing" their child's gender.[6]

A seven-year-old girl attended a school that had encouraged her parents not to confirm her gender! The parents claimed that their child was, obviously, a female when it came to her *sex*, but her *gender* had not been determined.[7] Had the school taken a stand, as other schools had done previously in similar situations (none of them this whacky), the decisions as to which clubs or sports the girl could participate in would have been made a couple of years before.

Imagine the difficulty of being seven and told that your parents, and the school, still had to determine if you are a boy or a girl. Like, a child's life at that age isn't already tough enough!

HOWL #4

The Thomas Fordham Institute published a report in 2016 about the difficulties college students are facing. This may sound shocking, but it seems that high school doesn't prepare all college bound students for higher education. A large gap exists between the minimum amount of knowledge that a student requires to earn a high school diploma, and what that student will need to succeed in college. Students enter community colleges (two-year programs) unprepared for even that level of schooling.

But educators tell kids that *everyone* should go to college. They "inspire" children by allowing them to become privy to the "secret": if they work hard, if they burn enough midnight candles, if they make enormous sacrifices in their jobs or their private lives, they will be able to go to college—and even *better*, they will succeed in college once they arrive. No matter what the culture, the economic conditions, the family environment, the innate intelligence level, the personality, the social surroundings of the individual—*anybody can succeed in college*. And *everyone deserves to be there*.[8]

HOWL #5

One elementary school tightened up its restrictions on the proliferation of bad health information by making certain the modeling of violent behavior was shielded from the eyes of the little ones. A mother at the school, a true crusader, who led the charge to protect the kids from images that could damage their psyche, passionately demanded a ban on . . . Superwoman lunch boxes. The mother said, "We have defined 'violent characters' as those who solve problems using violence. Superheroes certainly fall into that category."[9]

A conglomeration of isolated examples of political correctness does not constitute a trend; however, a whole series of books could be written, describing imbecilic policies that carry the pretense of protecting the emotional health of children or teaching kids not to offend others or hurt their feelings. The result of these policies is that they defy logic, creating an unadulterated mess of confusion in the minds of the young.

Not only has the letter of logic been scrapped, but the students' intuitiveness has been disregarded. Most people, even young folks, know instinctively that a Superwoman lunchbox isn't going to corrupt the peaceful nature of America's school children, or allowing red and green twinkling lights on a "holiday tree" isn't a threat to the inclusiveness of those that don't identify with Christianity. Kids aren't as brainless or fragile as some adults would have you believe.

What's weird is that more *teachers* aren't aware of the keen instincts of kids. The lack of maturity of some adults tends to blunt their ability to make clear judgments and *logical* choices; their absence of perceptiveness hampers their capacity to recognize bullshit as being nothing more, or nothing less, than bullshit. Your children, however, *know* that something ain't kosher.

Politically Correct *Speech*

The rampaging movement to protect feelings and establish decorum through hypersensitive actions and delicate speech has not been limited to schools; it has infiltrated the workplace, churches, government, law enforcement, and even the military. But the education establishment is on parade, and it is worth suffering a little personal blood boiling to check how the language has evolved into a politically correct series of jokes—*unintentional* jokes. Along the way, you have permission to chuckle—or cringe.

If you are following the latest round of politically correct speech, you will notice that it gets increasingly silly. Or so it sounds. Educators tell students that things *are* a certain way, and they need to be *said* a certain way, even if that certain way (the adjusted language) is not as specific or purposeful as they would prefer. And students know the schools are being dishonest. They understand that their teachers sometimes come off as demeaning and patronizing, even if the children don't understand what *demeaning* and *patronizing* mean.

Teachers often talk to their elementary school students in terms of gender specifics, but any teacher over the age of thirty can't help but slip up occasionally. They might refer to the *policeman* and then quietly correct that "grave" error by saying police *person* the next time. If the person is a woman, they use *policewoman*, but *cop* is gender neutral. Understand that your thoughts may be severely punished for even imagining a male-type while alluding to a *cop*.

In sixth grade classes, it is no longer unheard-of to open the possibility that men can have babies, although this is a terribly difficult concept to explain to kids. They know about Mom and Dad and hundreds of other male-female combinations making babies; in fact, the basic imagery of *anybody* making a baby may make it difficult for small children to understand or cope. It's tough enough for some *adults* to understand or cope with some of those images!

If you throw in that a *man* may make a baby, you'd better be able to explain how men have babies, too—which, of course, is the rub. Never mind the insanity of the idea. Simply toss out the words *mother* and *father* and replace with *parent*. And when you allude to a "parent" having a baby, refer to "her" as a *birthing person*,[10] as in, "My birthing person lived in Brooklyn for most of her life. Then she met her partner in Jamestown and they created a human person—me!"

Yashee wrote in *The Indian Express* in June of 2021, "Those who advocate the use of 'birthing people' say it is not just women who give birth. Trans men, a person assigned the female gender at birth but who identifies as a man, and genderqueer people, who identify as neither man nor women, also give birth."[11]

Your author has done some additional research on this subject and found *nothing* about biological birthing by a man. An embryo or a fetus may be planted in a warm balloon, and that balloon may be called a birthing . . . thing—or whatever. It's not hard to explain why some people get all worked up and defensive about these kinds of terms: Just hearing about them, like so much of political correctness, can be unbearably irritating. And if you're even mildly amused by all this, as opposed to agitated or confused, think about how tenth graders receive this information in their biology classes.

Children are now taught to avoid gender specific words. Don't say *manmade*, when you may easily say person made. Avoid *manhole;* simply use *hole*. You may still tell a child to call someone an *asshole*, if the kid doesn't specify a female *ass* or a male *ass*.[12]

Kids use the word *retard* all the time; you should remind them this word is insulting to people who are maligned because of their mental faculties. Some schools do not permit the use of the word *retardation*. A counselor described a kid as being socially retarded, and all hell broke loose. The counselor should have said, "Billy is limited in his social development," or depending on the specifics, "Billy messes up all the time when he tries to talk with other children [socially inept]."[13]

Don't call your friends *fags* or *homos*. Those are not proper words. Say *homosexual* or *gay*. And try not to say, "That's so gay!" which is an expression to use when something is lame. *Gay* is also what homosexuals prefer to be called. Just say, "That's so lame!"

See how much better that is.

While on the gay category, it is now unwise—abhorrent to some people—to refer to a person's sexual *preference*. When you talk about homosexuality, you are really describing a sexual *orientation*. Because people can't *choose* to be heterosexual or homosexual, they accept the notion that they are oriented one way or another. Cydney Adams of CBS News pointed out, "Sexual orientation is the inherent or immutable enduring emotional, romantic or sexual attraction to other people. Basically, it's who you are interested in dating and being intimate with. Someone can be transgender, but also be gay, straight, bisexual, asexual, or a whole host of other sexual identities that exist."[14] The most important thing to remember is that the attraction factor is not a choice. You are . . . what you are.

In a science class in a private Boston school, students were discussing the coronavirus and its effect on Major League Baseball after a long layoff. The question arose as to whether players that had been afflicted with the virus and were facing quarantine for a lengthy period would be put on the *Disabled List*. An argument ensued, because the players, though technically having contracted the coronavirus, were not sick, let alone disabled.

The debate lasted a couple of minutes, when a wise soul in the group rightfully pointed out that baseball no longer used a "Disabled List" to table players that had been injured but could return to active duty after a specified number of days. The former "Disabled List" is now called the *Injured List*, even though players on the so-called "Injured List" had not been injured; they had COVID.

The discussion transmogrified into a real hoot when a few of the students in the science class became offended—they claimed, on the behalf of others—because their classmates insisted on referring to the list of temporarily inactive baseball players as "disabled." This, some of them whined, was an affront to people in society who are physically impaired and cannot perform their normal, everyday activities.

The teacher sided with the students that loathed the term *disabled list* in favor of the politically correct, *injured list*. Evidently, if you are injured, you join a group of people that have managed to hold on to their personal dignity, guys that twisted their ankles while attempting to steal second base and had to sit out for a few games; on the other hand, if you are *disabled*, well, there's no athletic dignity in that.

Students should remind their parents that while they are traveling together, the woman that assists them on the airplane is the *flight attendant*, not a stewardess, which now carries those old, hackneyed sexual connotations. Remember the skit: "Hi, there, Big Boy! What would you like: coffee, tea, or me?" Apparently, only "stewardesses" would speak seductively and not *flight attendants*.

Some other warnings for students, especially the younger ones who don't really know any better but should be advised: Second graders who have male friends that have decided they would rather be girls may get *gender reassignment surgery*, not a "sex change operation," which, apparently, made the ordeal sound whacky.[15]

Remember to tell your friends that Beth has asthma and needs to sit on the sidelines during physical education classes. If you say that Beth is "afflicted with asthma," it somehow makes Beth a lesser person—being *afflicted*, that is, instead of simply *having* it.

Students are told that people who are strange or different could be *outcasts*, but they no longer should be referring to them as "black sheep." (Need that be explained?) No one is "fat" anymore; they are *overweight*. Not only is Marnie overweight; she is *hearing impaired*, (not "deaf," God forbid)! And her friend Miguel is not "blind as a bat"; he is *substantially visually impaired*. People are no longer "wheelchair bound" or "handicapped,"; they are wheelchair *users*.

Teachers would never suggest that a woman who trades sex for money is a prostitute; she is now the more honorable *sex worker*. And be careful about calling your unmarried Aunt Peggy a "spinster" or an "old maid." No way that she qualifies as one of those decrepit loser types! She is a *single woman*. Don't use the term "unmarried woman," as even "unmarried" could be easily interpreted as being less than married, and that would be a tragedy, though some married people would beg to disagree with that theory.

RUNNING A "RACE" OF POLITICAL CORRECTNESS

God help America!

In some parts of the country, and in a few random school districts, strict orders on how to refer to people that come to this country without the benefit of traditional immigration safeguards have been issued. Because a large segment of the school population is not made up of American citizens and children that have gone through the proper immigration channels, the delicacy of language can't be overstated. The truth is no matter what you say, or how you word it, you will offend someone.

American schools pride themselves on providing nurturing, safe environments for their students. Racial discrimination in a school may still happen, but *systemic* racial discrimination in America's schools no longer exists.[16]

Southern states that practiced racist, dehumanizing policies up until the late 1960s boast of the most stringent antidiscrimination laws. And they enforce them. Political science professor Rex F. Randall said the last place he would want to be accused of failure to yield to federal civil rights laws is in a state south of the Mason Dixon Line.[17] Yet, progressive—in a *positive* sense—civil rights accomplishments of the past have established legal precedents for equality and tolerance that triumph in today's inflammatory racial climate.

In Texas, California, and New Mexico, the numbers of students in the public schools that have come from Latin American countries, including Mexico, fluctuate; clearly, the percentages of school children from this population are rapidly increasing. The Pew Research Center showed this trend. In New Mexico alone, the proportion of the Hispanic population has climbed to 48 percent. Similar results can be observed in Texas and Florida.[18]

These trends do not take into consideration the hundreds of thousands of migrants that have *walked* to Texas from Central America during the last few months of 2021. The latest numbers of undocumented, unvaccinated, and untested people that have strolled across the Southern border or been flown or bussed to places around the United States are staggering.[19]

Most teachers don't care if a kid in their classrooms has citizenship papers, a green card, or a driver's license. An educator's job is to impart their subject matter to their students and help them feel safe and secure while at school. On the front lines, teachers stay far away from those bureaucratic decisions that make being a part of the education establishment a drag. It is the job of government to protect the border and enforce laws that help to do that.

A teacher may assume that all children in the schools have arrived by way of legally established channels. They will tell you that the easiest and least controversial thing to do is ignore the fuss that surrounds illegal migration, even now, while the U.S. does not have much of a border. And they are right. It is not politically correct—or legal—for a teacher to be concerned about, or questioning of, a student's immigration standing. Most teachers will adamantly tell you that it is not their business from where the kids in their classes have come. Their responsibility is to teach them.

Note that several hundred San Diego teachers escaped into encampments, in which migrant children waited for their parents while they hashed out their immigration status with border authorities. Teachers, free of charge, much of that time during their annual spring recess, volunteered to teach migrants. They went to crowded, ramshackle destinations, where young children, properly socially distanced and masks in place, eagerly awaited them.[20]

Teachers—good teachers—don't play politics, especially when children's futures hang in the balance. They do not indulge in protests and crusades. Their mission, their calling, is to *teach*. To a teacher, a migrant is an immigrant is an illegal alien. They don't care. To preserve the dignity of both their foreign and domestic students, they do the best they can to educate them, while shielding them from harassment and bigotry. *Classroom teachers do not proselytize on this issue*. Union leaders, political action committees, and boards of education are a different story.

Objectively speaking, purely from a factual standpoint, there is a difference in the official status of people that have come to this country in the past forty years or so. In the *old* days, an *immigrant* was a man or woman or child that arrived in the United States from another country. They followed immigration protocol, had a sponsor and a job waiting for them, and obeyed the laws of their new land. Their mission was to become a citizen of the United States of America, not to be a political foil or media talking point.

When that magical moment arrived, a judge swore them in before friends and family; they teared up, maybe sobbed aloud. They had achieved their dream by legally coming to America, assimilating into its culture, and obtaining the ultimate prize, citizenship.

An immigrant, *by definition*, may be in America for the purpose of work or education. They have a limited time on their visas. They may carry a green card to demonstrate their *legal* status, but they are not on a pathway to citizenship; at least, not yet. Maybe someday that will happen for them.

Woke schoolteachers have accused others of xenophobia for not using the "right" words to describe the immigration situation; their cries of "racism" never stop. Urged on by their union leaders, the job of teaching, rather than preaching, has become blurred. For these teachers, it is a sign of success when they see that their students can't distinguish between an *immigrant* and a *migrant*. They think it is a signal that their "tolerance" lessons have worked. All people are the same: the newly arrived migrants from El Salvador and immigrant steel workers in Detroit that have worked their tushes off in this country for fifty years—all the same!

The data are different when you know the distinctions. When politicians claim that *immigrants* tend to commit less crime than those who already live here, they are right; however, data independent of *illegal* immigrants is not considered. When you factor in illegal aliens, those stats fly out the window. When you include people that have come here for the sole purpose of causing trouble, like gang members, the reporting of the stats is skewed.[21]

And this is *precisely* why language matters. Using certain words or modifying artificial behaviors to refrain from hurting someone's feelings distorts reality. People are hurt by it. Yes, it seems kinder to refrain from noticing certain truths and realities. But words matter. They sometimes hurt; other times, they soothe and protect. Mostly, though—and many can't take *this* truth—using correct and precise expressions glorifies language, respects traditions, and clears up ambiguities.

Hans A. von Spakovsky, of *The Heritage Foundation*, wrote, "If we are going to discuss and debate the issue of immigration and what our public policy should be, we should at least use accurate, precise terms, and talk about, for example, *legal* aliens vs. *illegal* aliens."[22]

Advocates for illegal aliens want to stifle debate by making the false claim that if you are against "undocumented immigrants"—aka illegal aliens—you must be a racist, a nativist, or someone who hates all immigrants.[23]

This, of course, is a form of demagoguery. It is also a logical fallacy. But if you have an agenda to follow and a classroom of students to convince, you do what you can, while you can, to achieve your political, social, and educational goals, instead of teaching children what terms actually mean, such as "immigrant," "migrant," "border," and "citizenship."

Amanda Taub wrote in *Vox*, "[P.C. is] a sort of catch-all term we apply to people who ask for more sensitivity to a particular cause than we're willing to give . . . a way to dismiss issues as frivolous in order to justify ignoring them. The charge of 'political correctness' is often used by those in a position of privilege to silence debates raised by marginalized people, to say that their concerns don't deserve to be voiced, much less addressed."

The grave concerns of some appear frivolous to others; but rather than turn a blind eye to the grievances (however foolish) of a portion of the population that believes their worries are being unfairly dismissed, America's schools err on the side of political correctness. At the very most, some people respond very seriously and take what others perceive as constructive steps to help those who may be reaching out. At the very least, the rest of the population comes away from the situation with a hearty laugh.

NOTES

1. Any edition—or any dictionary, for that matter—offers an almost identical definition of *political correctness*.

2. This is my own haphazard division of political correctness genres. It doesn't matter; you know when someone is straining to be "politically correct" when you hear it.

3. *Merriam-Webster*, August 14, 2020. https://www.merriam-webster.com/dictionary/howl

4. Jane Ridley, "The 5 Most Outrageous Politically Correct School Rules," *The New York Post*, March 27, 2015. https://nypost.com/2015/03/27/the-5-most-outrageous-politically-correct-school-rules/

5. Todd Starnes, "School Bans Christmas Trees, The Colors Red & Green," Fox News, December 5, 2013. https://www.foxnews.com/opinion/school-bans-christmas-trees-the-colors-red-green

6. ibid. As a point of interest, in the summer of 2021, a couple in California burned down half the San Bernardino mountainside after lighting fireworks in celebration of their child's gender reveal party. I still don't know if the forever-stigmatized kid was "revealed" as a boy or a girl.

7. This is a fictitious scenario, an illustration of what *should* have happened.

8. Many school districts have used similar language in their mission statements: "*All students will qualify to attend a college of their choice.*" Yeah, right.

9. Jonah Goldberg, "Superheroes No More," *USA Today*, August 31, 2015. https://www.usatoday.com/story/opinion/2015/08/31/superheroes-moral-justification-violence-column/71459950/

10. At first, the term *birthing person* seemed so insensitive and detached from the miracle of motherhood, I didn't know what to make of it. And I didn't know what it *meant*. Having been given a clinical definition, I now think "birthing person" seems to be an even more depressing term than what I'd thought before. Where are the feminists?

11. Yashee, "Why Replace Mothers With 'Birthing People'?" *The Indian Express*, June 21, 2021. https://indianexpress.com/article/explained/explained-history-of-and-uproar-around-us-budget-document-using-birthing-people-instead-of-mothers-7351523/ (Go down to the third paragraph from the title.)

12. My conclusion: I am not sure if there is a source for that.

13. You may be amused (or not) by older television shows and films, in which this term is used casually and without malice.

14. Cydney Adams, "The Difference Between Sexual Orientation And Gender Identity," *CBS News*, March 24, 2017. https://www.cbsnews.com/news/the-difference-between-sexual-orientation-and-gender-identity/

15. *Purland Training*, "100 Politically Correct (PC) Euphemisms," August 15, 2021. There is a long list of humorous politically correct terms and words on these pages: purlandtraining.com/2020/08/01/100-politically-correct-pc-euphemisms/

16. Rick Esenberg and Daniel Lennington, "Critical Race Theory Has No Place in American Schools," *Real Clear Education*, June 14, 2021 (essence of article). https://www.realcleareducation.comarticles2021/06/14critical_race_theory_has_no_place_in_american_schools_110595.html

17. Alias Dr. Randall was a Professor of Communications at Whittier College. He spoke these words to a class in the spring of 1970. I remember them well. I wrote them down.

18. Jens Manuel Krogstad, "Hispanics Have Accounted For More Than Half Of Total U.S. Population Growth Since 2010," *Pew Research Center.* https://www.pewresearch.org/fact-tank/2020/07/10/hispanics-have-accounted-for-more-than-half-of-total-u-s-population-growth-since-2010/

19. The U.S, Border Patrol reports that from November, 2020, until September, 2021, the aggregate number is around 1,700,000! And it increased substantially after that count.

20. Ariel Zilber, "Outrage After Migrant Children In San Diego Get In-Person Classes From Teachers At A Temporary Immigrant Shelter," *Daily Mail*, March 30, 2021. https://www.dailymail.co.uk/news/article-9416981/Migrant-children-San-Diego-person-classes-school-kids-stuck-home.html

21. The exact number of homicides by these people is tough to come by; however, even if *one* illegal "immigrant" commits a murder, that's one more murder than should have happened—and would have *never* happened, if immigration laws had been enforced.

22. Hans A. von Spakovsky, *The Heritage Foundation*, "Undocumented Immigrant Is a Made-Up Term That Ignores The Law," July 30, 2018, https://www.heritage.org/immigration/commentary/undocumented-immigrant-made-term-ignores-the-law

23. ibid.

Chapter 11

Teaching Science: An Exercise in Hypocrisy

WHEN HOW THINGS WORK MADE SENSE

Science is the study of how things work.

Science can be difficult and confusing. Figuring it out is tough because things don't always work the way they're supposed to work. And *why* they work: that's something to ponder, too.

Teaching kids science can be either incredibly rewarding or endlessly frustrating. Most young people just want to see the end; they don't care that much about *how* they get to the end. Which is why children—their inherent curiosities having been deafened and deadened by the internet and social media—naively serve up their vulnerabilities to the teachings of science. They don't always care about the *why* and *how*; if they did, a lot of the dreck being shoved down their throats would be regurgitated before they had an opportunity to digest it.

Most people, no matter what their ages, don't fly into gleeful cartwheels after being subjected to new scientific theories and concepts. In bygone years, the nation's schools taught biology, chemistry, physics, and various subdivisions of science, like astronomy, which were thrown into a generic collection and called, "general science." Students were taught "settled science," which is the science of truth: *This is what is; this is why it is, and this is how it works*. All science, after being challenged and tested, should be "science of truth." But it isn't.

As you know from studying history (no longer an uncomplicated endeavor), the one-time, crazily disputed science of a few centuries ago evolved into the mundane, undisputed science of fifty years ago, concepts that hardly anyone rejects or questions; after all, science is . . . *science*. It explains stuff. Sometimes people *ooh* and *ah* over a new concept, after they have attended a particularly exciting lecture in a college science class (yeah, right), but they soon get over it. Galileo, Copernicus, Newton, and Einstein developed theories that are sometimes brutally difficult for school kids to understand; yet, everyone knows these scientists were right: they made sense.

Of course, science evolves. It is fair to say that even "settled science" may be changed one-day, after someone even more brilliant than an Einstein comes along and attracts a throng of obsessed followers. Those that truly succeed in changing science are accomplished in coaxing others to believe their facts and findings. They have credentials. These people are adroit; they have a unique brilliance that others can only envy. They can't be any ol' people or a bunch of nerdy science professors. They must come in the form of men and women that portend to possess the key to the future of civilization and have the moxie to attempt to prove it—and then *do*.

Sure, the past was replete with examples of controversy when it came to teaching science in the schools. But the evolution debate has lapsed into a state of repose. Religionists have lost, and anyone hardly cares that they have lost, or so it seems. For the most part, America has been all quiet on the western front inside the academic science arenas of its public schools.

Fairly recently, however, that changed. Like so many other areas of the curriculum, science is fluid. As of this final writing, here is the crux of the science lowdown. Here today, gone tomorrow is a worrisome adversary and a tough nut to crack.

CLIMATE CHANGE

In 2006, filmmaker Davis Guggenheim followed Al Gore on the lecture circuit, as the former presidential candidate campaigned to raise public awareness about the changes in the earth's temperatures.[1] At the time, the going hip term was *global warming* (and *global cooling*, go figure); the movie that hatched from the work of Guggenheim, Gore, and others is entitled *An Inconvenient Truth*.[2] It was *inconvenient*, because the manifestations of actually believing in the science of climate change would require an honest and moral person that believed in the climate change orthodoxy to make monumental sacrifices in order to *do* something about it.

Gore warned of melting ice and glaciers and temperatures that would cause the level of seawater to rise. His expertise was in politics. The *Vice President* Gore had been a presidential candidate at the turn of the century and lost one of the closest elections in history to George W. Bush.[3] The former vice president, under Bill Clinton, narrowly took it on the chin in the politically erratic state of Florida, which sealed his fate and ended his presidential aspirations.

The movie is engaging and, at the same time, frightening. The photography of what appears to be cataclysmic destruction is reminiscent of a horror movie from the 1950s, when mankind's main foe was the powerful forces of nature and, more frequently, the side effects of careless experimentation with radioactivity from the testing of nuclear weapons.

Here's the kicker, though: *An Inconvenient Truth* played its most popular runs on high school, middle school, and elementary school campuses across America. Perhaps, a million or more young Americans, some of them no older than six or seven, have watched *An Inconvenient Truth*, and it scared the ever-loving shit out of them![4]

But that's the point, isn't it? Play to *children*. Frighten *children*. Children run to their parents, and the parents console their kids, and the boogeyman waits in the closet until another day, when he is welcome to do his thing with lots more children. And it was *children* that promoted "climate change" to the forefront of the "popular fears" category for conscientious Americans. Kids were shown to be quite capable of influencing policy making.

Teen climate change activist Greta Thunberg didn't pull any punches at the United Nations when she accused world leaders of shameful indifference. She said in 2017, "I shouldn't be up here. I should be back at school on the other side of the ocean. . . . Yet you all come to us young people for hope. How dare you! You have stolen my dreams and my childhood with your empty words!"[5]

Thunberg goes even further, hinting those international leaders are evil. In a voice quavering with passion, she said, "You say you hear us and that you understand the urgency, but no matter how sad and angry I am, I do not want to believe that, because if you really understood the situation and still kept on failing to act, then you would be evil, and that I refuse to believe."[6]

Thunberg is still at it. Her clamorous tone at the Climate Accords in Paris last November came off not as bang but a whimper—a bit of a dud, actually; however, schoolkids—even some *college* students—see this teenage activist as a true fighter for humanity, a role model for future generations.

It's a shame when science morphs into political pabulum. The actual truth of the matter gets camouflaged, often tangled in a web of political infighting. But the issue of climate change is so overly advertised, hardly anyone takes it seriously anymore, unless forced to by a whiny child, a droning college professor, or an opportunistic bartender turned congresswoman.

The children are left to carry the heavy backpacks into battle; only it's not a fair fight. Kids are not equipped to resist, and their penchant for wanting to please others makes them ripe for the picking. So, refer to this handy guide on the teaching of climate change. If you observe this now, you should be able to share with your kids some options that the schools refuse to give them.

1. Climate change avoids principles of established science.

A funny thing has occurred in science during this century. People have invented new science to fit their political agendas. This is bad. This is not supposed to happen in a civilized, free society. Science is not a matter of opinion. When scientists conduct experiments, they do not manipulate the variables in order to control the outcomes. They do not lie while constructing their hypotheses. They do not interpret the conclusions of their experiments in some weird, unexplainable, and plainly bizarre way to get the reactions they wanted to get all along from fellow scientists.

If their experiment does not work, if their hypothesis turns bogus, they give it another try. Conducting experiments until they work, although not an exercise in expediency, communicates a quest for truth.

Science is objective and neat, like math. It takes a while, a long time in many cases, to get to a point where a "fact" may be labeled as a *fact*. It either is, or it isn't. It works either this way, or that way. Unlike mathematicians, scientists may get smarter or wiser as they investigate a topic, gather information, and correct their errors. "Facts" may change. But until the science has been settled, discussions and analyses and conjectures and debates continue, with all participants ostensibly striving to attain the truth. The next best thing would be to compromise on theories that most scientists can accept, while reserving the right to establish in the future this science as *actual* truth.

In the *Wall Street Journal*, Steven E. Koonin wrote, "The idea that 'Climate science is settled' runs through today's popular and policy discussions. Unfortunately, that claim is misguided. It has distorted public and policy debates on issues related to energy, greenhouse-gas emissions, and the environment. It also has inhibited the scientific and policy discussions that we need to have about our climate future."[7]

Koonin, a former climate change czar under President Obama, goes on to say, "[The media] lament on an allegedly broken climate and proclaim, yet again, that we are facing our 'last best chance' to save our climate from a hellish future. In fact, things aren't—and won't be anywhere near—as dire."[8]

The schools are where science flourishes; in fact, when there are controversies and knockdown, drag-out fights about contested science, it is usually at school board meetings, where the main debate over what should be offered to kids in the science curriculum takes place. Until recently, it had been peaceful; Al Gore mucked that up. *An Inconvenient Truth* warned five-year-old kids that they were going to die hideous, horrible deaths in a few years, unless people did something—those mean, nasty, selfish *old* people—to save them.

Greta Thunberg, after all, had traveled all the way to the U.N. from Sweden to punctuate that point of view.

2. Following the dictum of educators on climate change is simple: scare the kids.

For America to contribute to the forces dedicated to stalling the impending debacle of climate change, China, India, and Russia would have to play significant roles, which *they do not, and probably will not*. Those countries, and the United States, pollute the atmosphere with their targeted poisons. Unless *they* join the fight, anything America would do "to save the world" from the devastation of climate change signifies the U.S.'s acquiescence to the notion that something is better than nothing; unfortunately, "something" is purely cosmetic. America's impact is next to nil without, at least, China's and India's commitment to making huge economic sacrifices.

And then there's this: For America to pay even remedial attention to global warming, cataclysmic changes would have to be made in the national economy. The elimination of carbons is a stated goal. Such a policy would cripple industry. Because the airlines would cease to exist, forget about traveling any further on family vacations than your plug-in car will allow you to go.

Educators are informing your children that climate change is an existential threat, and everything else—all other issues—pale by comparison. Whatever needs to be accomplished to rid the planet of this blight should be at least *attempted*. Children, most of whom lack critical thinking skills of their own (a big thanks to the public schools for that one), fall into convenient niches of obedience—and, subsequently, concurrence—that have been carved out for them by their teachers.

An Inconvenient Truth captured the limelight and became a classroom gospel of science; educators' promises to take seriously their responsibility to present both sides of an important and controversial topic dissipated with each push of the play button on the classrooms' DVD players. Educators were no longer presenting science theories. Educators had latched onto the science of climate change as the *only* truth and, therefore, the *only* science. And for them to have done so, is counter intuitive to intellectual honesty, let alone good teaching.

Dennis Prager said, "Underneath the activism lies a simple truth: Young people are incredibly scared about climate change. They see it as a profound injustice and an existential threat to their generation and those that will follow." Prager goes on to explain that cramming into the hearts and minds of kids theories that have been camouflaged as established science is the *real* gross injustice.[9]

3. Prioritizing the fight against climate change would decimate the American economy.

Daniel Turner, executive director of Power the Future, capsulized the fears of some economists about drastically messing with the U.S. economy to promote a stringent climate change policy: "The Green New Deal would effectively destroy America's energy industry, and with it, our entire economy."[10]

On his first official day in office, President Biden signed an executive order to halt the Keystone Pipeline, removing seventeen thousand people from their jobs. John Kerry, the first United States special presidential envoy for climate, sloughed it off by saying the folks that worked on the pipeline could find jobs (someday) working in windmill and solar technology.[11] A month later, the state of Texas froze—literally—because it had run out of available electricity. The windmills that were supposed to supplement that electricity—the heavily touted windmills, an early indicator of the Green New Deal—froze, too. They were incapacitated. The cold in Texas during the winter of 2021 took no prisoners, and several dozen people died.

In the academic arena, you are not allowed to question a woke's reaction to climate change. "Established" science defies you to do such a thing!

One teacher in Florida tried to discuss climate change *reasonably* with his students. He was brought up in front of a disciplinary committee and barely managed to escape with his job. Joel Fox was forced to recant some of his statements regarding his displeasure with proposed climate change policies and the inevitable monetary consequences of those policies. He later apologized for stating his *opinion*.[12]

No fossil fuels mean no gasoline, which means no combustion engines. No cars would exist, unless you plug them in, and even that kind of car must get electricity from somewhere. Besides proposing the elimination of farting cows, AOC talks about no more airplanes, which translates to people having to walk to Hawaii if they want to visit their relatives there.[13]

GENDER SELECTION

It doesn't take a scientific genius to understand these five basic *facts* about sex and gender, what schools used to teach children:

1. There are two sexes (and two genders), male and female. Instinctively, this is what people believe, even children. Is that a surprise?
2. You are born either a male or a female. You don't get to choose. Maybe there are hormonal and genetic aberrations, and in rare circumstances, these abnormalities become both physically and psychologically

unbearable, and medical intervention is both necessary and desirable; however, this is not the norm. If small children are told otherwise, their already adolescent self-doubts may be magnified to a hyperbolic, and dangerous, degree.
3. Sex and gender may be different, but they are interrelated. You don't get to select your sex; to that extent, you don't get to pick your gender, either. It's not like walking around a car lot, kicking tires. Biology rules here. American kids used to be taught this. Not one five-year-old can explain to you the difference between binary gender and multiple gender biology, even after having "studied" gender selection for days in their first-grade classrooms!
4. One day a biological man may *feel* like a woman, but this doesn't make him a woman. It's weird, at *best*, for someone to announce he is a woman, after he has been a man all his life. What makes a man a man, and a woman a woman, is biology, not proclamations. The reason the kids' heads are buzzing is because to be told otherwise defies not only science but also what their parents have taught them—and common sense.
5. The curriculum of gender is driven by politics and special interest groups. It is not based on science. Definitions and interpretations of words may change; the *science* does not change. Children don't know this, of course. It's probably a good thing, too. They have a hard enough time understanding adults and all their other craziness.

Your humble author taught in the public school system for almost four decades. At the beginning of each semester, he received grade rosters with his students' names and a little bit of information about each kid. Part of the identifying information was a an "M" or an "F" by each name. Nobody ever thought anything odd about that. It's what the attendance office always did: supply the students' genders on the teachers' roll sheets. Frankly, some teachers relied on that identification, because with some of the students, it was difficult to distinguish by sight their gender. More than once he referred to a female by using a masculine pronoun, and vice versa. The kids laughed. Nobody cared. Nobody became huffy or indignant. Nobody ran to the ACLU over that.

Nobody revealed what their preferred pronouns were; nobody asked. Nor was your author obligated to provide his preferred pronouns to his students or administrators. He didn't *have* preferred pronouns. Other problems in the world clamored for headlines and attention; gender identification by stating pronouns wasn't one of them.

Yet, the critics forged ahead. *The Encyclopedia of Early Childhood Development* contended in 2013, "Teachers need training to recognize their own explicit and implicit biases, and how these biases affect their classroom behaviors. Additionally, teachers should receive explicit training in confronting children's biases, so they may reduce peer policing of normative gender activity."[14]

The schools are on it! Tiny kids must know that "normative gender activity" can't be handled by *them*. However, before the counselors and school psychologists begin their gender therapy sessions, it would be good for someone in authority to clarify what "normative gender activity" *means*.

GENETICS

The notion that there is an objective truth stymies those who would find insidious racial manipulations in the teaching of science to children. If "what goes up must come down" is true, racial exploitation of science should be irrelevant. And it should also be *impossible*.

Or so you would think.

The National Science Teaching Association sparked a discussion with this succinct observation: "Science has been used as a weapon against people of color."[15] The NSTA claims that (schools) foster a curriculum of "antiracist teachings in science." They continue, "We can introduce environmental justice topics, such as the Flint water crisis, to spark discussions about racism and *use science and policy to be actively antiracist*. Designing content is only one component of antiracist teaching; it also must be supported by the way we teach it" (italics added).[16]

These teachers proceed to give an example of how to be antiracist in their teaching methods: "Anti-racist teachers teaching predominantly urban Black students might allow them to use 'Black English' to communicate their scientific ideas. Doing so promotes a discourse of racial equity in which the linguistic identity of students is not silenced in favor of white discourses."[17]

Apparently, "white discourses" are always, and exclusively, composed of the proper grammar and syntax.

Racism in teaching science in the public schools had never been a point of contention. Imagine the millions of bigoted science teachers that had no idea how racist, sexist, transphobic, and homophobic they appeared to their students at the time they were spewing their bile! This causes one to shudder!

The teaching of genetics has taken a hit in the arena of racial sensitivities. Wokes have criticized science teachers for promoting the notion of genetic differences among races and concluding that it is those differences that lead to sociological disparities, especially in the areas of drug use, disease, homelessness, and crime. Some claim that various environmental and societal influences have profound effects on racial disparities, and children should not be taught that a race is inferior or marginalized based on *genetic* differences.

What wokes would do to the science curriculum is "fix" the way that science is *taught*, emphasizing environmental influences over, in some cases, scientific proof. Some educators refer to this as "a humane genetics education." The Wiley Online Library of California State University, Fullerton, concurs. "A humane genetics education helps students understand that inequality is not the inevitable product of genes, but it is socially constructed."[18]

Logically—sorry, for allowing logic to get in the way—one might suspect if there is an actual conclusion based on testing and experimentation, and the results are not satisfactory to the community, other ways to *change the results* of the research may be to approach the experiment with another methodology, redo the experiment, or flat-out manipulate the data (which is, to say, to fabricate the conclusions).

Or—a better way—minimize the conclusion by arguing in favor of external factors that have an effect, such as—oh—environmental influences that have a clearer causality to diseases than does the science of genetics. You begin that minimization by finding research conclusions that dispel the old notions about racial genetic differences, which have caused historic furor over the origins of the crudest forms of racism. Again, the National Science Teaching Association: "More recently, scientists studying human variation have provided evidence for why race is not inherently a biologically meaningful category."[19]

Most teachers argue against genetic influences on race. They blame disparities on societal ills that plague marginalized people: improper nutrition, poverty, incarceration, drugs, inadequate medical care, a lack of housing, and historical slavery—external factors over which they have had little or no control. There's a cool name for this: epigenetics. Genetic factors are altered by certain external influences, over which people do have control. A boy may have the genetics for strong muscle development or physical height, but if he does not eat well, his maximum potential for those beneficial genetic influences is stymied, or otherwise modified, in an unnatural way.[20]

This text does not take a position on the truth, or lack thereof, in genetic science. Citing genetic disparities based on race sounds peculiarly racist. But other considerations about genetic influence abound, such as that some cultures contract certain diseases at higher rates than other cultures, (which could also be external influences, such as diet). What about propensities towards certain types of athletic prowess? Are those due to environmental factors? Learning more about genetics in these realms may be helpful to everyone. Are certain areas of genetics education obsolete? Irrelevant? Racist? Again, let the scientists figure that out and then pass those truths along to your kids.

COVID-19

With the uncertainty brought about by the coronavirus pandemic, at the time of this writing, the *only* certainty seems to be that there is no certainty at all. (Is that a modern cliche?)

Whatever science there is, nobody pays any attention to it. Or they are confused by it and wind up reacting how they *wanted* to react in the first place. Their subsequent behaviors spring from their *desires* and not their adherences to the academics of science.

Lots of kids weren't in school at the beginning of the pandemic; they were home, supposedly on their computers, taking their classes virtually. Depending on their ages, most of these children received little or no disclosure as to how they wound up cramped inside their homes with the rest of their disgruntled families, disenfranchised from their teachers and, most important of all, from their friends.

Here's what the National Teachers Association wants kids to know about the coronavirus and the justifications behind their time spent being chained inside their homes: "The emphasis is on safety. Nothing is more important than our children being safe, and our staff knowing they are safe, too. [Distance learning] isn't ideal; it isn't preferred. But it is the safest form of learning right now . . . and for the immediate future."[21]

Consider those special habits, policies, bits of information, discoveries, and "truths" educators now must handle about the "science" of COVID-19. Introducing . . .

The Child's Covid Primer

1. Early on: masks don't work.
2. Later: masks do work, but do not protect the wearer.
3. Still later: masks work for the wearer, *and* they protect others.
4. Wear masks inside at large gatherings.
5. Wear masks inside at small gatherings.
6. Wear a mask if someone is in your house that doesn't belong there, like a BLM rioter.
7. Wear masks outside when around others.
8. Wear masks outside, even when you are jogging, playing soccer, or overturning a car and setting it on fire during a peaceful protest.
9. Wear a mask when you go to church, even at an outside service.
10. Do not sing at church; you may, however, softly hum, while wearing a mask.
11. Never mind. No church gatherings of any kind are allowed.

12. Wear a mask except while eating at a restaurant.
13. Wear a mask over your face at a restaurant between bites of food.
14. Going mask-less outside is appropriate if you are protesting for just causes like equity, diversity, and inclusion; and you may keep your mask off indefinitely if you can *define* equity, diversity, and inclusion.
15. You'll die if you go to school.
16. You probably won't die if you go to school, but you will kill your teachers.
17. You can catch the virus if you touch your face.
18. Never mind. The virus is not transmitted through the touching of stuff, like counters, door handles, and faces.
19. Never mind: Yes, it is.
20. *No, it isn't.*
21. You must stay *six* feet away from your friends at school.
22. When not at school, you must stay *three* feet away from those same friends.
23. It's okay to play baseball but don't touch the ball.
24. If you do touch the ball, you must rub it down with a concoction fit to kill all the germs in an urban landfill.
25. Never mind: playing youth baseball is not allowed.
26. Baseball is back but wear masks.
27. That funny looking Dr. Fauci *used* to work with President Trump.
28. Stupid Fauci!
29. That funny looking Dr. Fauci now works with President Biden.
30. Love Fauci.
31. Fauci is fading fast.
32. COVID-19 is the coronavirus. What either of those terms means, very few people know.
33. Whoops! Fauci's coming back!
34. Wear your mask while walking up to an MLB stadium, but you (wink, wink) may remove it inside the ballpark.
35. School graduations happened outside in 2021, and *in person*.
36. Except most college students that paid thousands and thousands of dollars to earn their degrees got only the digital treatment. Again.
37. You were ordered to stay inside, and then told going outside was better for you.
38. Exercise was recommended, especially for plump people, but then the gyms were shut down.
39. You were told that wearing two masks was better than wearing one mask. Three masks were the ultimate!
40. You heard that the coronavirus was racist.

41. Which didn't surprise you, because you've heard that virtually everything is racist. Still, you couldn't figure that one out.
42. You were taught that the virus came from animals in China.
43. Then you were taught that the virus came from a lab in China.
44. Maybe on purpose.
45. But don't get mad at China for this. Get mad at Russia for this, even though Russia had nothing to do with it.
46. Never mind: Blaming any country, other than America, is xenophobic.
47. You looked up *xenophobic* and figured you weren't that way, but people told you otherwise. And you felt bad.
48. It is xenophobic to refer to the variants by location: the Spanish variant, the Indian variant, the German variant? The Chinese "variant" is the *Big Kahuna*!
49. You were told the vaccine wasn't tried on kids your age during the experimental stages, and, therefore, might be dangerous. You just didn't *know*.
50. You were ordered to take the vaccine.
51. The vaccines work!
52. No, they don't.
53. If you are vaccinated, you may go mask-less.
54. Never mind. You must wear a mask, even if you have been vaccinated.
55. You need to get another shot, a *third* shot. Does it work? Humph!
56. Get vaccinated or lose your job.
57. It's okay for *certain* public officials to remain unmasked while in indoor crowds.
58. General Colin Powell died of the coronavirus.
59. No, he died of leukemia.
60. Is that recorded as a COVID death or a leukemia death—or both? Ahh!!!
61. The Delta variant is bad; it spreads.
62. Nobody can define the Delta variant.
63. The Omicron variant is worse than the Delta variant; it spreads and spreads.
64. Nope. The Delta variant is worse.
65. Teachers are hoping for a return of the original coronavirus.
66. So they can sound like they know what they're talking about.
67. Fox News presents many science conspiracy theories regarding the virus.
68. CNN ridicules Fox NEWS for their conspiracy theories.
69. Most children do not watch Fox or CNN; they care only about their pimples.
70. Should you wear a mask, like President Biden, while meeting on Zoom?

Teaching Science: An Exercise in Hypocrisy

This chapter had to be rewritten and updated a dozen times, because of the changing "science" of the coronavirus. Educators tell children that science is fact. But then they tell them to ignore facts if those facts aren't convenient truths, except of course, when it comes to Al Gore's book on climate change, because that book is about an inconvenient truth that should not be ignored. Get it?

When you look at the new science curriculum, it is not exactly a secret that the information being celebrated in the schools today is a science of fear: teachers scare kids about the impending doom of melting glaciers and searing temperatures and forest fires and hurricanes; they scare kids into thinking they were mistakenly born into a gender not of their *choosing*; they scare kids into thinking they are going to get sick and die because of this mysterious virus that kills mostly old people and people that are already sick or morbidly obese—but what the hell!—kids *might* get it anyway and die!

The ploy isn't to scare children into liking science. It isn't about helping children to soar to new heights that would make their country (currently about fourteenth in the world when it comes to children's knowledge of science)[22] proud. No, this is about much more. This is insidious and sinister and malicious. This is a manipulation of science that would have frightened even Copernicus. This is but one cog in the wheel of an evolving and changing curriculum in your schools. Somehow the mauling of the science curriculum leaves a particularly bitter taste because science is fact, and fact is security. Kids like security, and when educators mess with that, they do a greater disservice to your children than you could ever have imagined.

Ironically, teachers, politicians, and special interests challenged the settled science of gender and biology; in some cases, they mangled it at a time when the dubious science of climate change seemingly had been settled in the nation's schools. Your author does not claim to have the answers or understand the science. He has not received a revelation as to which science is right and which science is wrong. But the least that should be acknowledged is that the schools don't have all the answers, either. And they should not pretend as though they do.

Meanwhile, your children are in a tizzy about coronavirus science, because they don't know which information they hear is true, and which is phony. They are more than a tiny bit surprised when reputable, world-renown scientists are blocked or banished from YouTube, because they said the "wrong" things about mask wearing. During a March roundtable, several scientists discussed downsides to lockdowns, contact tracing, and children wearing face masks. YouTube pulled the video of what may have been an enlightening and invigorating discussion from its site.[23]

"Children should not wear face masks, no," Dr. Martin Kuldorff, a Harvard University professor of medicine, said at the roundtable.[24] YouTube cites *that* comment about face masks mandates for children and a second comment questioning face masks' overall effectiveness at reducing case rates as reasons for banishing the roundtable discussion from its platform.[25]

America stands up for its children. It does so in its schools; it does so in its restrictions and controls on the dissemination of information to those children, especially when it comes to science, and the "proper ways" to interpret it. Maybe science is no longer *science* to children. It's a bunch of confusing gobbledygook they are forced to learn now and to live with later. They feel compelled to follow the mandates of the so-called scientists; like good little sheep, they oblige their shepherds.

NOTES

1. Upon an initial examination, Al Gore does not *look* like much of a scientist; he appears to be a politician. But we have heard that Al Gore invented the internet; so, for him, wrestling with the science of climate change is a mere trifle.

2. *An Inconvenient Truth*, (Paramount Classics) 2006.

3. It is not surprising that after the high drama of ever-so-narrowly losing the 2000 presidential election, Vice-President Gore may have fallen off the deep end—at least, for a while.

4. I'm not sure if this would be considered a valid scientific principle.

5. *PBS News Hour*, YouTube, September 23, 2019. https://www.youtube.com/watch?v=KAJsdgTPJpU

6. She has quite the passion, this kid. Lately, she has been theorizing about COVID vaccines and their efficacy and the like. Why not? If she is an expert in greenhouse gases, she is probably also an expert on mRNA coronavirus shots. No?

7. Steven E. Koonin, "Climate Change Brings a Flood Of Hyperbole," *The Wall Street Journal*, Opinion Section, August 10, 2021. It may be worth repeating that Koonin is long-time climate change advocate and former advisor to President Obama. https://www.wsj.com/articles/intergovernmental-panel-climate-change-ipcc-un-united-nations-global-warming-floods-wildfire-stevens-palmer-koonin-11628631428

8. ibid.

9. Dennis Prager, *The LA Times* (on Twitter), September 20, 2019. https://twitter.com/latimes/status/1175112399021641728?lang=en

10. Jessica R. Towhey, "New Report Says Green New Deal Would 'Destroy' Middle Class," February 28, 2020. https://insidesources.com/new-report-says-green-new-deal-would-destroy-middle-class/

11. If you think John Kerry knows the difference between a wind turbine and a solar panel, I have some of that proverbial moon property to sell you.

12. Joel Fox is a pseudonym and represents thousands of teachers courageous enough to point out there may be another side to the science of climate change . . . and then recanted one statement after another under the threat of losing their jobs.

13. Adam Shaw, Fox News, "Green New Deal: Ocasio-Cortez Aims To Make Air Travel Obsolete," February 7, 2019. https://www.foxnews.com/politics/green-new-deal-ocasio-cortez-aims-to-make-air-travel-obsolete-aid-those-unwilling-to-work

14. Rebecca Bigler, "The Role Of Schools In The Early Socialization Of Gender Differences," *The Encyclopedia of Early Childhood Development*, December 2013. https://www.child-encyclopedia.com/gender-early-socialization/according-experts/role-schools-early-socialization-gender-differences

15. Peter A'Hearn, "White Science Teachers, Here's Why Anti-Racism Includes You," *National Science Teaching Association*, October 29, 2020. https://www.nsta.org/blog/white-science-teachers-heres-why-anti-racism-includes-you

16. ibid.

17. ibid.

18. Wiley Online Library, California State University, Fullerton, September 29, 2021.

19. Peter A'Hearn, "White Science Teachers, Here's Why Anti-Racism Includes You," *National Science Teaching Association*, October 29, 2020. https://www.nsta.org/blog/white-science-teachers-heres-why-anti-racism-includes-you

20. Centers for Disease Control, "What Is Epigenetics?" *Genomics and Precision*, December 21, 2021. https://www.cdc.gov/genomics/disease/epigenetics.htm

21. Corrine Sater, "What We Have Learned About Covid-19 And Resuming School," *NEA Journal*, November/December 2020, p. 6.

22. During the past 20 years, student subject proficiency polls have been all over the place. One consistent finding has been the K–12 rankings in science. American students have demonstrated deficiencies in all areas, especially chemistry, physics, and biological sciences. Just prior to the start of the pandemic, the results were a bit better. Most polls scored the U.S.A. at between 11–17; a few groups have ranked American students as high as ninth in the world in science.

23. Jake Stoffan, "DeSantis Fires Back After YouTube Removes COVID-19 Roundtable Clip," News4Jax, April 13, 2021. https://www.news4jax.com/news/florida/2021/04/12/desantis-fires-back-after-youtube-removes-covid-19-roundtable-clip/

24. Dr. Martin Kuldorff, "YouTube Pulls Video Of DeSantis Panel Discussion Urging No Masks For Children," *The Washington Post*, Technology Section, April 9, 2021.

25. Meryl Kornfield, "YouTube Pulls Video Of DeSantis Panel Discussion Urging No Masks For Children," *The Washington Post*, Technology Section, April 9, 2021.

Chapter 12

Graduate Woke

HATING YOURSELF FOR SOMETHING YOU DIDN'T DO

Democracy Prep, a Las Vegas charter school, has added a new high school graduation requirement. Of course, graduation requirements are nothing new; they have been around since the beginning of American education. But to graduate from this school, all white students must confess their privileged identity.[1]

Whatever *that* means; but no matter, "confessing their privileged identity" is required of a student to move on from this Las Vegas high school.

William Clark, a student at Democracy Prep, filed a lawsuit against the school. His lawyer argued that Clark should not have been compelled to take a course called Sociology of Change, which is compulsory for graduation.

Reporter Sam Dorman says that the course materials teach about interpersonal racism, and interprets this concept as, "what white people do to people of color." Teachers tell students that people of color *can* have prejudices against white people, but police, courts, and gangs of white people punish *these* prejudices. Moreover, any Black prejudice does not affect the rights of white people, and there is no such thing as "reverse racism."[2]

Just as they do with reading and writing and math, students must master "Sociology of Change," before they may escape high school into the waiting tentacles of their college teachers, where things get even worse. Like graduations, Baptisms, and Bar Mitzvahs, confessing your privileged identity has become a rite of passage.

HOLISTIC GRADUATION REQUIREMENTS

It's not enough that the wokes have barged into the nation's schools with screwed up, insane ideas about what to teach children; now, these ideas have formed into real classroom lessons, sometimes sustained over weeks or months. They taint all areas of the curriculum: math, science, health, history, government, speech, writing, and literature.

Extra woke courses—entire courses—have been added, some of them elective in nature, and others mandatory.

The most recent surges in woke curriculum have come from special interest groups that have gotten to the teachers' unions. Not that the teachers' unions must be "gotten to"; they don't. They're there for the taking and have been there for a long time.

Since the beginning of the summer 2020, America has undergone colossal changes. These changes were mostly philosophical and academic in nature; little in terms of meaningful legislation was passed during COVID and Trump's last year in office. After President Biden took the oath of office, the pillars of the status quo, for better or worse, began to tumble like the statues of historical icons the historically ignorant rioters had torn down.[3]

To fully appreciate the development of the new woke curriculum and what it portends for fully developed *courses*, one must examine how courses have been designed in the past, and the purpose of a carefully aligned curriculum, especially for high school students and those who may be graduating seniors.

The holistic approach with students has always worked best. With educators treating every aspect of a student's development, a young person is less likely to fall through the cracks. Teachers, counselors, administrators, nurses, and special guidance officers work together to nurture a child in as many aspects of her education (and personal growth) as feasible. By hiring these professionals, school districts get more cluck for their buck. They gather at the same sites and confer with each other. Districts pay them well, but when you add up the costs for the variety of services they render to students, the net result is a bargain for those schools that can cough up the money.

Setting practical and worthwhile graduation requirements is tricky. It used to be that teachers, parents, and students had conflicting views on what *practical* and *worthwhile* meant. For instance, in some corners, there was a push for more foreign language courses; in other places, graduation requirements committees mandated four years of physical education for a student to graduate high school.[4] Educators desired taking a holistic approach when deciding what was was best for students; the problem came in determining what this type of approach meant.

Graduation requirements vary by state and within a state. Men and women (and sometimes students) sit down and hash out the basics. How many credits will it take to graduate high school? Which areas of study should the schools require to earn a diploma? What do they want young people to *know* by the time they leave their district and march into adulthood?

During the past twenty years, state officials have pridefully boasted of hoisting expectations that every child go to college. Educators have since learned this is far from a realistic expectation. Schools operate more efficiently by stressing their ability to provide a variety of options for different types of kids, the main goal being that students graduate from high school with a meaningful education, and pointed in a direction that is suitable for each of them. Generally, these are the areas of study a student must navigate to receive a high school diploma:

Freshman—English, math, geography, science, elective, physical education
Sophomore—English, math, world history, science, elective, physical education
Junior—English, *math, U.S. History, *science, elective, physical education, fine arts, or industrial arts
Senior—English, *math, U.S. government, *science, elective **physical education
*not required
**may be replaced by a competitive sport

Students sought to take classes that would enable them to reach their goals. Electives were tailored to the kids' needs; for example, shop classes and other trade coursework could replace a foreign language or a higher-level math or science course. In addition, students could opt to take a course in speech, drama, music, or art as an elective or as part of an extended seven-period day, instead of a six-period day.

The philosophy of educators twenty or thirty years ago was mostly two-fold: (1) give students an opportunity to graduate high school and land a decent job OR attend a university (2) broaden the horizons of young people in all aspects of their education, and channel instruction for potential options into neatly structured courses. If any indoctrination took place, it was minimal and sporadic, certainly not because of a concerted effort by any group, political party, or band of aliens from outer space.

What is minimal indoctrination? Nods to Americanism are scattered throughout the tenure of a kid that attends a public school. The Pledge of Allegiance, the national anthem, deference to capitalism, democracy, and apple pie populated a child's day. The underlying tone—if not the message—was that America is a good place, a decent country, and its people courageous, strong, compassionate, and just. Patriotism was a given. The purpose of the classroom was not to make children gush with a sense of pride for their country. Schools were not in that business; they honored their implicit obligation to pass on to the throngs that trusted them the gratitude and respect educators held for the United States of America.

Parents shaped curriculum decisions; sometimes they became involved in the lesson planning of their kids' teachers. The involvement of parents helped to keep radical political influences by outside agencies—and, yes, that included teachers' unions—at bay. Currently, with a rush to ostracize parents from the process, "old-fashioned" support for parents' input is reemerging. Young journalist Jack Elbaum, wrote in October of 2021, "To tell parents that they do not have the right to have a say in what their children learn is to tell them that their children are nothing more than government property."[5]

A SCHOOL'S OBLIGATION

The June/July 2020 edition of *Educator*, an official periodical from the California Teachers Association, features a solid-black front cover. Inscribed in the center of that cover in bold yellow block letters is *Black Lives Matter*.[6]

Just below the *Black Lives Matter* head, in small golden letters, it says, "[California Teachers Association] calls for 'Racial Justice Now.'" The caption then directs the readers to page six, where a slew of short articles begin, all of them referencing the broadly brushed topic of "social justice."[7] Normally, this would not constitute an irritant for the many teachers in the CTA that do not subscribe to their in-your-face social justice pandering; however, several factors make this edition of *Educator* stand out:

This "Black Lives Matter" edition of the periodical came out during the midst of the coronavirus pandemic. One would have thought—perhaps, *should* have thought—the emphasis of the largest teachers' union in the country would have been on the many education challenges related to the pandemic. Most notably, their communication would have covered issues related to getting back to school and teaching their students while face-to-face.

Several issues of *Educator* during the early months of the pandemic were devoted to similar themes. This one, however (Volume 24) stood out for its brazen, unabashed praise for BLM and the positions this radical, outspoken organization has taken.[8] The parent organization of the CTA, the National Education Association, has taken similar stands in their reporting, and they, too, devoted little time during these months to traditional education issues. While the union reported experiences—mostly from individual teachers in their classrooms—about interesting and innovative strategies, inordinate amounts of time were spent with comments from teachers and others that featured a smorgasbord of bad things to say about America.

Mary Kay Linge, in the *New York Post*, May 22, 2020, felt compelled to summarize the views of authors of the 1619 Project: "Our national history is racist to the core, rooted in slavery and white supremacy." They fleshed out this concept in a 100-page magazine supplement that has already been added to the history curriculum in 3,500 U.S. high schools.[9]

Corrin Richin, a middle school teacher in Dayton, expresses more loathing for America: "It's hard to salute the flag and talk about 'liberty and justice for all,' when we all know America provides only liberty and justice for white people."[10]

Just wondering, Ms. Corrin, if this is 2022 or 1722?

While teachers, like others, are entitled to express their opinions and offer their personal takes on social issues, they frequently set themselves up as experts on the great problems of the day, many of which are not related to education. Their unions' journals are replete with teachers waxing philosophically about racial injustice and the shortcomings of American society: "We can't any longer deny history. White people that ignore the harms of White Supremacy, line up and be counted to repent." They never castigate white children that sit in their classrooms, but these teachers arm one another (with help from books like *White Fragility*) with a repertoire that they call their "lesson plans."[11]

Rarely, are educators with dissimilar views given a forum for their expression. These publications are massively bias and wholly inattentive to ideas from a conservative platform; in fact, there is no recognition that there *is* another side to the issue of *institutional* racial injustices in the United States. Any references to that thinking are purely pejorative.

If the schools are racially prejudiced, then why hasn't that been fixed by now? Teachers have run the show for decades. They have the clout of their unions behind them. Why hasn't their show been more racially just, more equitable? Teachers have control, no?[12]

The new woke curriculum has lopped along with the changing times, but it hasn't happened suddenly. It hasn't haphazardly, without direction, begun to fill file drawers and computer folders. Teachers are designing and controlling what is taught, the leaders of their unions and special interest organizations inconspicuously sitting at the helm.

Not *all* teachers are, in unison, conspiring against the kids of America—not by a long shot. The great silent majority of educators are looking on, wondering how they have gotten to this place; they are figuring out where to go from here. And they are embarrassed. Imagine being an educator at a time when union bosses were defending teachers lying on a beach and taking selfies, while they should have been zipping back to their schools and conducting classes.

Teachers' unions have taken over the public schools. They also have more political clout than any other collective body (except for government) in the United States. They are powerful entities. If they truly stood for what is best for children, it would be a courageous, beautiful thing. But they do not. They are mostly about salaries, working conditions, and health benefits for their members (like most unions). Since COVID-19, their irrationality has risen to the forefront with freshly illuminated selfishness and stupidity.

If you witnessed the modern dance number video, created and performed by the Chicago Teachers' Union, in order to convince the public that it was not safe for them to return to in-person teaching, you know about *stupid*. If you haven't seen that video, look it up.[13] Seriously. It's worth doing right now. You will cringe and laugh at the same time. Guaranteed.

GOING BERSERK

Curriculum and standards in public schools have been steadily changing for the past two years. The old ways are considered outdated and irrelevant. Worse, they are branded as racist and hopelessly out of touch. The emphasis on social justice has spearheaded movements not only to affect curriculum, but social justice has become an entire course of study unto itself. It has taken on a life of its own.

In 2019 in California, the legislature passed a bill that would have mandated a course in (social justice) as a high school graduation requirement. Surprisingly, Governor Gavin Newsom vetoed the bill. The California governor's reasoning had a lot to do with the lack of specificity in the legislation. He and others, most of the California legislature, voiced their concerns about the impulsiveness of the proposed law.

Those that opposed the new requirement were not sure of what the perspective course would entail. Great disagreement ensued. One faction wished that the course be informative about various cultures in America, presenting information from diverse groups, allowing them to express their views on the topics of the day, as well as offering counter views on history and government.

Another faction supported writing a section in the bill focusing on police brutality and systemic racism in law enforcement. In fact, the latter group wanted the course to be about race and cultural identity from the standpoint of conflict and oppression. This snapshot of American history ain't pretty. The teaching (and probably preaching) of Critical Race Theory and the institutional effects of slavery over the past three hundred years became a prominent feature of the new graduation requirement.

Educators and politicians couldn't agree or compromise, and the initial graduation requirement bill died in 2020.

Meanwhile, the state colleges put the public schools to shame by *adopting* a course that would be blended into the General Studies departments of the California State University system. The class would be taken during the freshman or sophomore years and would fulfill a part of the General Studies requirement, which was a huge deal for those that had pushed the culture studies course. This means that classes in speech, computers, argumentation, and basic communication may be sacrificed for underclassmen to take a course on something to do with social justice.[14]

Your author is privy to some of the proposed—and by the time you are reading this—*established* curriculum for a social justice or ethnic studies high school graduation requirement:[15]

- honoring the value of indigenous people
- the slave trade
- reparations for slavery
- the move West (and Custer doesn't come out looking too cool)
- the conflict with the majority (white) culture
- American imperialism
- internationalism vs. nationalism
- the criminal justice system (inherent racial bias)
- immigration and the plight of migrants
- white nationalism
- corporate greed (though Amazon and Google are given passes)
- an understanding of LGBTQs

In no way imaginable does this course present a favorable view of America. In fact, the curriculum exploits every opportunity to take a dump on this country.

Besides California, other states have gone berserk, implementing courses in cultural sensitivity. The Illinois State Board of Education in February approved a set of learning standards that ask teachers to assess their biases and "mitigate" their own behaviors that stem from "unearned privilege" and "Eurocentrism." Democratic governor J.B. Pritzker rubber-stamped a bill that established an "Inclusive American History Commission" to ensure the education of "non-dominant" cultures.[16]

A draft of the new ethnic studies curriculum in California *excludes* anti-Semitism from the examination of historically marginalized groups; however, it backs an anti-Israel boycott, divestment, and sanctions against the Jewish state, one of America's most committed allies.[17] The course also teaches students to "resist" the "Eurocentric neocolonial condition," which includes Christianity.[18]

Julian Peeples reported in December of 2020, "Schools are stepping up the fight to ensure that all students have a chance to see themselves and their ancestral legacies as a part of a well-developed curriculum."[19]

In doing so, students may identify with America's past and present that have been affected by their own cultural roots. Knowing these relationships isn't always comforting; it is one of the main reasons why educators have balked at cultural studies. Does this mean that *all* cultures would be discussed? And what constitutes a *culture*? Maybe most important of all, who would determine the curriculum and monitor the hefty biases that are certain to be exposed by individual teachers? What lends *any* credence to the assertion that cultural neutrality would be an assumption of the new course curriculum? (Hmm. . . . Maybe there is *no* assumption of cultural neutrality?): According to CTA President E. Toby Boyd, "State council approved an expanded ethnic studies policy that outlines guiding principles for the foundation of any adopted ethnic studies curriculum."[20]

Boyd is clearly reacting to the disappointment of several attempts by other states to implement ethnic studies courses like his own, imagined course, including the veto of Governor Newsom in his home state of California. He goes on to say, "We must show our Black and Indigenous students and students of color that we see them, that we see the systemic roadblocks in their path, and we will help them navigate this road until we can build a new one paved with opportunity for all."[21]

Almost everyone is in favor of equality, defined as equal *opportunity*. But Boyd keeps referring to *equity* in his non-ending stream of platitudes—not *equality*. You wonder if the president of the California Teachers Association knows the difference between *equality* of opportunity and *equity* in results.

Because these courses have arrived, it would be prudent to analyze—and carefully—the comments of the leader of one of the largest state teachers' unions in the United States.

"State council approved an expanded ethnic studies policy."

COMMENT: That is the State Council of the California Teachers Association. The CTA should not be confused with any other group of professional educators, legislators, or curriculum committee members. CTA leaders have reasons to be self-serving; it is *their* course, *their* set curriculum, and mostly *their* ideas.

"outlines guiding principles for the foundation of any adopted ethnic studies curriculum."

COMMENT: Blatant declaratory sentences such as this one give you the impression that Boyd is the ultimate authority, and the existing ethnic studies curriculum has been researched, analyzed, and filtered. What's left is Boyd's rendition of "guiding principles for the foundation of *any* adopted ethnic studies curriculum [italics added]."[22] He knows best; the cronies from the CTA, the NEA, and other teachers' unions have helped him out. They not only speak for all their union members; they speak for all people of the United States of America! *Obviously.*

> "Schools are stepping up the fight to ensure that all students have a chance to see themselves and their ancestral legacies as a part of a well-developed curriculum."

COMMENT: This line is from author Peeples, as she sets up the essence of Boyd's remarks, and his justification for this program. You *could* wonder where it had ever been stipulated or decreed that children had the right to learn about their own cultural roots (to see themselves and their ancestral legacies) at the expense of the American taxpayer. You would have thought that in an American school, students would learn about America—its warts and blemishes and all. But schools would still focus on *America*.

What happened to the Turks in their European struggles of some four hundred years ago—and there were a lot of exciting wars and battles to talk about, with the Turks losing almost all of them—might be a microscopic part of world history and an interesting tidbit in a European Studies course; however to assume that Turkish kids going to American schools have a *right* to learn about their Turkish culture and history is a bit presumptuous, and your author believes, obnoxious.

Parents who are passionate about passing along their cultural dynamics to their children could fill in—what they perceive as—very large gaps of information. And they could even take it further, making much of it personal, relating it to their own families. But giving such a sense of entitlement— *from the public* school—to all American families, and all children, seems off-the-charts unjustified.

The same could be said for Middle Easterners (their depth of history, much of it Biblical), and Russians (you know, those guys, without whom defeating Hitler and saving the world from Nazism may have been impossible), hundreds of thousands of whom migrated to Western countries in the 1970s, including the United States, to escape Soviet anti-Semitism.

Does a public high school in Flagstaff have a responsibility to teach children of Russian immigrants of their Russian heritage? Just for the record: most of those Russian immigrants were, well, just that. They were *immigrants*. They went through the established protocols, multilayered programs, and stringent policies to become American citizens. Obtaining citizenship after following through on all the legal procedures made these people *immigrants*; they should not be dumped into that cavernous category in which all people that came to this country seem to be lumped, whether they met their sponsors right off the boat, or they met their smugglers right after being let out of the back of a crammed minivan at the edge of a hot desert.

> "We must show our Black and Indigenous students and students of color that we see them, that we see the systemic roadblocks in their path."

COMMENT: This is a noble goal. One might wonder why it would be limited to only Black and Indigenous students. Poverty and indifference to education breed bad schools, bad teaching, and bad outcomes. That is not unique to people of color. White kids have also struggled with poverty and indifference to education. Do you not take notice of *those* kids? Or when it comes right down to it, are Ms. Peeples, Dr. Boyd, and other education "experts" boiling everything down to separations based on skin color?

People are now defined and judged, based on how they look.

> "we will help them navigate this road until we can build a new one paved with *opportunity* for all." (italics added)

COMMENT: Educators should stay carefully focused on the term *opportunity*. The president of the California Teachers Association may have offended some of his colleagues with this one. All we hear about from educators is diversity, inclusion, and *equity*. There is a marked difference between *equity* and equality, per Mr. Boyd's reference. *Equality* has to do with opportunity. *Equity* has to do with outcomes. Very few in society would argue that children should not have equal opportunity; many—maybe most—would contend that the outcomes of children's achievements should not be *fixed* to turn out the same.

It's a done deal. At the time of this writing, fourteen states have adopted a course in ethnic studies at the secondary level, and five of them have already confirmed that the class will be a graduation requirement. Undoubtedly, more are coming.

Many questions demand direct answers. And promptly. Or so you would think.

Who teaches the course? Does it meet the social studies requirement for high school graduation? What texts will be used? May a student opt out of *this* course in favor of a similar course? What if a particular class does not come close to being an ethnic mix? *What is an ethnic mix?* Which groups of peoples will be studied during the course? If there are no students of a certain group in a class, will studying that group be skipped over by the classroom teacher? Must the designated textbook(s) be used? What about guest speakers? Will they be allowed? Are LGBTQ groups one of the preferred groups for inclusion study?

Original concerns about antiwhite rhetoric might surface without an assumption of neutrality in the teaching of history or culture. Your author will go out on a limb and predict that any biases that appear in these courses will not be against people of color or marginalized gender groups. Look at white people to be at fault. It is a culture laden with racism. High school English teacher Josh Thompson thinks so. He said, "The idea of just sitting quiet and being told stuff and taking things in in a passive stance is not a thing that's in many cultures. So, if we're positively enforcing these behaviors, we are by extension positively enforcing elements of white culture. Which, therefore, keeps whiteness at the center, which is the definition of white supremacy."[23]

By the time this manuscript has been published, a number of these new graduation courses, including California's, will have been up and running. Like much else that goes on in education, the curriculum is experimental; the teaching is in its embryonic stages. When all is said and done, the *real* world will be the judge of these audacious decisions.

NOTES

1. Sam Dorman, "Instructed To Link Aspects Of Their Identity To Oppression," Fox News, December 23, 2020. https://www.foxnews.com/us/lawsuit-nevada-race-christianity-william-clark

2. ibid.

3. Massive changes have occurred since Biden's inauguration, not the least of which are unprecedented trillions of dollars in federal spending. In addition, the schools have fermented changes in the curriculum, as well. And as of this writing, America is borderless in the South.

4. The concept came down to this: All children should indulge in at least two years of rigorous exercise their first two years in high school; after that, students were *encouraged*, to perform in a competitive athletic activity. If not, the students were required an additional two years of physical education (exercise classes).

5. Jack Elbaum, "Should Parents Have Any Say Over What Their Kids Learn At School," *FEE Stories*, October 26, 2021. https://fee.org/articles/should-parents-have-any-say-in-what-their-kids-learn-in-school-virginia-voters-may-soon-decide/

6. *Educator* (cover) California Teachers Association, June/July 2020, Volume 24.

7. *Educator* California Teachers Association, June/July 2020, "CTA Calls For Racial Justice Now." Volume 24, p. 6

8. ibid.

9. Mary Kay Linge, "Public Schools Are Teaching Our Children To Hate America," *New York Post*, May 22, 2020 https://nypost.com/2020/02/22/public-schools-are-teaching-our-children-to-hate-america/

10. Corrin Richin is an alias. Interview conducted on July 23, 2021.

11. *Educator* pulsates with suggestions on how to embolden what they keep referring to as *"marginalized kids."*

12. The same logic goes for when power groups cry racism in inner city housing developments, or on police forces in urban communities. Those areas are controlled mostly by one of the two major political parties. They fell apart under the watch of that party. It is an abominable message, one of weakness and cowardice, to claim that they do not have the means to fix those problems.

13. I laughed so hard my ribs ached. You really must see this! If you keep in mind the Chicago teachers had serious intentions, it'll be even funnier. Enjoy!
https://www.facebook.com/watch/?v=642096529840296

14. Each university would have to work out the logistics, but the required course is the dictate.

15. I spoke with officials in local school districts and have perused ever-changing information concerning this graduation requirement. Courses and curriculum vary from district to district. Even the attitudes of the educators vary. Some are excited about these courses; others want to tie a noose around their necks and jump off the side of the nearest staircase.

16. Alex Nester, "Blue State Residents Oppose Woke Education," *Washington Free Beacon*, March 11, 2021. https://www.goacta.org/news-item/blue-state-residents-oppose-woke-education/

17. North Carolina Board of Education, "Democrats Push To Replace Current Standards With Radical Curricula," *Speaking About News*, March 20, 2021 (last full paragraph). https://speakingaboutnews.com/democrats-push-to-replace-current-standards-with-radical-curricula/

18. ibid.

19. Julian Peeples, "'All Power To Our Students, All Power To The People!'" *California Teachers Association*, October 26, 2020. https://www.cta.org/educator/posts/all-power-to-our-students-all-power-to-the-people

20. Toby Boyd, "'All Power To Our Students, All Power To The People!'" *California Teachers Association*, October 26, 2020. https://www.cta.org/educator/posts/all-power-to-our-students-all-power-to-the-people

21. ibid.

22. Whenever high-level educators render decisions, make evaluations, or offer hypotheses, the rest of the population is to validate those decisions, evaluations, and hypotheses Gospel.

23. Emma Colton, "Teacher Says Encouraging Behaviors Like 'Following Directions' Is White Supremacy," Fox News, September 14, 2021. https://www.foxnews.com/us/virginia-teacher-behavior-following-directions-white-supremacy

Chapter 13
COVID-19 Rides to the Rescue

THE SCIENCE IN YOUR FACE

The arrival of the coronavirus from China has forever changed education in the United States.

In March of 2020, schools around the nation shut their doors. Kids had to find ways to study. Many of them lacked the computers and other proper technology in order to learn online. Some students resorted to smart phones. Many children lacked any electronic device at all.

Parents had to stay home from work, because they could not set up safe daycare for their kids. Some parents couldn't afford *any* daycare.

Even among the more advantaged families, hardships surrounding equipment, physical space, and privacy reared their ugly heads. Families, many of them newly formed, blended, and disgruntled, were stuck together in small living spaces for months. Forming good learning habits, especially after a while, became practically impossible.

When society demanded that schools open again—from all quarters, well *past* the time for schools to open—large segments of the education community balked. Larger school districts, notably Los Angeles, Oakland, and Chicago, led by loud and obnoxious protesting teachers that instead should have been instructing kids in their classrooms, took to the streets.

Across the country, parents pleaded with the teachers. The *Wall Street Journal* in February of 2021 described parental frustration. "What this has really unveiled, this pandemic and how this situation has gone with schools reopening around the country, there's a bit of a power imbalance in terms of parents. We don't have representation in the bargaining room," said Meredith Willa Dodson, executive member of Decreasing the Distance, a group of San Francisco Unified School District parents who organized last year to reopen schools. "It not only impacts teachers, but it also impacts our children. First and foremost, our children's education is what we're talking about here."[1]

The public's disenchantment with educators, especially teachers, grew day by day. They accused teachers of being lazy, incompetent, and cowardly. Worst of all, the public, led by mass media—CNN, NBC, CBS, ABC, the *New York Times*, and the *Washington Post*—clamored in defense of the teachers' refusal to return to their classrooms. Virtual learning was indefinite.

The science supported that arrangement. Surprisingly, around the early spring of 2021, much of the science showed that children were safer at school than they were in their own communities, where people readily ignored social distancing and mask requirements. Children were often better off at school than at home, where large gatherings of people, many of them outside their own immediate families, routinely congregated for holidays. Physical contact among those attending private parties was inevitable. While at school, most children welcomed the policies of disinfecting the premises regularly, wearing masks, and staying at a distance from one another.

In addition to those safety protocols, "the science" explained that children were poor vectors of the coronavirus. They didn't contract it; they didn't spread it. So, yes, the actual school was the safest place for kids, while they were being guided by mature, self-disciplined adults; yet, *educators* implored their students to stay away.

DISGRUNTLED TEACHERS

Around the country, schools opened for business. Teachers, boisterous and vociferous, were the obstacles to getting things started again; it would take a while to get everyone back on track. And whether most individuals ever got back on track is famously open to debate and discussion. The question of "normality" became more complicated with the arrival of the Delta variant in the summer of 2021, and later, the havoc created by the highly contagious Omicron. Defining *normality* imposes an additional challenge. Unless there is massive agreement on the criteria for "on the right track," it is largely impossible to find a COVID-19 endgame when it comes to education, teachers, kids, the government.

Suffering by children, because of the gross disruption to their learning and family lifestyle, is documented in the *Mercury News*: "The closure of most California public school campuses since last March has been widely acknowledged to have hurt student learning, but a study this week brings that into sharper focus, finding significant loss in both language arts and math, and more in lower grades and disadvantaged kids."[2]

Teachers and students didn't unanimously welcome the awkward, rocky transition back to the real-life classroom. Having to teach with a computer screen in their faces, teachers forced themselves to navigate the dark, mysterious waters of hybrid instruction. Some taught from their desktops at home; others used laptops in their classrooms, while students sat at their own desks right in front of them! Ideally, the teachers that taught through a hybrid model utilized a camera, attached to a wall in their regular classroom, that followed them wherever they went, much like a futuristic surveillance system would be conceived to spy on innocent populations.

It got the job done. Sort of. A teacher's *in-classroom* instruction beamed out to her students, while the kids sat *at home* in their pajamas. Teachers boasted of their successes and mourned their failures. The *Washington Post* commented on the difficulty of hybrid learning: "The quality of instruction is dropping dramatically as teachers are being asked to manage in-person and remote learners at the same time. Other distance learners say it's hard to watch their returned classmates on camera and not feel jealous."[3]

School boards couldn't agree on which science to follow when it came to deciding whether to open the schools. There are many conflicting opinions and a multitude of "experts" that have varying positions when it comes to children, teachers, and schoolhouses. These differences are highlighted when one so-called expert disagrees with another so-called expert. Sometimes it becomes particularly dicey when the crux of the debate centers around politicians and teacher advocates who are trying to bolster their popularity or advance their agendas.

At the time of this writing, the controversies brought about by the coronavirus in the schools are, at best, confusing; and, at worst, debilitating. The mixing up of education modalities and the expectations that students and teachers adapt to the impulsive whims of administrators drive parents to their liquor cabinets.[4] Most people are well-intentioned. They want to go back to the way things were. They know the poor logistics of asking teachers to instruct students that sit live before them, while simultaneously intruding into the bedrooms of other students through the miracle of technology.

Lelac Almagor offered her verdict on distance learning and hybrid instruction in the *New York Times* on June 16, 2021. "Even under optimal conditions, virtual school meant flattening the collaborative magic of the classroom into little more than an instructional video. Stripped of classroom discussion, human connection, art materials, classroom libraries and time and space to play, virtual school was not school; it was busywork obscuring the rubber rooming of the entire school system."[5]

There are, literally, no winners; that is, unless you consider how politicians and teachers unions have conjured *images* of education goals being accomplished. School districts that sent their students back to school, or projected a *semblance* of sending their students back to school late in May of 2021, could claim that—hey!—*they got the job done*! They opened their doors before the school year had ended! No way did they prevent their students from returning to their hallowed halls of learning! Never mind that children were thrust into weird hybrid learning environments. They "went back to school" in many cases only for a few weeks, two or three days a week, and even then, for only a few hours a day. But they went back! Educators got the job done!

DEATH TAKES NO POLITICAL POSITION

During World War II, factions that cried out against American involvement in the war faded quietly into oblivion. They had been loud and ferocious. Public officials set straight those who believed the sacrifices that came because of the war were unjustified. After all, thousands of Americans were dying, and thousands more would die later. The notion that the pros and cons of the war—via the evils of Nazism—should be bantered about in the political arena was repulsive. Most Americans were revolted by the notion of a partisan discussions while there were serious life and death problems that had yet to be resolved.

Why then, was the arrival of an invisible enemy, the novel coronavirus, any different from any other moment in history, in which Americans banded together to defeat a common adversary, to repel an evil that threatened not only the United States but the entire world? How did this virus, this enemy, this opponent come to be looked upon in a different light—eventually, through a purely political lens—by the public and the leaders of the greatest democracy in the history of civilization?

Shana Gadarian, Professor of Political Science at Syracuse University commented, "We thought that the more worried people were about COVID, the more likely they were to be following public health officials' directives. And that's not what we found. . . . What we found was that the biggest divider in people's behaviors was not their age, not their demographics, not their education; *it was their partisanship*" (italics added).[6]

Here are five straight-forward reasons why the coronavirus, instead of becoming a rallying point for propping up America's collective strength, has become a political football, ending thousands more lives than would have been lost, if the virus had been managed as a true public heath crisis, instead of as a tug-of-war for power.

1. Early-on, political knives hurled toward their intended targets.

If you believe scientists in a Chinese lab in Wuhan manufactured this thing and then proceeded to unleash it on the world, while preventing it from spreading to the rest of China, then—yes, sinister forces had been at work; or clumsy and careless forces had been to blame. At a given point, however, Americans didn't know jack about this new virus, let alone where it came from or how to get rid of it.

In January of 2020, rumors became serious news stories. There was a novel virus out there. This virus had jumped from an animal to a person; person to person contact now could be deadly. A movie in 2011, called *Contagion*,[7] had already frightened millions of Americans by painting a portrait of a contagious, unrelenting bug that brought enormous numbers of people to their deaths. As bodies and corpses littered the streets of large cities, the movie-goer was left to ponder the sober question, "What if this *really* happened?"

Few answers about how to stop the virus were provided in the film. Only a series of unlikely coincidences and inane acts by a villainous character, played by Jude Law, and the courage of a cool dad, a regular guy, played by Matt Damon, provided reasons for hope. Alas, this film was fiction; sometimes in real life things don't turn out like in the movies, satisfying enough for us to sigh with relief . . . and then later head out for a cheeseburger.

At first, this country knew little about the virus, and the people had been dismayed and confused by the sparse information they had received. President Trump officially mentioned it in his annual State of the Union address, shown on international television, on February 4, 2020. This reference to a new virus came *after* the President had ordered a halt to all flights from China coming into the United States. The President issued that declaration as a reaction to his concern about the spread of the coronavirus.

For his move to ban Chinese travel to and from the United States, Trump was barbed by many, called a *racist;* presidential candidate Joe Biden and Speaker Nancy Pelosi labeled him a *xenophobe*. Pelosi then went on to tear to shreds, piece by piece, her copy of the President's State of the Union in front of a world-wide television audience. She did it slowly and methodically (although there were moments of unintentional comedy, with Speaker Pelosi appearing too weak to rip apart a pile of thin papers). So much for America's face of public concern about COVID.

2. The economic connection to the coronavirus opened eyes.

Most Americans root for a strong performance by the Dow Jones Industrials and other stocks. Even those who are not financially invested in industry and Big Tech companies care about the showing of these economic indicators. The durability of their pensions could rely on the success of the stock market, and the optics of a strong market cast favorable impressions on those in power.

In January 2020, as President Trump faced his first impeachment trial, one that ultimately ended in a failure, the coronavirus was creeping its away around the globe. Rumors of what may lie on the horizon caused the economy to behave erratically, and the market plunged. A yo-yo effect followed. Though the stock market was prone to react this way during times of volatility in the world, the sheer aggregate size of the market made its fluctuations appear even graver than they would have looked if the Dow had clocked in around 13,000, instead of 24,000.[8]

The stock market had been climbing steadily upward since Trump took over the presidency early in 2017. (It had begun to move drastically higher the morning after the 2016 election.) Unemployment in January of 2020 was at record lows. Things were looking good for blue-collar and white-collar workers. Americans projected an upbeat mood, but not so for the disgruntled masses that despised the Trump agenda, especially when it came to issues revolving around immigration, taxes, and dealings with China. Trump had to go. But his approval ratings roared higher, and most of the nation seemed content.

This weird disease, this new, mysterious virus, lurked. Americans didn't know much about it at the time; but when three deaths had been reported in a Washington nursing home, and a woman in Orange, California, had contracted the virus, it became apparent that the presently unknown would soon be taking its toll on America.

This toll would be measured in numbers of deaths, allegedly due to the coronavirus, but the dying and suicidal and poverty stricken would be heard from on the other side of the ledger, those that paid the price to *stop* a virus that killed, overwhelmingly, a small demographic of the population: *the average age of a fatality was seventy-nine*.[9] Never mind about the truth in that. Political expediency and a quest for power demanded that *all* Americans suffer in unprecedented ways, and the media devise means to scare people out of their wits.

3. Political forces mandate changes in the power structure of America.

If the presidential election had been held in October of 2019, Donald Trump would have emerged as a landslide winner. The same probably would have happened in early March 2020, despite an impeachment trial, based on allegations that Trump had a phone conversation with President Volodymyr Zelensky, in which the American president allegedly tried to convince the Ukrainian president to scoop up some political dirt on Hunter Biden, just in case the elder Biden would make a presidential bid, which, of course, he wound up doing. Despite having a transcript of a phone call that seemed to exonerate President Trump, his adversaries never proved offenses worthy of his removal from office, as ruled by the Senate after the impeachment trial.

Despite these distractions, Mr. Trump acted early in the crisis. *Hamodia* wrote on March 23, 2020, "Trump enacted travel and quarantine measures in late January and signed an $8.3 billion emergency coronavirus spending bill in early March. In mid-March, the World Health Organization declared the virus a pandemic and the president began to shift his rhetoric and warn Americans to take steps to limit the spread."[10] The president not only survived critical onslaught, which included impeachment, he took constructive steps in ways that nobody ever talks about on CNN or MSNBC to lay the groundwork for combating the virus.

Despite the Russian collusion investigation that went on for almost three years and eventually emerged with an abundance of hot air; despite continued attacks on Trump's honesty; despite unending barrages of negative commentaries and criticism from most of the media; and despite an impeachment trial, the bottom line for most Democrats was that President Trump had *survived*.

Media moguls and other Democrats had planned Trump's ouster from the presidency from the moment his victory had been announced. Some would go so far as to argue that plans were in the works to dump Donald Trump from office even *before* the 2016 election; schemes were in the works just in case Donald Trump would shock the nation with a triumph.

Those most worried about the 2016 election of Donald Trump did not waste time trying to get rid of him: everything from a three-year investigation of Trump's alleged associations with Russia (some even argued the president was a Russian spy), to his impeachment trial during a time the coronavirus first began to snake its way through America (which had been a devastating distraction from the pressing business at hand—to say the very least—including the seeking out of ways of minimizing the effects of the coronavirus). Besides their counterproductivity to the nation, these efforts had failed.

Enter COVID-19.

4. Many battled their own souls.

Of course, you already know all about this. The lingering effects of the pandemic on American education continue indefinitely. And very few benefit from the suffering of schoolchildren. . . .

Adjustment of those comments: *Many* may have benefited from the coronavirus and the impact it has had on America's school children. It's selfish. It's narcissistic. And it's spine-tingling. The virus, mysterious at first, became the focal point for manipulation by forces in this country that wanted—first and foremost—to get rid of Donald Trump. Trump's greatest strength was reflected in the percolation of the American economy. Poll numbers indicated that largely because of that strength Trump drifted toward reelection in 2020.

What to do? What to do?

Mayor Rahm Emanuel of Chicago echoed the thoughts of some in this country when he, unfortunately, publicly uttered, "Never let a good crisis go to waste."[11]

Little did Emanuel or anyone else realize just how many crises they would not "waste." Besides the pandemic and its related fears, the decimation of the economy as the result of poor decisions that had been made in order to fight the pandemic, the shutdown of American education in all its forms—except for the masses that would be hunched over a computer screen for a half-dozen hours a day—and costly riots and looting over race-related issues, all proved to be crises of epic proportions, true crises about which the former Chicago mayor could boast of for the rest of his life.

Despite the *groveling* of small business owners, most of America had remained closed into the early months of 2021.[12] Despite protests and demonstrations of civil disobedience that ultimately led to arrests and trials for the culprits that dared to keep their barbershops running or braved the hazards of keeping their gymnasiums available to their members, business owners were fined, arrested, and temporarily imprisoned.

Mounting suspicions overwhelmed the lives of ordinary Americans. Weird-looking, squeaky scientists told them to ignore the obvious. While 15 percent of the population stood at risk of succumbing to the deadly virus, the other 85 percent were burned by the "logic" of it all. For the first time in history, *healthy* people were told to stay inside and not go near others, and to wear cloth masks over their noses and mouths.[13]

Usually, a public disease is countered by measures that make sense. *Sick* people are told to stay inside; the weak and vulnerable are protected and given the best medical attention. With *this* virus, sick people were pushed into quarters with other sick people, and they died in clusters. Healthy people stayed at home, while their finances, their businesses, their jobs, their educations, their social lives crumbled around them.

Meanwhile, President Trump had signed an executive order barring Critical Race Theory training for federal workers; at the time, this news seemed rather innocuous, irrelevant to what was going on in the rest of the country. But it wasn't. It was *big*. Now, many of the Harvard elite, Google, and Alexandria Cortez-backed woke policies might be stopped in their tracks.

But not so fast. The coronavirus was methodically wrecking the economy. Or, at least, the collective reaction to it was wrecking the economy. In May 2020, President Trump urged Americans to get back to work, reopen their businesses, and send their children back to school. But schools, with a few exceptions—those states represented by conservative lawmakers—didn't reopen.

The teachers' unions' grip on the school districts made it apparent that the teachers' leaders had not prioritized the welfare of children. Union members stormed board meetings and made head-scratching demands—from contributing money to Black Lives Matter movements, to defunding the police—for reopening the schools. In Los Angeles, at a schoolboard meeting, Medicare for All surfaced as a condition for reopening the L.A. schools, as did, of course, defunding the police. The public questioned the dubious connection between returning fourth graders to their regular classrooms and withdrawing money from budget allocations to the city's police department.

The people wondered. They questioned teachers' unions about their annual national conventions. Why had they structured position platforms that called for the allowance of late-term abortions, reentry into the nuclear arms deal with Iran, abolition of the death penalty for capital murder, and marriage between consenting adults of the same sex?[14] What these had to do with improving education was anybody's guess.

For many, it still is.

Several L.A. County school districts have adopted a program called Social Emotional Learning (SEL). Teachers—rightfully so—have decided to bring an emotional and personal component into their various curricula. Here, they argue, students may disclose their thoughts and feelings and feel safe in doing this. Leave it up to the local teachers' union to distort what should have been a productive experience for children. Dena Simmons, a self-described SEL practitioner, wrote, "Teachers can [should] teach a unit on the relationship between identity and equity . . . how their identity helps or hinders their life opportunities . . . [question] their own power and privilege, as well as [American] racism, homophobia, sexism, and *other forms of violence* (italics added)."[15]

You might think it would be a wise, healthy, and professional goal to allow teachers to investigate their own hearts and souls to determine what kids need and which polices they wish to support or disdain. But their unions do not afford teachers that luxury anymore.

5. COVID's greatest hazards are its propensity for distraction and its proclivity for confusion.

America had been steadily climbing economically and militarily. Despite impeachment hearings in early January of 2020, Trump's State of the Union Address was met with widespread praise—at least, for Trump's future electability.[16]

Covid would ride to the rescue: On one hand, it diverted America's eyes off problems that required immediate attention; on the other hand, it threw every bit of the nation's attention on—as if he needed it—President Donald J. Trump. The wishful thinking among the masses to throw Trump from office now seemed more than a pipe dream; it became a strong possibility. And as time marched on, that possibility turned into a probability.

The media did not take too kindly to the federal government's initial handling of the coronavirus. They persisted in their grumbling, along with their Chicken Little fear-mongering. During the previous five years, Trump had been blamed for everything bad and rarely given credit for anything good; in fact, what would generally be considered a "positive" under the tutelage of any other President, was turned into a "negative" if it had been associated with Donald Trump (think prison and bail reform measures).

If only President Trump could be blamed for COVID-19 . . .

Hmmm . . .

Through this coagulation of politics and disease and destruction, America's schools were, for all intents and purposes, put on hiatus. Classes were cancelled, buildings closed, while a few teachers traveled to San Lucas and Cancun and posed in their bikinis for selfies. A hauntingly harmful curriculum was seeping into various subjects at the public schools. Progressives, bonded together by similar ideas about how to attain power and change America, were umbrellaed under the announced objectives of teachers' unions (and other special interest groups). They had already slowly begun their missions. The coronavirus, along with the tumult of the summer of 2020, bolstered their pace.

While teachers took to the internet to simulate teaching, parents stayed home with their kids. Many of those parents saw what their kids were being taught. They stuck their heads in front of the computer, next to those of their children, and watched.

They received an eyeful.

The rhetoric of COVID has screened the citizenry from what is happening in its most basic of institutions. That 2 + 2 no longer *necessarily* equals 4 throws up a red flag. For decades, people have laughed at the contention that math could be subjective. Now, however, academia has suggested that pushing objectivity in math makes educators white supremacists and agents of the patriarchy.

What has happened? Where is the courage, the logic of the past—the connection to reality? Have these been squashed under the gravity of political extremism? The resilience of Americans to adversity is not a secret: after Pearl Harbor; after 9/11; after the Great Depression. But now the demagoguery and the eccentric rantings of educators and politicians have managed to tear the hearts and souls out of a people known for their ability to fight for what is good and right. It rubs off on the kids. They see faces of fear, not of valor—of submission, not of resistance.

The coronavirus has brought much to fear, but legitimate hysteria should be aimed at those who are using your children to change America: first, by getting you to question your time-tested values; and second, by guiding you to hate the country you have always loved.

NOTES

1. Chris Maher and Jennifer Calfas, "School Reopening Pits Parents Against Teachers: 'Is There a Word Beyond "Frustrating"?'" *The Wall Street Journal*, February 16, 2021.

2. *The Mercury News*, "Coronavirus: California Data Show Substantial Learning Loss, Inequity," January 27, 2021. https://www.edpolicyinca.org/news/coronavirus-california-data-show-substantial-learning-loss-inequity

3. *The Washington Post*, "Kids Are Returning To Their Classrooms, But What Will Happen To Those Who Stay At Home?" Editorial, April 21, 2021. https://www.washingtonpost.com/local/education/kids-are-returning-to-classrooms-but-what-will-happen-to-those-who-stay-at-home/2021/04/06/26df73a0-8cdf-11eb-a730-1b4ed9656258_story.html

4. This confusion has been intensifying, and so has the bitterness on all sides on this issue. Sometimes I think if everyone could find a way to sit down and talk things through, they might work it out. It's kind of like when warring Native Indians sat down together and puffed away on their "peace pipes." Whatever they had stuffed inside those pipes helped to settle everyone down for a bit.

5. *The New York Times*, "Why Remote Learning Is A Failure," Opinion/Editorial, June 16, 2021. https://www.nytimes.com/2021/06/16/opinion/remote-learning-failure.html

6. Shana Kushner Gadarian, "Why Did COVID-19 Become Partisan?" *Syracuse University News*, September 13, 2020. https://news.syr.edu/blog/2020/09/13/why-did-covid-19-become-partisan/

7. *Contagion*, Warner Bros. Pictures, 2011.

8. At the time of this writing, the DOW had gone up to around 35,000!

9. *Statista*, "Number Of Coronavirus Disease 2019 (COVID-19) Deaths In The U.S. As of August 18, 2021, By Age," August 18, 2021. https://www.statista.com/statistics/1191568/reported-deaths-from-covid-by-age-us/

10. *Hamodia*, "Impeachment 'Diverted the Attention' of Administration From Coronavirus Response" March 31, 2020. https://hamodia.com/2020/03/31/impeachment-diverted-attention-administration-coronavirus-response-mcconnell-says/

11. Rahm Emanuel, "Never Let A Good Crisis Go To Waste," (Jerry Bellune) *Lexington Chronicle and Dispatch News*, July 31, 2021. https://www.lexingtonchronicle.com/business/never-let-crisis-go-waste

12. Small businesses, malls, department stores, restaurants, movie theaters, sporting events, TV productions, concerts, and personal services, such as massage parlors, gymnasiums, barber shops, and nail salons had all shut their doors.

13. Certain political elements in this country used the virus to make changes they had been wanting to make for decades. Control is what they needed; control is what they got. Somehow we were convinced to shut our healthy selves up, ruin our economy, and postpone health care for our other ailments.

14. These were not informal theoretical discussions. Both the National Education Association and the American Federation of Teachers have constructed platforms around these social policies at their annual national conventions during the past couple of *decades*.

15. Dena Simmons, "Why We Can't Afford Whitewashed Social-Emotional Learning," *ASCD Education Update*, Vol. 61 Number 4, April 2019.

16. S.E. Cupp, "What Trump's Reality Show Speech Revealed," CNN, February 5, 2020. https://www.cnn.com/2020/02/04/opinions/sotu-commentary-roundup-opinion/index.html

Chapter 14

Under the Gun, Getting It Done

MAINTAINING CALM WHILE THE STAKES ARE HIGH

Although I am not presumptuous enough to think I can *start* a movement, I believe that I can *join* a movement.

When I write, I occasionally like to be somewhat ambiguous. But not this time. I would sacrifice style and literary craftiness for clarity. This material isn't about a frolic at the beach or having a beer at a bachelor party. This stuff is *serious*. The last thing I want to do is play a game with readers. The stakes are too high.

The frustration I feel is palpable. It sometimes leads to unattractive, undignified word barrages on my part. But I get through phases of emotional explosiveness by reminding myself that I'm not alone. Concerned educators, political leaders, and parents throughout the country are working to combat the infestation of woke ideas into America's schools.

And then I read this: "Just half of parents support teaching critical race theory in schools, even though the theory's main premise is that racism continues to permeate society."[1]

That was printed in *USA Today*. Frankly this sort of inadequate analysis of CRT is disturbing—and it is unacceptable.

Sitting for a while in silence, I verified in my own mind why these words were so distressing—*because they're not true*! That CRT's main premise is that "racism continues to permeate society" is a fabrication of what CRT is all about. Critical Race Theory is not about reminding people that racism is still alive and well; *CRT is about putting down white people*. They are the oppressors. They are responsible for the slave trade, from which all Black people—not just American Blacks—still suffer. White people are racists and insidiously so . . . particularly when they deny their own racism.

Others are frustrated and angry. They fear for their children; they worry for their country. Wokes have made inroads. Contrasts and comparisons of changing curriculum and pedagogy have clarified these fears. The most constructive thing we can do now is to move forward, foster a positive attitude, and join alliances with groups and individuals that share our concerns for our children and, ultimately, our nation.

For your consideration, I humbly present to you a description of activities revolving around the challenges of the new progressive curriculum in our schools. In addition, I offer important concrete suggestions for taking further action.

WHAT'S BEING DONE

As it has turned out—a *lot*!

I can't keep up with it! It's exciting . . . dismaying and frustrating, too . . . but *exciting*!

1. Teachers have balked at the new curriculum.

Maybe not enough of them—for *certain* not enough of them—but educators are not all of one mindset. Because so much of what has happened to affect curriculum is *political*, we should be reminded that there are *two* major political parties in this country. *Still*. At least, for now. Not all educators have the same mindset. Yes, one party is dominant in the teachers' unions, but there are plenty of open-minded, fair-minded teachers of all races out there that do not—and could never—subscribe to the notion that white people have been sent by the Devil.

Consider these (edited) comments from three different teachers when they were asked questions about *White Fragility*, White Supremacy, and how these ideas have been formally (and informally) included in the subject matters that they teach every day to kids.[2]

> When my district suggested core books for students, I noticed all three of those books had to do with police brutality and how the police are racists out to hurt Black people. My first impression was that the literary quality of the writing was *awful*. I didn't use the books with my students. I didn't tell anyone. I didn't protest. I just kept quiet about it and went back to the books I had been teaching for years. (Joyce, A.P. English teacher, grade 12)

> I refused to teach most of the ridiculous ideas the district committees had set up for us to teach [in science]. There are only two sexes, male and female. I

couldn't lie to kids. I couldn't confuse them at such a young and impressionable age. When I talked privately with other teachers, my colleagues, about these things, we all laughed and agreed. When we spoke, there was a mixture of horror and humor. But during formal meetings, many of the teachers clashed on these subjects. There was a lot of emotion, and some of that emotion had turned into anger. (Raul, biology teacher, grade 11—a former local teachers' union president)

You know when I finally saw the light? When I had to present material online to fourth grade students about homosexuality, transsexuality, and the like. I thought, hey, the *parents* of these kids are probably listening in to most of this (Zoom classes). What are they thinking? All I knew was that if I was a parent and watching a teacher talk about sexual liberation, honoring the sexual you, and not being afraid to experiment with different sex ideas—because, hey, try it; you might like it—I would be all over that teacher! I went back to the classroom this past fall. We'll see what I can do to bring back some sanity into health education for *fourth graders*! (Marcy, fourth grade teacher)

Paul Rossi, who teaches mathematics at the posh Grace Church High School in New York City, spoke up. "As a teacher, my first obligation is to my students. But right now, my school is asking me to embrace 'anti-racism' training and pedagogy that I believe is deeply harmful to them and to any person who seeks to nurture the virtues of curiosity, empathy and understanding."[3]

2. Unions are being pulverized.[4]

Okay, *pulverized* may be too strong of a word here, especially because the unions still have enormous amounts of power and control, and without the cooperation of the big teachers' unions, politicians and special interest groups would have no power to make changes.

Not enough is being done to stick it to the teachers' unions, although there have been roots of change that look very promising. For one thing, the Supreme Court in 2017 concluded that teachers (all public employees) were not required to join their public employees' unions. Nor did they, as pursuant to previous policies, have to pay a nominal agency fee after they opted out of union membership.[5] This was *big*.

Before that Court decision, teachers forked over union dues, whether they liked that idea or not. The truth is that not all teachers subscribed to the same political views; nor did they like where their dues was going. Much of it flowed to political candidates in the Democratic party. Millions of dollars were donated to Planned Parenthood and pro-choice (on abortion) funding. Union leaders bragged about these causes at their national conventions. What withdrawing economic and military aid from Israel has to do with American *education* issues is beyond the understanding of most normal people (which, of course, excludes leaders of the National Education Association and the American Federation of Teachers, the two largest national teachers' unions in the United States).

Teachers have gotten on board. They have spoken out. During the last few years, an increasing number of teachers refused to join their local or state unions. *Education Week*[6] reported the declining numbers. The major complaint: teachers didn't like the way they were portrayed in the media during the coronavirus pandemic. Union leaders appeared selfish, obnoxious, and a little crazy. That was the rub. When enough of the rank-in-file apply sensible pressure and emphasize common sense in union decision-making—or else!—positive things happen.

3. Political leaders have awakened.

Just to hear them speak out is invigorating, especially for yours truly, after having researched and discussed this scary material. I realized I am not alone in my quest to restore levelheadedness in our schools. Leaders from both political parties have lent some vociferous criticism of woke impositions in school curriculum.

Maybe the guy that best nailed it was Senator Ted Cruz of Texas: "They've been living their lives, raising their kids, and suddenly they're finding out that their local school is teaching them that America is fundamentally racist, that all white people are racists, that every issue we have in America, it is all about us fighting on racial lines that whites and Blacks hate each other and have to hate each other. And that's all a lie. That's all poison and it's being poured into the minds of our kids."[7]

Some of the most outspoken proponents of force-feeding children a woke curriculum have found their lives more difficult lately. Admittedly, they haven't had it difficult enough, but the tide is turning in some sections of the country. Even blue states, like Illinois, have rebelled against these changes in our schools.

Roger Morris, teacher and former union executive, had the courage to say, "It is embarrassing to be a part of a culture where children are being brainwashed like this. Did I say 'embarrassing'? I should have used the word *horrifying*. This has to stop. It will stop. I see the signs of discontent, and they are encouraging."[8]

As this thing has dragged on, political office holders have weighed in on its merits. The most recent responses are deafening. Congressman Bob Good has been working on legislation that makes the teaching of Critical Race Theory illegal. He may not get there, but his sentiment sounds like it's in the right place. Rep. Good said, "What we hope to accomplish is to advance Martin Luther King's principles, which were to judge people by the content of their character and not by the color of their skin," he continued. "We don't believe that race defines a person."[9]

The wokes may try to stop politicians from doing the right thing; from time to time, they succeed. But they can't stop *you*—not *all* of you. And they can't stop ordinary Americans from believing in the words of Dr. King.

4. Parents are joining together in shows of strength.

The reports coming out of the school systems of Portland, Oregon, and its suburbs are, to say the least, dismaying. Children are being taught the narrative that America is fundamentally evil, and the rioters who continue to wreak havoc on that once-beautiful, quiet city are held up as heroes. Christopher Rufo reported, "The schools [in Portland] have self-consciously adopted the pedagogy of the oppressed as their theoretical orientation, activated through a curriculum of critical race theory and enforced through the appointment of de facto political officers within individual schools."[10]

The ever-growing truth is that parents have had it with this pedagogy. They have been speaking up. Newly formed parent groups, such as Parents Against Critical Theory (PACT), have actively engaged across the country, and are increasingly standing together to erect a wall against the woke invaders.[11] Parents don't want their children taught that they are oppressors because they have the wrong skin color. Teaching white kids that they are evil because of their race is wicked, just as it was when the worst schools of our past taught Black children that they were intellectually inferior because of their race.

The *New York Post* clarified what turned out to be misinformation or a lack of understanding. Liberal talking heads and politicians are trying to pretend these parents want to stop schools from teaching about slavery or Jim Crow. That's simply untrue. "Every viral speech of a parent speaking out against CRT shows how clearly they understand what CRT [really] is."

Very few parents want their children immersed in a one-sided racial vendetta that seeks to blame seven-year-olds for the acts of people with their same skin color from past generations. This is racial scapegoating, growing from the same depraved ideology that has dispersed guilt and shame on entire groups of people based solely on skin pigmentation.

School districts seem oblivious to the fact that they are losing not just conservative parents, but the great bulk of the middle-of-the road families who want their children to get a quality education.

Parents don't want their children sexualized; they are against a constant discussion of gender fluidity and other concepts that were considered mental dysfunctions just a few years ago, and whose treatments are still fiercely debated by medical experts around the world. Parents, rightfully, snarl at so-called "experts" who advise other people's children to consider their gender as only temporary, for "they might change their mind." Parents possess enough wisdom to know a boy is a boy, and a girl is a girl. And guess what? The science backs them up on that.

Karen England of the Capitol Resource Institute recorded in *Daily News*, "The kindergartners came home [from school] very confused, about whether or not you can pick your gender, whether or not they really were a boy or a girl."[12]

Another parent of a student in the same class said, "My daughter came home crying and shaking so afraid she could turn into a boy."[13]

And the Heritage Foundation suggested in February of 2021, "Americans are rallying around the Promise to America's Children, which is dedicated to protecting children from the harms of destructive gender ideology as well as the equality and safety of girls and women's sports."[14] Parents of female athletes are outraged that their daughters are losing spots on varsity teams to biological males who have subjectively identified as females. "It's their kids' lives and their mental health that the schools are fucking with," said one father, after his daughter was trounced by a transgender boy in a sprint at a high school track meet in Southern California.

I am wondering where the feminists are on this one. Why are they silent? Transgender boys defeating biological girls in sports? Feminists? Hello? My daughter runs races in college, and if something like this happened to her, I'd be throwing a few punches. Okay . . . maybe not. But I would at least write a book about it.

5. People like you are talkin' about it.

Individuals that have worked in education for a long time know some things about the inner workings of the system. They are familiar with the secrets. They have encountered the furtive little creeps that run the show, but hardly anyone else knows about them.[15] Sometimes when we refer to "they," there is no face, no real person, to confront. The makings of frustration come from a lack of communication and a dismal amount of attention paid to the visibility of political decision-making.

Teachers are a unique breed. They like control and are uncomfortable when they can't call the shots. It is part of the reason—maybe the *major* reason—they had elected to be a part of the teaching profession. They see what's happening; they either take risks to change it, or they eventually manage to become comfortable inside their own skin, while succumbing to the illness of indifference. Some teachers that find their hands have been tied become physically ill because of their inability to sustain control in their environment.

Many educators wish their realities away. Unfortunately, the forces for change in the schools are relentless; what makes the relentlessness dangerous is its insidiousness. They sneak up on you. Before you know it, the wokes are here; they have done damage. And in the places where they have dug in their heels, a bias, slanted deterioration of the curriculum has become painfully obvious to parents.

Lately, though not entirely transparent, wokeness in the schools has gradually been growing. Like the Blob, as it moves about, it increases in its strength and size and manages to leave destruction in its path. As treacherous as it has become, wokeness creeps up quickly. People hardly notice.

But that's over now. People like you *are* noticing.

WHAT CAN BE DONE

The rebellion is ongoing. The tasks are never-ending. In addition to the impressive work that that has been accomplished, America has a long way to go. Here is a quick look.

Parents

Show up at school board meetings, and regularly. If they forcefully kick you out, you will get some cool airtime with Tucker Carlson and Laura Ingram.[16] Your seeming misfortune will not turn out to be a misfortune at all.

Talk to your children's teachers about the parts of the curriculum you don't like. No mother or father *wants* to be that irritating putz of a parent that constantly gets berated in private when teachers have their lunchroom conversations about annoying parents. But if your objections are legitimate, they will secretly respect you—and might even be a little afraid of you.

Schedule meetings with the administrators at your child's school. After you have had a discussion with the principal, keep going. Hold a meeting with the district's superintendent or a level administrator.

Speak with parents of other children in your kids' classes. Or you could contact parents of children with whom your child does not share a class. Later, you may want to start support groups, gripe tribes, or you can go for the gusto by organizing loud protests and rallies. Get a feel for other parents' enthusiasm.

Send by regular mail letters to other parents at the school. Include administrators and teachers in this mailing. You could supplement the hard copy postal letter with emails to those same parents. Use high quality paper. Type cleanly and ask around for editing help. Suggest a time for a meeting at a local library. Provide refreshments. This initial organization is critical. You will determine how much work you must do to pump up the enthusiasm. Much of that effort will be in the form of disseminating information. Once parents *know* about you, and what you are trying to accomplish, they will respond.

Fend off resisters. Some parents like to act contrarily. Others won't see the issues the way that you do. Be polite with them. Do not engage in harsh public squabbling. Yes, the issues involved matter a lot; and, yes, the stakes are high. But sometimes the art of passivity gets better results than aggression. You won't convince these people. They won't convince you. Place your energies elsewhere. And stay classy.

Write a few more letters. By postal mail, address the school board. (They *will* read your letter, at least, in a private session.) Send to the superintendent of schools (your child's local district but the county superintendent, as well). At a given point, you could contact the state superintendent of schools and the governor of your state. For all the good it would do (which is little or none), you could write to the education secretary in the current administration. Contact your congressional representative and senators. Each state has a slate of legislators that has eyes and ears, especially in an election year, which this is. Keep in mind, you don't have to be the only one writing. This may be one of the tasks of the parent groups.

Host politicians. You would have to find a suitable venue, of course, but there are plenty of private organizations that would be happy to assist you, especially if your speaker is a popular or influential lawmaker.

Do fundraising and/or donate. The money could be used to run a campaign against the slimy lawmakers that are a major source of the woke curriculum problems. Even if the dough doesn't get to a live, breathing campaign, just the threat of your raising money to throw the bums out of office is likely to influence the way they approach their agendas in the future.

Teachers

It is practically impossible for most normal people to imagine that your everyday, run of the mill, hard-working teacher endorses this garbage. The problem is that polls and surveys don't always tell a true story; neither do public discussions and formal discourse within the earshot of those who wield the power. Teachers can get fired for saying the wrong thing. It didn't used to be that way, because of tenure laws. Today, the irony is that the unions that protect teachers from unwarranted job dismissals frequently find themselves at great odds with comments and actions that have put those teachers on the firing line. Talk about a quandary!

Be transparent in your views and actions. If you are being asked to do or say something that clearly goes against what you know or believe to be right, *then you must speak up*!

We joked before about being fired and then doing a gig on cable television. That may not be too far offtrack. You already know that it is not healthy or wise for schools to condone gender change surgery for small children. You already know that it is not appropriate for little kids to be encouraged to explore their pleasure areas before they learn how to spell them. So, you must speak up. The elephant in the room must be exposed. Smart, conscientious educators should not be forced into situations in which fear intimidates them into remaining silent, and they later feel like cowards.

More teachers should volunteer to have curriculum input, serve on committees that establish graduation requirements, and determine the identities of the guest speakers in front of the children. If you see or hear something at a scheduling meeting that runs contrary to what you believe, engage. This is the benefit of volunteering for these kinds of positions. Does it require more of your time? Yup. Can you get your hands a little dirty? Yes, especially when you have to push back on those whose imbecilic ideas make absolutely no sense whatsoever but *would* do a lot of harm to children.

The benefits of becoming involved may be greater than you ever thought possible. Going out on a limb is never relaxing, but it is often exhilarating. Lots of people spend their whole lives wondering if they will ever make much of a difference in the world. The good news is that most teachers don't have that problem. Here's your chance to make one *huge* difference.

Fight your unions. Be clear. Tell your local union leaders (maybe later, state and federal, too) that you don't like woke ideas; that bringing their curriculum and philosophies into the schools hurts kids and debases our country. But be specific. School board meetings around the country have turned into cage matches. They capture attention. This is primarily a good thing. Go to meetings in which they extend to you a platform.

Eventually—sooner, rather than later—you will be confronted, so be prepared. Ultimately, as this thing continues to go on, and unions actively continue to work for unfortunate distortions in school curriculum, you may have to decide whether or not to remain a dues paying member of the teachers' union. Collective bargaining by your union is done in the name of *all* teachers. Even if you stomp out of the union hall after claiming moral reasons for having done so, you still benefit from the protections and salaries of the union's collective bargaining negotiations. Don't let anything else that you hear convince you otherwise.

One of the most contentious arguments about compulsory union membership has to do with non–union workers reaping the same rewards as those that have actually paid their dues. The unions have structured the system that way, so some states have passed laws and stipulations like contingency fees in lieu of regular union dues. The Janus Decision by the United States Supreme Court warned the unions they could not *require* membership as a condition of employment. The upshot of requiring membership is that the unions use the collected fees in order to support their degenerate political whims, including scary woke curriculum alterations.[17]

Teachers should not allow their unions to hold them over a barrel. They have more control than they think. Union leaders must run for office every year or every other year, and the officers are subject to reelection or removal.

There is a given point at which a teacher should attend a local union meeting (or a leadership council meeting, where the bigwigs of the union exercise some of their subterfuge). You can stand at the microphone, speak loudly and clearly, and say your piece about what you know to be true about this curriculum. Just think. After you remind the audience that believing 2+2=4 is not a racist postulation, there will be a bit of silence in the room. People won't know whether to laugh or cry. That came from *you*. You exercised your power to leave them speechless for a moment!

Convince your site bosses that you have a better way. Most schools now participate in shared decision-making processes. These alternative organizational structures exist because teachers got tired of always taking orders from the top and winding up with little say in their school's policies. Often those collectively created ideas were laden with foolishness. Teachers—the smartest ones, the more experienced ones; hence, the wisest ones—felt frustrated because they simply knew better than the less enlightened teachers how to problem-solve; they also knew better how to lead. With asinine ideas permeating curriculum committees and threatening long established state standards and graduation requirements, site administrators, like the principal and her assistants, are ripe for the convincing.

Only a *portion* of educators have bought into woke. Of those, a smaller number has bought in completely. At this writing, which may change every time I edit this page, the news is spreading. What began as more covert methods for changing policies became flagrant with the publication of *White Fragility* and vociferous praise for the 1619 Project.[18] When educators began using terms like *antiracist* and *systemic bigotry*, they let the proverbial cat out of the bag, and it was hard not to notice what they were doing, where they were heading. These concepts were new to most teachers, men and women that use their own brains and ways of viewing the education world. Honestly, there was no reason to flock together and be readied for the slaughter.

Speak up at faculty meetings. All schools conduct them; they are normally dull, a waste of precious time that could be spent helping children. Considering the weighty issues involved with the new woke curriculum, and the disparate opinions on those issues; your meetings with colleagues may get testier. And hotter. This is where your resolve comes in, your determination.[19] When woke teachers are confronted, they fight back like nasty cats. It is your job not to give an inch. Too much is at stake. And remember, you are *right*.

Readers have been informed. Direction has been given. Even without my humble snippets of sarcasm and haughty addresses, the mere acquaintance of readers with the activities that have been carried on in the names of *equity, diversity, inclusion,* and *social justice* are enough to generate change, to cease the America-hating diatribes, antiscience rants, and antiwhite racism being promoted in the schools.

NOTES

1. Erin Richards and Elia Wong, "Parents Wants Kids To Know About Ongoing Effects Of Slavery ..." *USA Today*, November 3, 2021. https://www.usatoday.com/story/news/education/2021/09/10/crt-schools-education-racism-slavery-poll/5772418001/

2. These teachers wish to remain anonymous.

3. Paul Rossi, "NYC Teacher: We're Damaging Kids With 'Critical Race Theory,'" *The New York Post* (Opinion Section), April 13, 2021.

4. Not literally, but I like using this word. The unions aren't being "pulverized," either. Some of them have taken some body blows, but the heads remain intact.

5. John Fensterwald and David Washburn, "High Court Ends Mandatory Fees Collected By Public Unions," *EdSource*, June 27, 2018. https://edsource.org/2018/high-court-ends-mandatory-fees-collected-by-public-unions/599702

6. Liana Loewus, "Participation In Teachers Unions Is Down, And Likely To Tumble Further," *Education Week*, October 12, 2017. https://www.edweek.org/leadership/participation-in-teachers-unions-is-down-and-likely-to-tumble-further/2017/10

7. Senator Ted Cruz, "Ted Cruz Warns Against The Dangers Of Critical Race Theory Infiltrating America," Fox News, June 27, 2021. The quotation from Senator Cruz is in the second paragraph. The awful use of punctuation is not my fault.

8. In an interview conducted in June, 2021.

9. Matt Leach, Joe Schoffstall, "Legislation Seeks To Make Teaching CRT . . . A Civil Rights Violation," Fox News, September 28, 2021. https://www.foxnews.com/politics/legislation-crt-schools-civil-rights-violation

10. Christopher F. Rufo, "The Child Soldiers Of Portland," *Education, the Social Order*, Spring, 2021. https://www.city-journal.org/critical-race-theory-portland-public-schools?wallit_nosession=1

11. Karol Markowicz, "Kudos To Black And White Parents . . ." *New York Post*, June 23, 2021. https://nypost.com/2021/06/23/kudos-to-black-and-white-parents-mounting-an-uprising-against-race-theory/

12. Kathy England, *Las Vegas Review Journal*, (executive director of the Capitol Resource Institute testifies), 2021 (exact date unknown). review journal.com

13. ibid.

14. Jared Eckert and Emilie Kao, "Promise To America's Children Warns Of Destructive Equality Act LGBT Agenda," *The Heritage Foundation*, February 19, 2021. https://www.heritage.org/gender/commentary/promise-americas-children-warns-destructive-equality-act-lgbt-agenda

15. These "furtive little bastards" seem to make the same mistakes over and over; they then recycle ideas that repeat the original guffaws. Nothing in the past measures up to the antichild decisions administrators, school boards, and teachers' unions are making today.

16. Sean Hannity and Dan Bongino might also pay you some attention.

17. Brian Miller, "Unpacking The Janus Decision," *Forbes*, January 27, 2018. https://www.forbes.com/sites/briankmiller/2018/06/27/unpacking-the-janus-decision/?sh=7f17a0d041a4

18. *White Fragility* gives de facto praise for the 1619 project.

19. I do not suggest that you get involved in fistfight; however, should this occur, be sure that you go bare knuckle, as opposed to wearing sissy boxing gloves.

Bibliography

A'Hearn, Peter. "White Science Teachers, Here's Why Anti-Racism Includes You," *National Science Teaching Association*, October 29, 2020. https://www.nsta.org/blog/white-science-teachers-heres-why-anti-racism-includes-you

About Photography. "Story Behind The The Terror of War: Nick Ut's Napalm Girl," https://aboutphotography.blog/blog/the-terror-of-war-nick-uts-napalm-girl-1972

Adams, Cydney. "The Difference Between Sexual Orientation And Gender Identity," *CBS News*, March 24, 2017. https://www.cbsnews.com/news/the-difference-between-sexual-orientation-and-gender-identity/

Akhtar, Allana. "Google Prioritizes 'Authoritative' Results To avoid Leading Users To Misinformation," *Insider*, June 10, 2021. https://www.businessinsider.com/google-does-not-auto-complete-searches-wuhan-lab-leak-theory-2021-6.

Alan, Peter. "White Science Teachers, Here's Why Anti-Racism Includes You," *National Science Teaching Association*, October 29, 2020. https://www.nsta.org/blog/white-science-teachers-heres-why-anti-racism-includes-you

Anderson, Monica. "A Majority Of Teens Have Experienced Some Form Of Cyberbullying," *Pew Research Center*, September 27, 2018. https://www.pewresearch.org/internet/2018/09/27/a-majority-of-teens-have-experienced-some-form-of-cyberbullying/

Baker-Bell, April (2020). *Linguistic Justice: Black Language, Literacy, Identity, and Pedagogy*, Chapter 1, (Taylor & Francis).

Barth, F. Diane. "Why Are Some Men So Terrible?" *Think*, July 28, 2018. https://www.nbcnews.com/think/opinion/why-are-men-so-terrible-what-can-we-do-about-ncna895306

Becker, Hollee Actman. "You Have to Watch This 8th-Grader's Viral Apology for His #WhiteBoy Privilege," July 12, 2016, *Explore Parents.* https://www.parents.com/toddlers-preschoolers/everything-kids/you-have-to-

Belge, Kathy & Bieschke, Mark (2011). *The Ultimate LGBT Guide for Teenagers*, (Zest Books).

Bigler, Rebecca. "The Role Of Schools In The Early Socialization Of Gender Differences," *The Encyclopedia of Early Childhood Development.* December 2013.

Blackburn, Mollie & Miller, Kathy (2017). "Equity by Design: Teaching LGBTQ-Themed Literature in the English Language Arts Classrooms," *Midwest & Plains Equity Assistance Center.*

Bolt, Ewe. "The New Age Of American Imperialism," *The Globalist,* May 11, 2018. https://www.theglobalist.com/united-states-donald-trump-iran-nuclear-deal-imperialism/

Bova, Chris. "Racial Slurs In Literature Spark Conversation Between Educators, Students And Parents," Fox 17 News, February 24, 2020. https://www.fox17online.com/news/local-news/kent/racial-slurs-in-literature-sparks-conversation-between-educators-students-and-parents

Boyd, Toby. "'All Power To Our Students, All Power To The People!'" *California Teachers Association*, October 26, 2020. https://www.cta.org/educator/posts/all-power-to-our-students-all-power-to-the-people

Brainy Quotes. "Jacqueline Woodson Quotes," August 8, 2021. https://www.brainyquote.com/quotes/jacqueline_woodson_633497

Brinkley, Collin & Stobbe, Mike. "Vaccinated Teachers and Students Don't Need Masks, CDC Says," *AP*, July 9, 2021. https://apnews.com/article/lifestyle-science-health-education-coronavirus-pandemic-a65c9c0375ce441fcd10866eb8ea990b

Brooks, Billy. November 26, 2021. https://br.ifunny.co/picture/when-regular-math-is-too-difficult-so-you-introduce-africentric-7W3630Wd8

Brooks, David. "The Nuclear Family Was a Mistake," *The Atlantic*, March, 2020 Issue, p. 1.

Burke, Ted. "Was e.e. cummings Racist," *Like It Or Not*, June 30, 2011, par. 2. https://www.ted-burke.com/2011/06/was-eecummings-racist.html

Burnett, John. "Confederate Statues Coming Down Around Us But Not Everywhere," *NPR*, October 20, 2020. https://www.npr.org/2020/10/06/919193176/confederate-statues-come-down-around-u-s-but-not-everywhere

Calfas, Jennifer & Maher, Chris. "School Reopening Pits Parents Against Teachers: 'Is There a Word Beyond "Frustrating"?'" *The Wall Street Journal*, February 16, 2021.

Camera, Lauren. "Boys Bear The Brunt Of School Discipline," *U.S. News and World Report*, June 22, 2020. https://www.usnews.com/news/articles/2016-06-22/boys-bear-the-brunt-of-school-discipline

Carlson Tucker. "Pilot Ability No Longer Matters To United Airlines, Skin Color Does," *Real Clear Politics*, April 8, 2021, posted by Tyler Stone. https://www.realclearpolitics.com/video/2021/04/08tucker_carlson_pilot_ability_no_longer_matters_to_united_airline_skin_color_does.html

Centers for Disease Control. "What Is Epigenetics?" *Genomics and Precision*, December 21, 2021. https://www.cdc.gov/genomics/disease/epigenetics.htm

Coard, Michael. "Anyone Celebrating Columbus Day Is Racist, Ignorant, Or Both," *The Philadelphia Tribune*, October 12, 2020, Op-Ed, par. 2. https://www.phillytrib.com/commentary/michaelcoard/coard-anyone-celebrating-columbus-day-is-racist-ignorant-or-both/article_5efc4464-05c5-5130-9f55-4fa87889e2d9.html

Coates, Ta-Nehisi. "The Case For Reparations," *The Atlantic*, June 2014.

Colton, Emma. "Math Professor Claims Equation 2+2=4 'Reeks Of White Supremacist Patriarchy,'" *Washington Examiner*, August 10, 2020.

Colton, Emma. "Teacher Says Encouraging Behaviors Like 'Following Directions' Is White Supremacy," Fox News, September 14, 2021. https://www.foxnews.com/us/virginia-teacher-behavior-following-directions-white-supremacy

Columbus, Christopher & Strauss, Valerie: "3 Things You Thought He Did That He Didn't," *The Washington Post*, October 14, 2013.

The Columbus Dispatch (Staff Writer). "Statue Decision Is Insulting To Me As Columbus State Alum," June 23, 2020, editorial page, par. 3.

The Conversation. "Teen Suicide Prevention During COVID-19," January 28, 2021. https://theconversation.com/teen-suicide-prevention-during-covid-19-how-parents-and-kids-can-have-honest-and-safe-conversations-152485

Conway, Allie. "The Righteous Survivor," *PBS News Briefs*, September 28, 2018.

Corley, Cheryl. "Do Police Officers In Schools Really Make Them Safer?" *NPR*, March 28, 2018, "Special Series: Justice Collaborative." https://www.npr.org/2018/03/08/591753884/do-police-officers-in-schools-really-make-them-safer

Cornfield, Meryl. "YouTube Pulls Video Of DeSantis Panel Discussion Urging No Masks For Children," *The Washington Post*, April 9, 2021.

Cronin, Mattimore. "*Parable: The Emperor Has No Clothes*," Mattimore Cronin, August 16, 2019, Origin: Hans Christian Andersen (1837).

Cropsey, Seth & Halem, Harry. "Now Is The Time To Think About The Character Of Our Armed Forces," *Hudson Center*, March 20, 2021. https://www.hudson.org/research/16744-now-is-the-time-to-think-about-the-character-of-our-armed-forces

Cruz, Ted. "Ted Cruz Warns Against The Dangers Of Critical Race Theory Infiltrating America," Fox News, June 27, 2021.

Cupp, S.E. "What Trump's Reality Show Speech Revealed," CNN, February 5, 2020.

DiAngelo, Robin (2018). *White Fragility: Why It's So Hard For White People to Talk About Racism*, (Beacon Press).

Dennon, Anne. "The Value of Trade Schools in Today's Economy," *Best Colleges*, April 29, 2020. https://www.bestcolleges.com/blog/the-value-of-trade-schools/

Dictionary of American History. "Teachers' Loyalty Oath," August 9, 2021.

Dier, Chris. "My Students Still Have Questions About The Capitol Riot" *Education Week*, January 5, 2022.

Dodd, Christopher. "Franklin Child Development," *The Franklin Health Department*, 2021. franklinchild development.com.

Dorman, Sam. "Florida Mom Gets Standing Ovation," Fox News, October 8, 2021. www.foxnews.com/us/florida-mom-virginia-mass-exodus-public-schools

Dorman, Sam. "Virginia Moving To Eliminate All Accelerated Math Courses Before 11th Grade As Part Of Equity-Focused Plan," Fox News, April 22, 2021. https://www.foxnews.com/us/virginia-accelerated-math-courses-equity

Eckert, Jared & Kao, Emilie. "Promise To America's Children Warns Of Destructive Equality Act LGBT Agenda," *The Heritage Foundation*, February 19, 2021. https://www.heritage.org/gender/commentary/promise-americas-children-warns-destructive-equality-act-lgbt-agenda

Educator California Teachers Association. June/July 2020, Volume 24 (cover).

Educator California Teachers Association. June/July 2020, "CTA Calls For Racial Justice Now." Volume 24, p. 6.

Emanuel, Rahm. "Never Let A Good Crisis Go To Waste," (Jerry Bellune) *Lexington Chronicle and Dispatch News*, July 31, 2021. https://www.lexingtonchronicle.com/business/never-let-crisis-go-waste

Esenberg, Rick & Daniel Lennington. "Critical Race Theory Has No Place in American Schools," *Real Clear Education*, June 14, 2020.

Espelage, Dorothy. "Sexual Harassment Common Among Middle School Children," *Erekalert!* December 9, 2016. https://www.eurekalert.org/news-releases/920812

Essenberg, Rick & Lennington, Daniel. "Critical Race Theory Has No Place in American Schools," *Real Clear Education*, June 14, 2021 (essence of article). https://www.realcleareducation.comarticles2021/06/14critical_race_theory_has_no_place_in_american_schools_110595.html

Fazio, Ryan. "Young Americans Need To Appreciate The Good Fortune They Take For Granted," *The New York Post*, July 3, 2021 (opinion section).

FBI Crime Report, 2001.

Fensterwald, John & Washburn, David. "High Court Ends Mandatory Fees Collected By Public Unions," *EdSource*, June 27, 2018. https://edsource.org/2018/high-court-ends-mandatory-fees-collected-by-public-unions/599702

Finkelstein, Hans Roscoe (2019). *For Whom the Grammar Bells Toll*, (Chain Publishing), pp. 6–7.

Foskett, Janelle. "Firefighters Attacked, Apparatus Damaged During Civil Unrest," *Fire Rescue 1*, June 2, 2020. https://www.firerescue1.com/firefighter-safety/articles/firefighters-attacked-apparatus-damaged-during-civil-unrest-9AfaNiScSHVXhNTC/

Frankl, Viktor E. (1946). *Man's Search for Meaning* (Beacon Press).

Franklin, Teryl. "Who Was Hans Heg? Whose Statue Was Torn Down In Madison?" *Wisconsin State Journal*, September 27, 2020.

Fregni, Jessica & Zing, Laura. "Shaping An Anti-Racist School Culture," *One Day*, September 11, 2020. https://www.teachforamerica.org/one-day/top-issues/shaping-an-anti-racist-school-culture

Gadarian Kushner, Shana. "Why Did COVID-19 Become Partisan?" *Syracuse University News*, September 13, 2020. https://news.syr.edu/blog/2020/09/13/why-did-covid-19-become-partisan/

Gevirtzman, Bruce J. (2011). *Audacious Cures for America's Ailing Schools*, p. 267 Rowman & Littlefield.

Goldberg, Jonah. "Superheroes No More," *USA Today*, August 31, 2015.

Goldberger, David. "The Skokie Case: How I Came To Represent The Free Speech Rights Of Nazis," *The American Civil Liberties Union*, March 2, 2020. https://www.aclu.org/issues/free-speech/rights-protesters/skokie-case-how-i-came-represent-free-speech-rights-nazis

Gonzales, Mike & Wood, Dakota. "The Woke Takeover Of The US Military Endangers Us All," *The New York Post*, May 23, 2021. https://nypost.com/2021/05/23/the-woke-takeover-of-the-us-military-endangers-us-all/

Gottbrath, Laurin-Whitney. "US Vote 2020: Why Women Decide Elections," *Al Jazeera*, November 1, 2020. https://www.aljazeera.com/news/2020/11/1/us-vote-2020-why-women-decide-elections

Graham, Tim. "Bill Maher WHACKS Google, Facebook For Banning All Lab-Leak Questioning," TalkFest, June 21, 2021. https://talknest.com/2021/06/bill-maher-whacks-google-facebook-for-banning-all-lab-leak-questioning/

Greene, J.P. & Shock, Katherine. "Adding Up to Failure," *City Journal*, Winter 2008. https://www.city-journal.org/html/adding-failure-13072.html?

Gustini, Ray. "Noted McCarthyite e.e. cummings Also Apparently Racist," *The Atlantic*, May 25, 2011, www.theatlantic.com/culture/archive/2011/05/noted-ideolog

Hamodia, "Impeachment 'Diverted the Attention' of Administration From Coronavirus Response" March 31, 2020. https://hamodia.com/2020/03/31/impeachment-diverted-attention-administration-coronavirus-response-mcconnell-says/

Herrmann, Zachary. "Finding What's True," *Harvard Graduate School of Education*, May 17, 2020. https://www.gse.harvard.edu/uk/blog/finding-whats-true

Ho, Sookhan (2006). "Are You Multiculturally Mindful?" *Virginia Tech Research Magazine*, Vol 1, p. 1.

Hollyfield, Amy. "Who Should Replace Christopher Columbus Statue At Coit Tower?" *ABC 7*, June 22, 2020. https://abc7news.com/san-francisco-christopher-columbus-statue-removed-sf-coit-tower-replacement/6260070/

Horwitz, Juliana Menasce. "Race in America 2019," *Pew Research Center*, April 9, 2019. https://www.pewresearch.org/social-trends/2019/04/09/race-in-america-2019/

Howard PhD, Monica. "How To Know If Your Child Is Being Bullied," *Child Mind Institute*, August 12, 2021, par. 4. https://childmind.org/article/how-to-know-if-your-child-is-being-bullied/

Howicker, Heather. *ABC News Tonight*, August 15, 2020.

The Indian Express. "Why Replace Mothers With 'Birthing People'?" June 21, 2021. https://indianexpress.com/article/explained/explained-history-of-and-uproar-around-us-budget-document-using-birthing-people-instead-of-mothers-7351523/

James, Tom. "Spotlight: Building an Anti-Racist Math Curriculum," *Impact*, December 10, 2020.

Jones, Dave. "Rahim Reed Retires From The Community He Helped Build," *UCDavis*, July 19, 2021.

Keene, Houston. "Virginia Parents Torch Loudoun County School Board," Fox News, May 12, 2020. https://www.foxnews.com/politics/lcps-torched-parents-critical-race-theory

Keller, Jeremy. "Is The War In Vietnam Properly Taught In American Schools?" *Quora*, December 12, 2019. https://www.quora.com/Is-the-Vietnam-War-properly-taught-in-American-schools

Kelly, Austin. "5 Ways To Build Equity In Your Math Lessons," *We Are Teachers*, August 5, 2019. https://www.weareteachers.com/equity-math/

Kimmel, Michael. "When Middle Schoolers Say #MeToo," HuffPost, December 15, 2017, par. 3. https://www.huffpost.com/entry/sexual-harassment-in schools_b5a32 b145e4b00dbbcb5bb530

Kornfield, Meryl. "YouTube Pulls Video Of DeSantis Panel Discussion Urging No Masks For Children," *The Washington Post*, Technology Section, April 9, 2021.

Krogstad, Jens Manuel. "Hispanics Have Accounted For More Than Half Of Total U.S. Population Growth Since 2010," *Pew Research Center*. https://www.pewresearch.org/fact-tank/2020/07/10/hispanics-have-accounted-for-more-than-half-of-total-u-s-population-growth-since-2010/

Kuldorff, Dr. Martin. "YouTube Pulls Video Of DeSantis Panel Discussion Urging No Masks For Children," *The Washington Post*, Technology Section, April 9, 2021.

Lake, Asante. "Analysis, Meaning and Summary of Carl Sandburg's Poem *Nigger*," April 1, 2020, Comments Section, 2nd par. https://www.americanpoems.com/poets/carlsandburg/nigger/

Lambda Literary. "Supporting LGBTQ Writers In The Schools," July 26, 2021. https://lambdaliterary.org/lgbtq-writers-in-schools/

Leach, Matt & Schoffstall, Joe. "Legislation Seeks To Make Teaching CRT . . . A Civil Rights Violation," Fox News, September 28, 2021. https://www.foxnews.com/politics/legislation-crt-schools-civil-rights-violation

Leef, George. "A Racially Woke Agenda Is Now Hardwired in Public Schools," *Minding the Campus*, November 4, 2019. https://www.mindingthecampus.org/2019/11/04/a-racially-woke-agenda-is-now-hardwired-in-public-schools/

Linge, Mary Kay. "Public Schools Are Teaching Our Children To Hate America," *New York Post*, May 22, 2020.

Lixico (2021). https://www.lexico.com/en/definition/social_engineering

Loewus, Liana. "Participation In Teachers Unions Is Down, And Likely To Tumble Further," *Education Week*, October 12, 2017.

Loudon Public Schools, Newsletter. "Update: LCPS Offers Parents Options In Selection Of Reading Materials," May 19, 2021.

Markowicz, Karo. "Kudos To Black And White Parents . . ." *New York Post*, June 23, 2021. https://nypost.com/2021/06/23/kudos-to-black-and-white-parents-mounting-an-uprising-against-race-theory/

Martino, Barbara A. "How Marketers Target Kids," *Media Smarts*, 2008, par. 1. https://mediasmarts.ca/digital-media-literacy/media-issues/marketing-consumerism/how-marketers-target-kids

Mathias, Christopher. "Over 100 Confederate Symbols Removed Or Renamed Since George Floyd Killing," HuffPost, October 14, 2020. https://www.huffpost.com/entry/100-confederate-symbols-removed-since-george-floyd_n_5f86255cc5b681f7da1c9d04

McBreen, Kelen. "Furious Parents Read Vulgar Material Assigned By Public School," *News War*, August 12, 2021. https://www.newswars.com/furious-parents-read-vulgar-material-assigned-by-public-school-she-sucked-my-dck/

McCaffrey, Kevin. "Arthur Miller's Empathy for the Common Man Has Never Felt More Timely," *The Telegraph*, June 9, 2020. https://www.telegraph.co.uk/theatre/what-to-see/arthur-millers-empathy-common-man-has-never-felt-timely/

Mercury News. "Coronavirus: California Data Show Substantial Learning Loss, Inequity," January 27, 2021. https://www.edpolicyinca.org/news/coronavirus-california-data-show-substantial-learning-loss-inequity

Merriam-Webster, August 14, 2020. https://www.merriam-webster.com/dictionary/howl

Meyer, Katie & Rizzo Emily. "Don't Discuss The January 6 Insurrection With Students," *PBS, BBC World Service*, January 5, 2022. https://whyy.org/articles/dont-discuss-the-jan-6-insurrection-with-students-a-bucks-school-district-tells-teachers

Meyers, Lori. "California Promotes 'Dismantling Racism In Mathematics' Guidance In Draft For Statewide Framework," Fox News, April 14, 2021. https://www.foxnews.com/us/california-racism-math-framework

Miller, Brian. "Unpacking The Janus Decision," *Forbes*, January 27, 2018.

Mind Fuel Daily, August 10, 2021. https://www.mindfueldaily.com

Minichello, James (2020). "AASA Issues Statement On Recent Events And Racial Inequality In Our Nation," *The School Superintendent's Association.*

Mulrine, Anna."Are Boys the Weaker Sex?" *U.S. News & World Report*, July 30, 2001, 131 (4), 40–48.

National Council of English Teachers (2017). "Resolution on Strengthening Teacher Knowledge of Lesbian, Gay, Bisexual, and Transgender (LGBT) Issues," Resolution (Items 1–6), p. 1.

National Speech and Debate League website. Comments thread, November 22, 2021. NSDL.com

National Speech and Debate League website. Comments thread, September 21, 2020. NSDL.com

Naverette, Kathy. "Review of *Queer*" Kalamazoo Public Library, 2021. https://www.kpl.gov/catalog/item/?i=ent://ERC_215_348/0/OVERDRIVE:f10e6ea7-389f-4365-ad92-375f2e14219d

Nester, Alex. "Blue State Residents Oppose Woke Education," *Washington Free Beacon*, March 11, 2021. https://www.goacta.org/news-item/blue-state-residents-oppose-woke-education/

New York Times. "Why Remote Learning Is A Failure," Opinion/Editorial, June 16, 2021.

Newman, Lagra. "Examining The Why Behind Every Policy And Practice," *One Day*, September 11, 2020. https://www.teachforamerica.org/one-day/top-issues/shaping-an-anti-racist-school-culture

Newman, Leslea (2003). *Heather Has Two Mommies*, (Alyson Publications).

Nolf, Al. "Is The War In Vietnam Properly Taught In American Schools?" *Quora*, December 19, 2019. https://www.quora.com/Is-the-Vietnam-War-properly-taught-in-American-schools

Noone, Sean. "Twitter Suspends 70,000 Accounts Following US Capitol Riot," *WKBN27*, January 11, 2021. https://www.wkbn.com/news/national-world/twitter-suspends-70000-accounts-following-us-capitol-riot/

Norberg, Johan. *Johan Norberg Quotes.* https://quotefancy.com/quote/1664967/Johan-Norberg-Capitalism-has-given-people-both-the-liberty-and-the-incentive-to-create

North Carolina Board of Education. "Democrats Push To Replace Current Standards With Radical Curricula," *Speaking About News,* March 20, 2021.

Omole, Mojola. "The Case For Teaching Kids About #MeToo In Elementary School," *Quartz*, January 14, 2018. https://qz.com/1182842/the-metoo-movement-should-begin-in-elementary-school/

Paine, Thomas. "The Crisis Number One," *Common Sense*, January 10, 1776, located at SE corner of S 3rd St. & Thomas Paine Place (Chancellor St), Philadelphia.

A Pathway to Equitable Math Instruction. "Dismantling Racism in Mathematics Instruction," May, 2021. equitable math.org

PBS News Hour. YouTube, September 23, 2019. https://www.youtube.com/watch?v=KAJsdgTPJpU

Peeples, Julian. "'All Power To Our Students, All Power To The People!'" *California Teachers Association*, October 26, 2020.

Pew Research Center. "Blacks Upbeat about Black Progress, Prospects," January 20, 2010. https://www.pewresearch.org/social-trends/2010/01/12/blacks-upbeat-about-black-progress-prospects/

Pineda, Dorany. "In Burbank Schools, A book-Banning Debate Over How To Teach Antiracism," *Los Angeles Times*, November 12, 2020. https://www.latimes.com/entertainment-arts/books/story/2020-11-12/burbank-unified-challenges-books-including-to-kill-a-mockingbird

Prager, Dennis. *The LA Times* (on Twitter), September 20, 2019. https://twitter.com/latimes/status/1175112399021641728?lang=en

Price, Michael. "European Diseases Left A Genetic Mark On Native Americans," *AAAS,* November 15, 2016. https://www.sciencemag.org/news/2016/11/european-diseases-left-genetic-mark-native-americans

Prigge, Matthew. "What You Might Not Know About Carl Sandburg's Milwaukee Roots," *Milwaukee Journal*, May 31, 2018, Culture section.

Prior, Ryan. "Vandals In North Carolina Set Fire To Gen. Lee Statue, But Not The Confederate One," CNN, February 21, 2019. https://www.cnn.com/2019/02/21/us/general-lee-statue-north-carolina-trnd/index.html

Purland Training. "100 Politically Correct (PC) Euphemisms," August 15, 2021. There is a long list of humorous politically correct terms and words on these pages: purlandtraining.com/2020/08/01/100-politically-correct-pc-euphemisms/

Rantz, Jason. "Melinda Gates Foundation Bankrolls 'Math Is Racist' Lunacy," *The Jason Rantz Show*, 770 KTTH, February 19, 2021.

Rantz, Jason. "The Tucker Carlson Show," Fox News, interview with Tucker Carlson, October 5, 2020.

Reilly, Wilfred. Kentucky State University, "The Tucker Carlson Show," Fox News, November 26, 2021.

Reimann, Matt. "Dead White Guy Author John Steinbeck Actually Invented The Woke Apology," *Timeline,* September 14, 2016. https://timeline.com/john-steinbeck-woke-apology-dcafe114855f

Reuters, Thomson. "Racial Discrimination," *FindLaw*, 2021. https://www.findlaw.com/civilrights/discrimination/racial-discrimination.html

Richards, Erin. "Math Scores Stink In America," *USA Today*, February 28, 2020.

Richards, Erin & Wong, Elia. "Parents Wants Kids To Know About Ongoing Effects Of Slavery . . ." *USA Today*, November 3, 2021.

Richardson, Valerie. "PragerU Fights YouTube Over 'Censoring' Of Conservative Videos," *The Washington Times*, August 28, 2019.

Richie, Don. "9/11 Is History Now," *Time*, (History/Education), September 10, 2019. https://time.com/5672103/9-11-history-curriculum/

Ridley, Jane. "The 5 Most Outrageous Politically Correct School Rules," *The New York Post*, March 27, 2015.

Riley, Naomi. "'The 1619 Project' Enters American Classrooms," *Education Next*, Vol. 20, No. 4. https://www.educationnext.org/1619-project-enters-american-classrooms-adding-new-sizzle-slavery-significant-cost/

Rosenberg, Sari Beth "How I'm Teaching My Students About The January 6 Insurrection . . ." *Parent*, January 6, 2022.

Rossi, Paul. "NYC Teacher: We're Damaging Kids With 'Critical Race Theory,'" *The New York Post* (Opinion Section), April 13, 2021.

Rufo, Christopher F. "The Child Soldiers Of Portland," *Education, the Social Order*, Spring, 2021. https://www.city-journal.org/critical-race-theory-portland-public-schools?wallit_nosession=1

Saavedria, Maria. "5 Reasons To Defend Christopher Columbus," *The Hispanic Council*, October 2019. https://www.hispaniccouncil.org/5-reasons-to-defend-christopher-columbus-today/

Salter, Michael. "The Problem With A Fight Against Toxic Masculinity," *The Atlantic*, February 19, 2019. https://www.theatlantic.com/health/archive/2019/02/toxic-masculinity-history/583411

Salvatore Cianci, Susan. "Civil Rights in America: Racial Voting Rights," *National Park Service, Office of the Interior*, 2009. https://www.nps.gov/subjects/tellingallamericansstories/upload/CivilRights_VotingRights.pdf

Sater, Corrine. "What We Have Learned About Covid-19 And Resuming School," *NEA Journal*, November/December 2020, p. 6.

Seitz, Amanda. "Image Distorts Rep. Omar's 9/11 Remarks," *AP News*, September 11, 2019. https://apnews.com/article/archive-fact-checking-7354840002

Shaw, Adam. Fox News. "Green New Deal: Ocasio-Cortez Aims To Make Air Travel Obsolete," February 7, 2019. https://www.foxnews.com/politics/green-new-deal-ocasio-cortez-aims-to-make-air-travel-obsolete-aid-those-unwilling-to-work

Simmons, Dena. "Why We Can't Afford Whitewashed Social-Emotional Learning," *ASCD Education Update*, Vol. 61 Number 4, April 2019.

Simmons, Rachel. "When Middle Schoolers Say #MeToo," HuffPost, December 15, 2017.

Soave, Robby. "Chicago Teachers Union: 'The Push To Reopen Schools Is Rooted in Sexism, Racism, and Misogyny,'" *Reason*, June 20, 2020, https://reason.com/2020/12/06/chicago-teachers-union-reopen-schools-sexism-racism-misogyny/

Sommers, Christina Hoff (2000). "The War Against Boys," *The Atlantic*, Issue, par. 1. https://www.theatlantic.com/magazine/archive/2000/05/the-war-against-boys/304659/

Sprinkle, M.K. "Racist Mathematics Or 'Racism Propounded As Antiracism'?" *The Baltimore Sun*, March 13, 2021.

Starnes, Todd. "School Bans Christmas Trees, The Colors Red & Green," Fox News, December 5, 2013. https://www.foxnews.com/opinion/school-bans-christmas-trees-the-colors-red-green

Statista, "Number Of Coronavirus Disease 2019 (COVID-19) Deaths In The U.S. As of August 18, 2021, By Age," August 18, 2021. https://www.statista.com/statistics/1191568/reported-deaths-from-covid-by-age-us/

Staviridis, James. "Here's Why Trump Has Lost So Much Support In the Active Duty Military," *Time*, October 9, 2020.

Stoffan, Jake. "DeSantis Fires Back After YouTube Removes COVID-19 Roundtable Clip," News4Jax, April 13, 2021. https://www.news4jax.com/news/florida/2021/04/12/desantis-fires-back-after-youtube-removes-covid-19-roundtable-clip/

Taub, Amanda. "The Truth About 'Political Correctness' Is That It Doesn't Actually Exist," *Vox*.

Teach Woke, July 24, 2021, par. 1. https://www.teachwoke.com

Time, October 9, 2020, Ideas Politics. https://time.com/5898258/trump-lost-support-military/

Towhey, Jessica R. "New Report Says Green New Deal Would 'Destroy' Middle Class," February 28, 2020. https://insidesources.com/new-report-says-green-new-deal-would-destroy-middle-class/

Trumbo, Dalton (1939). *Johnny Got His Gun*, J.B. Lippincott, p. 49.

Turner, Michael. "Why We Should Teach Students Patriotism At School," *Whereyat*, August 10, 2021. https://whereyat.com/why-we-should-teach-students-patriotism-at-school

Umbot, Parter. "The Explorer In The Silly Hat," Peter Houston, *KABC 790*, July, 1999. The date of this interview with Mr. Umbot is an approximation.

Urevig, Andrew. "How Should Climate Change Be Taught in the Schools?" *Ensia*, July 10, 2019. https://medium.com/ensia/how-should-climate-change-be-taught-in-schools-across-america-4c22a577644b

USA Today. "Is Math Racist?" December 7, 2021, via Lindsay Kornick, Fox News, December 9, 2021. https://www.foxnews.com/media/usa-today-mocked-asking-is-math-racist

Various Authors. "A Longitudinal Examination Of Homophobic Name-Calling In Middle School: Bullying, Traditional Masculinity, And Sexual Harassment As Predictors," *American Psychological Association*, August 14, 2021. https://psycnet.apa.org/record/2016-62668-001

Vitti, Nikolai. "Superintendent Says Detroit Schools 'Deeply Using Critical Race Theory,'" Fox News, December 1, 2021. https://www.foxnews.com/us/superintendent-says-detroit-schools-deeply-using-critical-race-theory

von Spakovsky, Hans A. *The Heritage Foundation*, "Undocumented Immigrant Is a Made-Up Term That Ignores The Law," July 30, 2018, https://www.heritage.org/immigration/commentary/undocumented-immigrant-made-term-ignores-the-law

Washington Post. "Kids Are Returning To Their Classrooms, But What Will Happen To Those Who Stay At Home?" Editorial, April 21, 2021.

Wehrie, Roy. "What Went Wrong In Vietnam?" *Illinois Times*, News and Opinion, October 19, 2017.
Wiley Online Library, California State University, Fullerton. September 29, 2021.
Wineburg, Sam. "Why Historical Thinking Is Not About History," *Sam Wineburg's Keynote Address*, 2015. http://on.aaslh.org/Wineburg2
Zilber, Ariel. "Outrage After Migrant Children In San Diego Get In-Person Classes From Teachers At A Temporary Immigrant Shelter," *Daily Mail*, March 30, 2021. https://www.dailymail.co.uk/news/article-9416981/Migrant-children-San-Diego-person-classes-school-kids-stuck-home.html
Zoppo, Avalon. "N.J. Student Says He Was Kicked Out Of Class Over Trump Banner," October 30, 2020, *True Jersey.* https://www.nj.com/ocean/2020/10/nj-student-says-he-was-kicked-out-of-class-over-trump-banner.html

Index

The Adventures of Superman, 33
Almagor, Lelac, 183
An Inconvenient Truth, 154–55, 156, 157. *See also* Gore, Al
Anthony, Casey, 92

Barth, Diane, 85
Biden, Joe: appointment of Kristen Clarke, 54; cutting Keystone Pipeline, 158; Google search engines, bias toward, 135; Hunter, 186–87; military directives regarding diversity, 56; on mixed gender bathrooms, 39, 49; policy changes begin, 170
Bizarro, 33–34; then and now social policies, 35–39
Black English, 160
Black Lives Matter: denouncing the nuclear family, 48; on forbidden classroom speech topics list, 27–28; teachers' unions support for, 172–73
The Blob, 199
Bovia, George, 18
Boyd, E. Toby, on ethnic studies course, 176; equity vs. equality, definitions of, 176
Breaking Bad, relevance to math, 63
Brooks, David, 5

Burke, Ted, on e.e., Cummings' racism, 19

cafeteria lunches in schools, 5
Calley, William, My Lai Massacre, 37
Camera, Lauren, 97
California Teachers Association, 176
capitalism, attitudes of teachers on, 7
Carlson, Tucker, 56, 199
Cather, Willa, 15
censorship, list of banned books, 42–43
Chicago Teachers' Union, dance by, 113–14; on reopening schools, 10
The Child's Covid Primer, 162–63
Cisneros, Sandra, 20
Civil Rights Laws of 1964, 40, 53, 146
Clark, William, lawsuit by, 169
Clarke, Kristin, 54
climate change: forbidden topic, 131; hypocrisy in science, 43; in kindergarten, xviii; pushed in schools, xix–xx. *See also* science
Coard, Michael, 105
Cohen, Leonard, 13
Columbus, Christopher: defense of, 106–8; defined as a white man, 105; woke perspective on, 105–6
Contagion, 185
Conway, Allie, 21

Corley, Cheryl, 36
coronavirus: arrival of, 181, 184; average age of mortality, 186; Delta variant, 64, 182; effects on stock market, 186; Pelosi, Nancy, at State of the Union, 185; politics of, 185; schools, effects on, 181–82; science regarding, 181–82; in State of the Union Address, 185
crime, concepts taught in schools, 44
Critical Race Theory, vii–xxii; comments by teachers about, 194; graduation requirement, 174; inaccurate premise of, 193; parental support for, 193; Parents Against Critical Race Theory, 196–97; true premise of, 193. *See also* 1619 Project
Cropsey, Seth, 55
Cruz, Ted, on Critical Race Theory, 196
Custer, George Armstrong, 102

Dean, John, on the importance of children, 1
Decker, Richard, teaching on 9/11, 115
Democracy Prep School, 169
DeSanctis, Ron, 137
diversity: airplane pilots, among, 55–56; among the NBA, 52–53; definition of, 51–52; dilemma concerning, 52; in education, 57; and equity, 176; the military, Department of Diversity, 57; Mr. Lu, comments by, 58; ROTC, 55; Trump vs. Biden, under, 56–57
"diversity, equity, inclusion," xxi–xxii, 53, 163, 178
Dorman, Sam, 179

Educator (teachers' union monthly journal), 172
Edwards, Ross, 52
Emanuel, Rahm, 188
The Emperor Has No Clothes, allusion to, 51
England, Karen, 198

equity vs. equality, 48, 70, 128; gender relevance, 70; math relevance, 67–71
Espelage, Dorothy, 92

Fazio, Ryan, 134
fear mongering, 190, 191
Fifty Shades of Gray, 96
First Amendment, woke reaction to, 129–33
Frankl, Viktor, comparison to Martin Luther King, 40, 59
freedom of speech: college professors, contentious about, 131–32; dilemma concerning, 123; in Disneyland, 133; effect on children, then and now, 125–28; offensive speech, topics list, 130–31; parents, influence of, 123–24; speaking out, fear of, 138

Gadarian, Shana, 184
Game of Thrones, 38
Gascon, George, 44
gender prioritized language, 25–26
gender selection, basic facts of, 58–59
genetics: anti-racism teaching of, 160; racism, in the teaching of, 160–61
genocide, 106, 114
Ginsberg, Allen, 13
Goldman, Bernard Rabbi, 101
Good, Bob, 196
Gore, Al, 59–60, 154, 156, 165
"Grab Tits Tuesday," 92
graduation requirements, 170–71
grammar, teaching of, 25

Haber, Benjamin, 15
Heather Has Two Mommies, 22
Heritage Foundation, 198
Hiato, Senator, 92
history of the United States, woke view of, 103
Howard, Jamie, 95

Ilhan, Omar, commentary on, 9–11, 115

illegal aliens, differential definitions of, 27, 149, 150
institutional racism, xi, 10, 44, 46–47, 69, 129, 148, 173–74. *See also* slavery; systemic racism

January 6, facts about, 116–17; teaching about, 116
Janus Decision, by Supreme Court, 201–2
Jefferson, Thomas, 109, 120, 125
justice, definition of, 44

Kavanaugh, Brett, 27, 91–92
Kennedy, John Fitzgerald, xxvi, 40, 112
Kerry, John, 158
Keystone Pipeline, cutting of, 158
Khrushchev, Nikita, 64
Kidfluence, 9
Kimmel, Michael, 93
King, Martin Luther: birthday celebration of, xvii, 40; famous words of, xvi; philosophy of, 59, 197. *See* Frankl, Viktor
Koonin, Steven E., on climate change, 156
Kuldorff, Martin, 165–66

Lady Gaga, 15
LGBTQ: adding books about, 17; authors of, 21–22; definition of, 23; gay clubs in schools, 22; miscellaneous materials, 23; overview, 21. *See also* Whitman, Walt
Linge, Mary Kay, 173
Loudon County Schools, provocative reading list, 90–91

Mahr, Bill, on Google searches, 135–36
Major League Baseball, 133, 146, 163
man-slut, 91
Man's Search for Meaning, 40
Martin, Christina Sanchez, 41

math: advanced classes, elimination of, 66; and China, 65; dummies group, 67; minority groups, relevant to, 67; objectivity of, 63–64, 65, 68–69; racism in, 63, 68; racist standardized test questions, examples of, 72; subjective pedagogies, 66; white supremacy, likened to, 63, 68. *See also* equity
McCaffrey, Kevin, on Arthur Miller, 19
Media Smarts, 9
men and women, differences between, 38–39; separate organizations for, 38. *See also* Frankl, Viktor
Me-Too at school, 89, 91, 93, 97
Meyers, Lori, 68
military, U.S., attitudes against, 37–38; Vietnam War, 36–37, 38
Miller, Arthur, *Death of a Salesman*, 20; "greatest American playwright in history," from *Telegraph*, 20
Miller, Mark, 37
Morris, Roger, 196

National Council of Teachers, 23
National Science Teaching Association: on the coronavirus, 162; on genetics, 160
National Speech and Debate League, accusatory posts, 28–29
Newsom, Gavin, 44
Norberg, Johan, 46
9/11, teaching of, 114–15
nuclear family: argument for, 4, 48; condemned by, 5, 48; definition of, 15
N-word, reinforcing racism, 20; by Cummings, 19; by Sandburg, 14–15; by Steinbeck, 18; in *To Kill a Mockingbird*, 20

Obama, Barack, election of, 40
old dead white men, 15; misogyny, 16; sexism, 16
Omicron, 164, 182

Ortega, Philip D., 18

parents, influence of, 172; PACT, 197; rebellions by, 10, 197–98; suggestions for, 199–200
Pascoe, C. J., *Dude, You're a Fag*, 94
patriotism, 3–4
Peeples, Julian, 176
Pilgrims, 102, 105
Pledge of Allegiance, xxvi, xxiii, 2–4, 28, 106, 171
police: as a career, 83; chants against, 36; as civil servants, 35; on George Floyd, xv; of January 6, 116, 121
political correctness: behaviors, examples of, 142–44; definition of, 141; on immigration, 148–49; legitimate concerns, 150; speech, examples of, 144–47
Powell, Colin, 164
Prager, Dennis, 60
protests/riots, 45–46

Randall, Rex F., 148
Rantz, Jason, xi, xxii, 73
Revere, Paul, 102
Revolutionary War: deaths from, 108; justification for, 109; and white supremacy, 109
Ritchie, Don, 115
Rossi, Paul, 195
Russia, as a world power, 177–78; immigrants to U.S. from, 177–78

Saaverda, Maria, 106
Sahliti, Angela, 91
the Salem Witch Hunts, 92
Sandburg, Carl: accusations of racism, 14; anti-war philosophy, 13; censorship of, 14; poetry of, 13–15; *Silver Plaque* winner, 13. *See also* n-word
Schenck vs. the United States, 127
science: definitions of, 153; of fear, 165; fluidity of, 154; settled science, 42

SEL (Social Emotional Learning), 189
Seltzer, James, 17
sexual harassment, 92
shutdowns, effects of, 189
Simmons, Dena, 189
Simmons, Rachel, 89
1619 Project, 41, 110, 173, 202
Skokie, parade by National Socialist Party, 132
slavery: Civil War, cause of, 11; long-lasting effects of, 110; reparations, 110
social engineering, 2; traditional, nature of, 3–8
socialism vs. capitalism, 46–48
social justice: definition of, 174; established curriculum, 175, 185; graduation requirement course, 174–75; questions about, 179
social media, as private companies, 137–38
Sommers, Christina, *The War on Boys*, 77
Soto, Gary, 20

von Spakovsky, Hans A., 150

speech and debate, in schools, 28–29; Facebook posts, 29; forbidden topics list, 26–28
State of the Union Address (2020), 189
statues, destruction of, 117–18
Steinbeck, John, as a racist, 18; *Tortilla Flat*, 18
suicides, by teens, 85–86

Tang, Amy, 20
targeting children, reasons for, 8–9, 11
Taub, Amanda, 150
teachers: dance by, 174; reactions to woke movement, 201; selfies on the beach, 190; suggestions for, 201
Teach Woke: justification for, 10; workshops in, 10
Thomas Fordham Institute, 143

Thomer, Nancy A., 8
Thompson, Josh, 179
Thunberg, Greta: at Paris Climate accords, 155; at United Nations, 155
To Kill a Mockingbird, censorship of, xiv, 20, 138, 212
toxic masculinity: definitions of, 84; symbols of, 85; teachers' adjustments to, 93; whiteness factor, 93; woke warnings about, 94–98
toxic teaching, 84–85
transgenders in sports, 198
Trumbo, Dalton, *Johnny Got His Gun*, 109
Trump, Donald: coronavirus, handling of, 185; racism, 185; State of the Union, 185; xenophobia, 185

Umbot, Parter, 106
unions: demands by, 189; Janus Decision (2018), 201–3; policy positions of, 189; power of, 173–74. *See also* Chicago Teachers' Union, dance by

war on boys: academic effects of, 82–83; options of boys during 1960s, 78–79; relationships with women, 81. *See also* Me-Too; suicide; toxic masculinity; toxic teaching
Washington, Eric, 18
Wehrie, Roy, 113–14
Westin, Dan, 33
White Fragility, xv–xvi, 27, 173, 194–95, 202, 204–5
whiteness, at the center of culture, 41. *See also* 1619 Project, discussion of
white supremacy, pervasiveness, 41; American Revolution, 109–10; as controversial writing subject in the classroom, 27; destruction of statues, 117; labeled as, 46; in math, 66, 68, 73; slavery, symptomatic of, 173–74; teachers, handled by, 194–95
Whitman, Walt, 15
Wineburg, Sam, 101
Woodson, Jacqueline, on diversity, 51
World Health Organization, 187
World War II, reference to, 184
writing, teaching of, 24

Young, Tim, 63
Youngkin, Glenn, election of, 91

Zelensky, Volodymyr, 186

About the Author

Bruce J. Gevirtzman has written several books on education topics, but none of those books is as provocative—or important—as this one.

He currently teaches in the Human Communications Department at California State University Fullerton. He taught English in the public schools for nearly four decades. He coached high school baseball, directed theater, and ran the speech and debate program.

Bruce is the *one* to write this book. His vast experience in education affords him a unique perspective. He looks out from inside the system and then steps back, where he wrestles with the enormity of the many challenges in today's schools.

Awarded "District Teacher of the Year," Bruce was elected CTA/NEA (teachers' union) representative from 1992–2004 and served on the body for developing California Education Standards in English. He worked on the committee to develop and align twelfth grade course development, while designing Language Arts Curriculum for the International Baccalaureate Program.

Other books by Bruce J. Gevirtzman: *Shaking Hands with Aliens: An Intimate Understanding of America's Teenagers*; *Straight Talk to Teachers: 20 Insane Ideas for a Better Classroom* (Rowman & Littlefield, 2009); *From the Inside: Audacious Cures For America's Ailing Schools* (Rowman & Littlefield Education, 2011); *Frustration of Shame: In Defense of America's Teachers* (Rowman & Littlefield Education, 2016); and *Going on Autopilot: The Baseball-Mind Connection*.

Bruce currently resides in Brea, California, with his hard-working teacher wife and two disillusioned college student children.

www.ingramcontent.com/pod-product-compliance
Lightning Source LLC
Chambersburg PA
CBHW020123240426
43673CB00038B/573